LOUIS VAN GAAL:

DUTCH COURAGE

ANDREW J KIRBY

ISBN: 150533697X
ISBN-13: 978-1505336979

ALSO BY THIS AUTHOR

Fergie's Finest: Sir Alex Ferguson's First x11 (Endeavour Press, May 2013)

The Pride of all Europe: Manchester United's Greatest Seasons in the European Cup (Endeavour Press, June 2014)

PRAISE FOR *DUTCH COURAGE*

From Ajax to Man United, via Bayern Munich, Andrew J Kirby plots the rise of this indomitable, complex figure with verve and great insight. Despite not being a Manchester United fan, Van Gaal's extreme personality has long intrigued me. Kirby captures it on the page with an uncanny accuracy. This book is exhaustively researched, and offers great psychological insights into the man, as well as the world of football. Most books about football are poor- Kirby's is an exception, and is written with a ferocious intellect that matches its subject matter. A must-read for fans of United, and those of us interested in this colossus of football.

Guy Mankowski, author of *How I Left the National Grid*

PRAISE FOR *THE PRIDE OF ALL EUROPE*

The book succeeds in encapsulating the hopes, dreams, disappointments and joys of so many different eras. Just the right time to re-live them! A great read for any red.

Manchester United fan review on Amazon

A great read. Highly recommended.

Manchester United fan review on Amazon

Andrew J Kirby

PRAISE FOR *FERGIE'S FINEST*

A brilliant look at the finest players we've seen during Fergie's reign, and indeed, the club's entire history. A must read for any red.

Scott the Red, Editor: Republik of Mancunia United Blog

As a Manchester United fan I found it really interesting and the author knows his stuff. I recommend reading it.

Angela Bowman, Manchester United fan

This book takes an intelligent, thorough and witty look at the players who served Fergie during his reign at Man United. The perfect gift for the red devil in your life!

Sam Sharp, Manchester United fan

I definitely recommend this to anybody interested in football in general and Manchester United in particular. Buy it now!

Michael Hopkins, Manchester United fan

Andrew J Kirby

FOR OUR MARCH GIRL

Andrew J Kirby

CONTENTS

INTRODUCTION –

"THE DEVIL HIMSELF"

Barring a few notable exceptions, films featuring football are dreadful. Perhaps the greatest of those exceptions is Ken Loach's 1969 drama, *Kes*. Though not strictly a football film, for most, the truly memorable scene – the comedy-filling in a bleak, kitchen-sink sandwich of a film - is the one featuring Brian Glover, acting out his Bobby Charlton fantasies on a school playing field as he competes against a battalion of disinterested kids.

Glover doesn't just play to the stereotype of the bullying, overly competitive, whistle-happy PE teacher. He goes above and beyond. He turns a simple PE lesson into a war. We watch him, our jaws agape, as he elbows children out of the way, sending them flying so they'll flop face-down onto the muddy, playing-field turf; as he awards himself non-existent penalties and then takes them himself; as he tramples the fragile egos of the conscientious objectors – such as the film's hero, the perennial last-pick Billy Casper, who just wants to swing from the goalposts – under his studs.

Lyn Newton writes engagingly about the stereotype of the PE teacher in her blog on Familes.com. She asserts that the role of the PE teacher *used* to be in order to "prepare students for the military. They prepared students for physical endurance." She describes these early PE teachers as "drill sergeants" whose job was to "humiliate and demean the students." In other words their job was to break 'em down and build 'em back up again, *fight-ready*.

Though the role of the PE teacher has now changed, the stereotype persists.

Talking of stereotypes, the appearance and demeanour of the new manager of Manchester United has over the years led to his being pigeon-holed. The epithets most frequently used to describe him are: arrogant, uncompromising, authoritarian, brutal. He's a control freak. A disciplinarian. A "fundamentalist".

Sid Lowe, in his excellent book *Fear and Loathing in La Liga*, talks of the manager's "size, his powerful jaw, and boxer's nose, his sometimes blunt manner" which make it "too easy to portray him in an almost demonic light. In the hands of the critics (in Spain), he literally became a caricature."

Enter, to boos and hisses, the man who, to many, is a pantomime villain. Enter, rolling his shoulders, and cracking his neck left, then right, adjusting his "Michael Portillo quiff", one Aloysius Paulus Maria van Gaal. Yes, that's right, it's something of a mouthful of a name. But he's something of a mouthful of a man too.

We know him as Louis van Gaal.

Or maybe we don't know him at all.

Maybe we only know the myth.

We know that – yes - Van Gaal is a trained PE teacher, "spending 11 years at the celebrated Don Bosco school in Amsterdam". In Ian Chadband's profile piece for *The Telegraph* upon Van Gaal's announcement as the next Manchester United supremo, the journalist spoke with Van Gaal's old friend John Haen, who remembers Louis "running the epic street matches between the vast families of Van Gaal and Haen kids. 'Even then, he would make himself mostly the captain,' says Haen."

Which brings us back to Brian Glover, on that grubby playing field in Barnsley, making like Bobby Charlton. Indeed, take away Van Gaal's Steve Bruce-nose, and the Dutchman's burly, square-shouldered, slightly paunchy exterior does resemble the *Kes* actor's. And he *accessorises* like the stereotypical PE teacher too. In a feature on the Dutchman in September 2014's *FourFourTwo* magazine, Uli Hesse notes that at Bayern Munich, "he (LVG) carried a whistle and a stopwatch – 'old-fashioned accessories' as the *Suddeutsche Zeitung* put it". What's more, in his early appearances in the Manchester United dugout Louis was never without his clipboard. No new-fangled tablets or mobile phones for *this* Dutchman then.

We know this. We've seen it.

And we know that even his former players quake at the mention of his name. Zlatan Ibrahimovic remarked that under Van Gaal's tutelage players were treated like "soldiers". Franck Ribery's bottom lip wobbled like Billy Casper's when he described his treatment by the Dutchman at Bayern: "When the coach always speaks badly about you, when he keeps on putting you down, then it is tough," he moaned.

Lucio, the poor dear, says: "Van Gaal hurt me more than anyone else in football."

Christian Nerlinger, who was sporting director at Bayern Munich during LVG's time as head honcho, calls him "scary".

We know that Louis van Gaal has clashed with players, particularly senior ones, practically everywhere he has managed. At Bayern there was Ribery, and the Italian Luca Toni. Barney Ronay writes in *The Guardian:* "Van Gaal had insisted from the start on two major protocols at team meals: players must eat in the same space every day and they must sit up straight. A few weeks later Van Gaal spotted Luca Toni slouched in his seat at lunch and began to shout across the canteen. When Toni took no notice Van Gaal marched across, grabbed him by the collar (he is 6ft 1in, Toni 6ft 3in) and yanked his centre-forward up and almost out of his seat before walking back to his lunch in silence. Nobody slouched after that. Least of all Toni, who left on a free transfer before the year was out."

At Barcelona, he fell out with both Hristo Stoichkov and Rivaldo. Sid Lowe writes: "Rivaldo, in particular was a problem and he was also Barcelona's best player. His relationship with Van Gaal would become increasingly fraught. Increasingly public, too." Van Gaal later countered Rivaldo's complaints: "He doesn't want to think for the team, he wants to think for himself. For the first two years he was not a big problem. I invested a lot of time in him, but he thinks he is bigger than the coach."

This was at *more than a club* Barcelona. And Van Gaal's problem was not the typical one: player thinks he's bigger than the *club*. It was the fact that Rivaldo clearly thought he was bigger than *Van Gaal*.

Eventually the clash of egos (allied with the typical Barcelona 'nest of vipers' boardroom squabbling, and a media vendetta) saw a galled Van Gaal leave the club. Sid Lowe writes: "When he (LVG) eventually did depart he did so with the message: 'Barcelona is nowhere near as important a club as everybody here thinks it is. You have not won much. *I* won more in six years at Ajax than Barcelona have won in one hundred.'"

Later, after *more* boardroom shenanigans, Van Gaal was appointed for an ill-fated second spell at Barca. Of this, the then president Gaspart said: "I should have known that sequels are never any good... It was like *the devil himself* was returning."

Louis van Gaal, he of the cloven hooves and the horns on his forehead.

And yet, according to some, the Dutchman sees himself as the exact opposite. Uli Hoeness said: "His problem is that Louis doesn't think he's God, but God the Father. Before the world came into existence, Louis was already there. But the world doesn't work the way he sees it.'"

Saint or sinner, Louis van Gaal, the new leader of the Red Devils. LVG the *HGV*: a heavy goods vehicle crashing into Old Trafford, shaking the very foundations of that famous old stadium. LVG, the "volcano" (Nerlinger) who runs on LPG, also known as propane or butane (a flammable mixture of hydrocarbon gases at any rate) ready to explode at any given moment.

This is the man who, when unveiled as the new man at the Bayern Munich helm in 2009, described *himself* like this: "I am what I am; self-confident, arrogant, dominant, honest, industrious, innovative."

Inflexible. This is the man who, when he was in charge at Barcelona, was portrayed in the Spanish equivalent of *Spitting Image* as "a brick topped by a mop of hair".

At Bayern Munich, according to Nerlinger, he "infamously pulled down his trousers in a team talk to make a point".

Paul Wilson, writing for *The Guardian,* observes that LVG has a "penchant for confrontationalism. Van Gaal has his own way of doing things. People disagree with him and say so, but few can ever get him to change his mind."

Which, of course, brings to mind Brian Clough – another famous football disciplinarian whose character closely resembles that of Glover in *Kes* – and in particular Cloughie's famous soundbite on dealing with player disagreements: "We talk about it for 20 minutes and then we decide I was right."

It also brings to mind Sir Alex Ferguson, who, by proxy, via the dog-leg angled detour of David Moyes, Louis van Gaal succeeds in the Old Trafford hotseat.

The more you hear about Van Gaal, the closer he comes to Fergie. He is stubborn, hard-nosed. He likes "to provoke and challenge". He can be, Wilson writes, "very aggressive with the media, when he considers criticism is not constructive" (In a press conference after leaving Barca for the first time, he declared: "Friends of the media... I am leaving. Congratulations.") Then there's the buried hatchets – many of which have found their way into the backs of his former players.

Like Ferguson, indeed, like nearly *all* successful leaders, Van Gaal has one of the main qualities of a winning manager. He is a likeable psychopath. (Paul Scholes, after witnessing the Dutchman from close quarters, said: "he's a bit like a mad genius… he looks a bit crazy to me"). He is also, according to Wilson, "a highly intelligent man who understood that some players are more individualistic and needed different treatment. He did not expect everybody to behave the same way but he demanded respect for the basic ground rules, for the framework of collective work. If you did not get in line, you had a problem."

Like Ferguson's teams, Van Gaal's sides work to a rigid code. Zlatan was right when he compared the players to "soldiers". LVG has his trusted lieutenants. And his cadets. He places great faith in youth because young players are more easy to mould, are not set in their ways. Can be made *fight-ready*.

Like Ferguson's (earlier) United teams, there is a wholehearted commitment to attacking football. It is almost as though LVG has heard the clarion call of the Stretford End when United are chasing a game: *Attack, attack, attack-attack-attack!*

Attacking has become Van Gaal's *credo*. Barney Ronay writes of this other aspect to the LVG stereotype: "If there is a cartoonish element to the details of the Van Gaal myth – here he comes, this wild-eyed Don Quixote, gripped by the unreconciled obsessions of extreme discipline and creative attacking football…"

Here he comes, this man who will sacrifice all for his principles, his vision of how football *should* be played. Here he comes, the blinkered "drill-sergeant", the over-inflated PE teacher.

Philipp Lahm, in his outspoken autobiography, writes: "Louis van Gaal can be credited for implementing a playing philosophy, which made us (Bayern) very successful in the first season. But he refused to acknowledge the deficits of his philosophy in the second season and he refused to eliminate them. Our game was completely geared towards offence and this saw us concede a lot of goals in Van Gaal's second year. I pointed out some of our areas of concern to Van Gaal and he listened to me, but then he would do what he wanted to do."

He would do what he wanted to do.

He's Louis van Gaal, he does what he wants, to paraphrase another famous Manchester United fan ditty.

But there's been one thing missing from this caricature of the new man to take up the managerial reins at the Theatre of Dreams thus far in, and that's his other obsession. Winning.

As head coach of the Netherlands in the 2014 World Cup, he led them to within a whisker of the final, beating world champions Spain *5-1* along the way, before his young Dutch charges were finally beaten on penalties by Argentina.

In terms of his *club management,* he is even more of a heavyweight: Van Gaal has won a combined seven league championships across Europe: back home in the Netherlands he won the Eredivisie crown three times with

Ajax (in 1993-94, 1994-95, and 1995-96), and then with unfashionable AZ Alkmaar (in 2008-09); in Spain he was victorious with Barcelona in La Liga (in 1997-98 and 1998-99: Sid Lowe notes that in doing so he "became the first Barca coach to win the title in both his first seasons since the legendary Herrera" in 1958-59 and 1959-60); and then in Germany, where he led Bayern Munich to Bundesliga glory (in 2009-10). His 'domestic' trophy cabinet also contains the KNVB Dutch Cup (in 1992-93 with Ajax), and a hat-trick of Johan Cruyff Shields, in the Dutch equivalent of the Charity Shield; the Copa Del Rey with Barcelona (in 1997-98); and the German Cup (DFB Pokal) as part of a domestic treble, along with the Bundesliga and DFB Supercup in 2010 with Bayern Munich.

In Europe also his teams have been successful. Van Gaal's Ajax won the UEFA Cup in 1991-92, and the UEFA Super Cup (along with the Intercontinental Cup) in 1995. And the Dutchman's Barcelona won the Super Cup two years later.

Individually, he's won honours: he was the World Soccer Manager of the Year and Onze d'Or Coach of the Year in 1995. He was the recipient of the Rinus Michels Award (as best Dutch coach) in 2007 and 2009, and in 2010, was named German Manager of the Year.

But perhaps his most celebrated victory came in the Champions League, when his Ajax "Babes" - with an average age of 23 - became kings of Europe in 1995, beating a brilliant AC Milan side in the final (they were also runners-up the following year).

Which brings me back to that other crucial piece of the jigsaw which makes up the complex personality of Louis van Gaal: his faith in youth (which bodes well for Manchester United).

Christian Nerlinger says: "Van Gaal, with his experience and great touch for youth development, is the perfect man for the (United) job."

Barney Ronay agrees: "Van Gaal is a master of player development and fearless in his promotion of talented youth. Historically, this is the United way. Van Gaal is a manager who puts down foundations. In his time at Bayern they won a league title and reached a Champions League final, but just as significantly Van Gaal installed some key components of their subsequent successes. He signed Arjen Robben, converted Bastian Schweinsteiger into a central midfielder and helped ease David Alaba, Thomas Müller, Holger Badstuber, Toni Kroos and Mats Hummels into the first team. At Ajax, he revamped the academy and helped a generation of players to bloom. At Barcelona, he gave Andres Iniesta, Xavi, Carles Puyol and Lionel Messi a concerted start."

Louis van Gaal is, we have seen, no respecter of reputations. Even in his role as the boss of the Dutch national side LVG proved he was not one to fall back on the same old tried and tested. In the *World Cup Preview 2014: Four Four Two* magazine, Swansea stopper Michel Vorm was asked about the difference between previous coach Bert van Marwijk and the then incumbent Van Gaal. Vorm said: "Van Marwijk had been manager for quite a while. With him, there was quite soon a default starting line-up. Now, it doesn't matter whether you're Wesley Sneijder or Bruno Martins Indi, you have to prove yourself every week. That's why a lot of young guys are still in the frame for the Dutch team. Everybody holds a chance."

This was borne out in the stats. "Since the start of his second reign (…) Louis van Gaal" handed out "debuts to no fewer than 25 players, most of whom" plied "their trade in the Eredivisie." And, "with a new, young team, the talk of dressing room unrest that marred the Euros (in 2012, where the Dutch exited, disgraced, in the group stages) faded away quickly".

It is all kinds of easier to exert an iron will over younger, hungrier, *more grateful* players.

9

But over the years his commitment to young players has proved no passing fad. What he accomplished at Ajax in 1995 with that famous young team, brimming with youth team graduates, he attempted to replicate wherever he went. Indeed, so zealous was LVG in his belief in giving youth its chance, it was to him Sir Alex Ferguson turned *in* 1995 when he was considering a "controversial switch in his thinking and contemplating breaking up his '94 'Dream team'".

Stuart Mathieson, in the *Manchester Evening News* writes that it was LVG who "helped rubberstamp Sir Alex Ferguson's conviction that a mini revolution was a must at United in 1995. The Class of '92 were knocking on the first-team door and Paul Ince, Mark Hughes and Andre Kanchelskis were the candidates to become victims in the upheaval. As Ferguson mulled this contentious idea that he knew would be greeted with some howls of derision from critics and fans alike he watched the European Cup final from Vienna.

Milan were a Euro super power and Champions League holders but they were beaten by Van Gaal's Ajax in the Ernst-Happel Stadion. The Dutch side was full of players from Ajax's famous Academy. Match winner was substitute Patrick Kluivert was 18-years-old.

In the side were 19-year-old Clarence Seedorf, 22-year-olds Michael Reiziger and Marc Overmars. Goalkeeper Edwin van der Sar was just 24 and the De Boer twins Frank and Ronald were 25.

Their success against the Italians convinced Fergie that David Beckham, Gary Neville, Nicky Butt and Paul Scholes should be given their heads and join Ryan Giggs as regular seniors. From squad members they became the core of Fergie's XI and within a season were League and FA Cup double winners.

Fergie would have gone forward with his plans anyway but Van Gaal's blueprint gave him the final seal of approval.

Van Gaal's blueprint was the primary factor in his appointment at Barcelona, two years after his *Oh Vienna* moment. He told Sid Lowe: "The reason they wanted me in 1997 was that they identified with the Ajax style. We'd just been World champions and Nunez (the then Barca president) liked our ideas. He wanted me to educate the kids, to be involved in youth development, bringing passing, attacking football back... For the Barcelona directors, it was logical to turn to me. I was selected because of the style and because that Ajax team had an average age of nineteen or twenty."

Lowe notes that it was Van Gaal who re-established the "blueprint for youth development at La Masia (the Barca academy)" and "gave debuts to Xavi Hernandez, Carles Puyol and Gabri and later, when he returned for a brief second spell in charge in 2002, to Victor Valdes and Andres Iniesta, as well as Pepe Reina and Thiago Motta."

Barcelona's golden generation came into fruition after Van Gaal had left the scene (devil's tail between his legs), and indeed, until recently "His spell (as Barcelona manager) is not regarded with particular fondness; rather, it is often forgotten... Critics had accused Robson (who he replaced at the helm) of being too soft; now they accused Van Gaal of being too hard... The day he walked away he admitted, 'yes, I am arrogant'."

And he was. Is. Arrogant enough to dream. According to Lowe, early on in his reign at Camp Nou "Van Gaal had announced that his dream was to win the European Cup with a team of Catalans." However, in 1999, the dressing room "included eight Dutch players."

"Dutch dominance became a kind of running joke but for many Catalans it was no laughing matter. A banner at Valencia read: 'Welcome to Mestalla, Ajax.'" And "...a poll showed that 63 percent felt the club was losing its identity..."

Now, however, his spell is undergoing some revisionism, and LVG is being given at least some of the credit for establishing the foundations upon which Barcelona could become one of the greatest club teams the world has ever seen.

Revisionism or not, Van Gaal is not one for modesty. He's more than happy to take the credit for his contribution to the evolution of Barcelona. Speaking to Lowe, he said: "It's not normal to bring so many through. Those players are the backbone of Barcelona and a model for football in Europe. That's *my contribution*. They are polite and educated, modest, they think about the team, and they can influence the others."

And they sound a lot like another abnormal strain of youngsters at another club – Scholes, Beckham, the Nevilles, Butt and Giggs and Manchester United's Class of '92 – whose greatest night of triumph came *at* Camp Nou, Barcelona, whilst the *blaugrana* were managed by Van Gaal.

Talking of Champions League victories, two of the key players in Bayern Munich's 2013 success at Wembley were Thomas Muller and David Alaba. Those were two of the fruits of the Bayern youth development squad deemed ready for promotion by Van Gaal and trainer-coach Herman Gerland during LVG's brief spell in charge of the German powerhouse club. LVG says: "I always want to know what is below in the youth. The players who are talented. He (Gerland) is the one who said to me (Thomas) Muller, (Holger) Badstuber and (David) Alaba. He said to me these are the players you can maybe use. I observed them and let them train with us and then decided where to play them."

Often Van Gaal's ideas on *where* to play these young players was crucial. Alaba, for example was converted from fair-to-middling midfielder to marauding left-back, and was a revelation (in much the same way that

Guardiola's recent redeployment of full-back Philipp Lahm as a midfield pivot was an eye-opener).

The Dutchman sees things other coaches do not. He has a totally new perspective. "I'm not the kind of coach who just goes out and buys players for the sake of it," he says. "I'm a coach who wants to – and can – improve players." He is analytical; "a sitting-down coach, not a standing-up coach", but even sitting down, he inspires true loyalty. Robin van Persie, the captain of his Netherlands team in Brazil for the 2014 World Cup declares: "I will walk on fire for him if I have to."

Players appreciate the tweaks he makes will turn them into *better* players.

Andres Iniesta says: " 'Victor, Xavi, Puyi, me... our generation is very grateful to him.

Xavi insists: "People see him as arrogant and aloof but he's really not."

So who is he then, this Louis van Gaal, and what can he bring to Manchester United, that most vaunted of clubs?

Hugo Borst, a one-time Van Gaal confidante says Louis is: "a special, brilliant person but a walking paradox. You're never really comfortable with the guy. Sometimes, so social, so lovely and laughing. Then times, a dictator, arrogant, gets so angry. I've experienced both sides of him. There's never a dull moment."

On this everyone seems to concur. Christian Nerlinger predicts that Van Gaal's United reign will be anything but predictable: "one thing is for sure: it will not be boring."

Daniel Harris, writing for *The Guardian*, said of Sir Alex Ferguson: "crucially, he recognised that Manchester United must never be boring – and really, there exist few more damning insults in any context.

Indeed, since survival became more assumption than objective, much of the human project can be viewed as a treatise against exactly this. Broadly speaking, boredom is why sport was invented, its name taken from an archaic word that meant 'a source of amusement and entertainment'. Nowadays, people seek it relentlessly in almost everything that they do, a mania illustrated by the presence of books in toilets and smartphones in pockets.

Under Van Gaal, Manchester United will not only amuse, but entertain. He is aggressive, imaginative and charming and his teams are aggressive, imaginative and charming, reliably serving their principal purpose: captivating a captive audience."

There you have it: aggressive and charming, open and honest and at the same time inspiring a siege-mentality wherever he goes, angry yet laid back. This is a man who is in touch with his feminine side. He openly admits: "I cry almost every day. There's always something that touches me." And yet at the same time, almost in the same breath, he brands some of his players "wimps", and wrings his hands because Arjen Robben is not man enough to play a game without wearing leggings. "I've never worn leggings like Robben does. I'm never cold because I'm warm bloooded. My wife says so too. We always sleep spooning."

Louis van Gaal is a paradox from top to toe. Hell, even when you get down to the brass tacks of it. His nickname in Holland is The Iron Tulip.

This book will attempt to reach an understanding of the Iron Tulip by studying his philosophy, and his character. It will follow him through his managerial career from Ajax to Manchester United. It will aim not only to amuse, but entertain, like the man himself. If it has not succeeded, don't blame the Iron Tulip, but rather the writer who aimed to grasp his petals and read what was inscribed on them.

Has Van Gaal the stones to be a success at Old Trafford? Most definitely. The only slight doubt is the fact that *despite* his bolshy claims on leaving Barcelona that first time (*I've won more than you, ner ner ner*) in the following years the fountain of his success *might* be starting to dry up. After all it is a long time since 1995 and that night in Vienna. Nearly 20 years in fact. United's own *annus mirabilis* of 1999 seems like an age ago, but was more recent than the Year of Van Gaal.

Much also depends on how you *define* success. Success at Manchester United (much like it is at Barcelona) does not solely depend on winning trophies. It is as much about style, about promoting talent from within the ranks, about doing things in a certain way. Make no mistake about it, Louis van Gaal's tenure at United will have initial rocky spells (so did Fergie's). But behind it all there will be a plan, a blueprint. The Reds looked directionless, rudderless, dare I say it *boring* under David Moyes.

Louis van Gaal is the exact opposite. A fair-to-middling player - certainly he was no Cruyff - he drills his players to act out his Bobby Charlton fantasies on the pitch, and will do so again at the Theatre of Dreams.

I – "FOOTBALLING UTOPIA"

AJAX (1991 – 1997)

When the biggest club in Dutch football offered the untried, untested Louis van Gaal his first coaching contract, Van Gaal did not fall to his knees and begin showering the Ajax director's feet with grateful kisses. No, the ever-so-humble young LVG instead gripped the director's hand and pumped it, hard. Then, fixing the director with an arrogant glare, Louis said in all seriousness: "Congratulations on signing the best coach in the world."

Such pride often comes before a great fall.

But, surpassing all expectations, Louis van Gaal did become for a spell in the 1990s, if not *the* best coach in the world, at least one of the select few who might be considered for the role. In November 1995 Van Gaal's Ajax, the reigning Champions of Europe, silenced the Bernabeu with a scintillating display, eventually running out 2-0 winners (the scorers were Litmanen and Kluivert). In the aftermath of the game, the then Real Madrid coach Jorge Valdano spoke in hushed, awestruck tones about the Dutch club's level of performance. "Ajax", he said, "are not just the team of the nineties, they are approaching football Utopia."

Pep Guardiola concurred. "My jaw dropped when I saw Van Gaal's Ajax play," he cheered in his autobiography. "They did everything a football team should do perfectly in my eyes."

Van Gaal himself was in no doubt as to the fact that his team had reached the pinnacle. In 1995, after adding the Intercontinental Cup to Ajax's voluminous trophy cabinet, he bellowed: "We are the best! We are the best! And not just of Amsterdam. But also of Rotterdam. And Eindhoven. And Europe… And now we are the best of the…. *world!*"

Such metaphorical chest-beating would find its echo in 2010, when after winning the league with Bayern Munich the Dutchman yelled: "Who has the best defence? FC Bayern! Who has the best attack? FC Bayern! And that's why we are *champions*! And not just in Munchen. Also in Gelsenkirchen! And also in Bremen. And in Hamburg! We are the best of Germany. And perhaps soon: of Europe!"

But by then *some* people had stopped listening. At Ajax, however, the whole of the footballing world *had* sat up and taken notice of Louis van Gaal and his extraordinary young team.

Van Gaal seemed to have come from nowhere.

One could *almost* have understood it if it had been, say, Johan Cruyff. Cruyff was, and is, the personification of Dutch football philosophy, and a symbol of Ajax.

JC was the saviour, the figurehead, the star for Ajax during the most successful spell in the club's history. He was top-scorer for seven consecutive seasons between 1965-66 and 1971-72, during which time they won five Eredivisie titles and two European Cups (they also won a third European Cup a year later, though JC did not top-score). But he was about so much more than that: Cruyff was the man who gave Ajax their glamour, their swagger. He was the man who carried their name across the globe.

JC was their prophet and demigod all rolled into one.

JC and his disciples in those 1970s Ajax and Netherlands teams played Utopian football, dominating matches with their passing style, their constant circulation of the ball, the interchangeability of the players, and, of course, with flair and tricks (generally provided by Cruyff, he of the famous 'turn'). They set the bar totally high. Set expectations totally high too, so that just like everybody wanted Brazil to play 'like Brazil' (which meant the way they'd wowed the world in the 1970 World Cup), so the Netherlands, and Ajax, had to play *the Dutch way*. Which meant Total Football.

And after nearly two decade of the Dutch playing in a decidedly *un*-Dutch fashion, suddenly they'd regained their mojo again. Ajax in the mid-nineties were Total Football all over again.

But it wasn't JC who worked the miracle of Vienna, securing *that* improbable triumph against Milan in the Champions League final of 1995, thereby bringing Ajax back from the (European) dead.

It was Louis van Gaal.

As a player, LVG wasn't exactly Johan Cruyff. As a manager, Van Gaal and Cruyff are closer. Their managerial careers have spun webs across some of the greatest names in European football: they both list Barcelona and Ajax on their respective CVs. But as a player, Van Gaal was more of a *Jordi* Cruyff (Johan's hard-working but rather less *stellar* son, who turned out for Barcelona and Manchester United in the nineties).

Ian Chadband, in a profile piece for *The Telegraph*, noted: "As a footballer, his intelligence and fine passing could never quite make up for his slowness: his only first team appearance at Ajax came in a friendly because Johan

Cruyff was injured. Many believe his whole subsequent coaching career, from Amsterdam to Barcelona, has been about trying to eclipse Holland's greatest footballing brain and never having the flair and creative genius to quite pull it off. The pair, famously, do not get on."

There's nothing like a grudge to get the creative juices flowing, and there's nothing quite like the grudge between the two leading lights of Dutch football.

Who started it?

Both claim it was the other to blame.

Van Gaal traces it right back to 1989. In a piece in *The Telegraph* Jonathan Liew notes: "the story goes that Van Gaal was having dinner at Cruyff's house, left abruptly because he was informed that his sister had died, and Cruyff got offended. Cruyff, for his part, describes this as rubbish. 'You wonder whether he has one or two screws loose,' Cruyff said of Van Gaal in 2009. However it started, the tension between the two is very real. In 2011, the Ajax board tried to hire Van Gaal as a technical director. Cruyff, a fellow board member, went berserk when he learned of the appointment, taking Ajax to court in an attempt to block it on the grounds that he had not been consulted. Cruyff won, and the appointment was overturned."

The pair of them could argue all day about who started it, but for the purposes of this book it is useful to take a mature view; to consider Louis van Gaal's career through the lens of his rivalry with Cruyff because it is Van Gaal's intense desire to emerge from Cruyff's shadow, to cease being portrayed as 'the ugly sister', to *trump* him, which has helped him to maintain focus and desire, which has driven him to succeed time and time again.

Liew says: "Cruyff and Van Gaal were both steeped in Ajax tradition and share many of the same ideas of football, not least a steadfast belief in 4-3-3 and quick passing. But there is one fundamental difference between them.

Cruyff won pretty much everything there was to win at club level, played in a World Cup final, *charmed an entire generation.* Van Gaal, an enterprising and cerebral midfielder six years his junior, joined Ajax in 1972 with hopes of emulating him. He left after a year without making a single first-team appearance. Despite spending almost a decade at Sparta Rotterdam, his playing career was unremarkable. By his own lofty standards, it was a failure."

After Sparta Rotterdam, Van Gaal saw out the twilight of his playing career at struggling AZ Alkmaar. He played 17 games in his final season – 1986-87. (His overall career statistics, taking in spells at Royal Antwerp in Belgium, Telstar, Sparta, and AZ, was 34 goals in 333 games over 16 years as a professional). But by this time he was already beginning to move into coaching. He'd been named assistant coach at AZ in 1986, but the club was in disarray. Co-founder (and owner) Klaas Molenaar had left the club in 1985, putting the final full-stop on an heretofore unprecedented period of success for the club which had culminated in a Dutch championship in 1981 and an appearance in the UEFA cup final (where they lost on aggregate to Ipswich Town). Star players were departing and were not adequately replaced.

1988 was a great year for Dutch football: in West Germany the Netherlands' team, led by Marco van Basten, Frank Rijkaard and Ruud Gullit, and bossed by Rinus Michels, were crowned champions of Europe by winning UEFA '88 (still their best performance in a major international tournament), putting an end to 14 years of hurt after their so-near yet so-far performances in the World Cups of 1974 and 1978. 1974's defeat to West Germany had particularly hurt. Throughout the tournament, no side had found an answer to the Netherlands' Total Football, and its key exponent, Johan Cruyff. Now Cruyff-less, the Dutch had finally vanquished a few ghosts.

But 1988 was also a great year for Louis van Gaal. For that was the year he was coaxed back to his beloved Ajax in order to become manager Leo Beenhakker's assistant.

In truth, it wouldn't have taken much coaxing. In 1988 AZ had reached their lowest ebb: they were relegated from the Eredivisie. And for Van Gaal, the dangled carrot of being able to work under and learn from Beenhakker, a much-respected coach who was returning to Ajax after three years in the Real Madrid hotseat (he'd won La Liga in his final season), allied to the fact that he (Louis) would be coaching players of the calibre of Arnold Muhren, Aron Winter, John Bosman, Jan Wouters, and John van't Schip - all of whom had made the Dutch squad which had brought back the Henri Delaunay trophy from West Germany - meant it was all too easy to jump ship.

But things weren't quite as rosy in the Ajax garden as they might have seemed. Even Dutch football's biggest club was not immune to losing its star players and of that triumphal Euro '88 squad, the true stars – its Cruyffs – had plied their footballing trade outside of the Eredivisie. Gullit and Van Basten were at Milan; Rijkaard was at Real Zaragoza. Most of the Ajax contingent *in* West Germany had been either ageing players heading towards retirement (such as former Manchester United star Arnold Muhren) or youngsters (Aron Winter; who would himself move on, to Italy, where he'd turn out for both Lazio and Inter).

In 1987-88, PSV Eindhoven completed a hat-trick of consecutive Dutch league titles, and although Ajax had come second in each season, the gap between this 'big two' of Dutch football was increasing. In 1988, PSV won it by nine points. Allied to this, *unlike* Ajax, PSV featured some Euro '88 stars who were at the height of their powers, including Ronald Koeman and Wim Kieft. And though Ajax won the European Cup Winners' Cup in 1987, supporters were becoming increasingly impatient for domestic glory.

And although the new double-act at the helm at Ajax – it was a typical *big man- small man, good cop-bad cop* duo comprising the statesmanlike Beenhakker and the boxer-a-like Van Gaal – began to get Ajax playing like Ajax again, still, in 1988-89, PSV Eindhoven retained their Eredivisie crown (they also won the KNVB Cup, to complete the double).

Still, the Ajax way thing was important, for it was also the *Dutch* way. Jonathan Liew says: "The Ajax and Holland sides of the 1970s sometimes played what could be classed as a 3-4-3. Ruud Krol would play as a sweeper, occasionally mopping up behind the defence, occasionally stepping into midfield to form the base of an attack. It was an attacking system, based on possession and smooth transitions."

Total Football, in other words.

Over the past few seasons, it was *PSV* who'd started to look more like the archetypal *Dutch* team – in 1987-88, they'd scored a whopping 117 goals in 34 games – and Ajax fans didn't like that. Not one bit.

Finally, in 1989-90, Ajax wrestled the Eredivisie title back from Eindhoven, but this time it was the Ajax *fans* letting the *team* down. The Amsterdam club found themselves banned from European competition for a year after an incident in a 1989 UEFA Cup game in which the Austrian 'keeper Franz Wohlfahrt was hit by a bar thrown by the Ajax supporters. There was to be no European Cup campaign for Ajax in 1990-91.

This disappointment seemed to carry through into the next season. PSV reclaimed their Eredivisie crown on goal difference from the Amsterdam giants, thanks in no small part to the magical goalscoring feats of the Brazilian, Romario. Romario had top-scored a season earlier too, but this time he was joined at the top of the charts (with 25 goals) by a new *Dutch* tyro: Dennis Bergkamp, of Ajax.

Bergkamp was schooled by Ajax from an early age (11) and was steeped in the history and philosophy of the club. Cruyff had handed him his debut as a 17, back in 1986. He scored his first senior goal in 1987, but struggled for a regular place in the team until a year later, by which time Beenhakker and Van Gaal were in charge.

Jan Mulder, the Dutch former footballer, now football writer and presenter, describes Bergkamp as possessing the "finest technique" of any Dutch international.

Under Van Gaal's tutelage, Dennis Bergkamp would hone his talents, *improve* as a player. Bergkamp says: "He will never admit it, but the football Van Gaal propagates is the football of Cruyff, and Wenger. Only the methods differ. Cruyff's coaching is based on how he was as a player: adventurous, spectacular and offensive. He doesn't analyse so much. It's more instinct and technique. Van Gaal is didactic. Louis gives his players instructions they need to perform to make the system work. And the system is sacred."

Even as a coach under Beenhakker, Van Gaal was beginning to develop his blueprint, and it was all about the system, about the good of the team. Precisely because Van Gaal was *not* Johan Cruyff as a player, he declared (in an interview with Fifa.com): "Players count for nothing, the team is everything. I set more store by a player's character than by his on-field qualities, and particularly whether he is willing to give everything to the cause. There are some incredibly talented players who haven't got the character or the personality to suit my methods.

You need the right mindset, and it depends on how the players see the coach and vice versa. The coach is the focal point of the team but you need to have an open mind, and so do all the players. Everyone needs to work together to achieve a common goal. Preparing your tactical formation is essential. Each player needs to know where he has to be, and that is why there needs to be mutual understanding because you need absolute discipline. This is a sport played by 22 men, and there are 11 opponents out there playing as a team. Each individual needs to know who he has to beat and be there to support his team-mates."

Liew agrees: "Cruyff played Total Football in its purest form, with 10 outfield players all theoretically interchangeable in their roles. It required outrageous talents, thrilling individuality and pure instinct. To play the Cruyff way, you had to pack the team with gifted individuals and allow them to 'feel' their way through the game.

For Van Gaal, stars were of secondary importance. The system was king. If a player didn't fit into the system, or didn't want to fit into the system, he was out. This is why Van Gaal is such a fiercely divisive character amongst players: like Jose Mourinho, he decides very quickly whether he wants you or not. If you're his guy, great. If not, it might be worth a quick call to your agent."

Bergkamp adds: "All players are equal to Van Gaal, big names do not exist for him, and everyone is subordinate to the team and the system, his system. Cruyff being a great player encourages individualists because they can decide matches. He challenged them. Johan was himself the greatest of all. Others played in the service of him. Van Gaal could not do that. It would also go against the team he is building. Subordinate. But what if you have ten mediocre painters and Rembrandt? Do you tell Rembrandt he does not have to imagine, and that he doesn't represent more than the others? Or are you going to give him the feeling that he is special and let him display it, so he can produce his finest work."

At the end of the 1990-91 season, Leo Beenhakker departed Ajax in order to take over at Real Madrid again. Louis van Gaal was promoted to manager and immediately began to put his blueprint into action. His credo: the team, the team, and nothing but the team. His ambition: to entertain. His moral duty: to provide attacking football. But above all else, the system, and the team. "You have to play as a team and not as individuals," Van Gaal says. "That's why I'm always going back to the vision, then the team, and then which players fit in my system, a 4-3-3, because I'm always playing that."

In LVG's first season as a manager, Ajax finished as runners-up (again) to PSV Eindhoven, despite the sterling efforts of Bergkamp who top-scored with 22 goals. But Van Gaal was to announce himself – in his own inimitable way - on the European stage in Ajax's triumphal UEFA Cup campaign. Though Ajax had won a hat-trick of European Cups during the 1970s, this was Ajax's first ever UEFA Cup title, and they won it by defeating Torino on away goals in the final.

They'd also defeated Italian opposition – in the form of Genoa, who'd beaten Liverpool in the quarter-final – in the semi-final, and in both games it was their goalscoring feats away from Amsterdam which had seen them through. Against typically robust Italian defending, Ajax had scored two in the final, first-leg at the Stadio delle Alpi, and three in Genoa. Though Dennis Bergkamp top-scored with six in the campaign, the team as a whole showed no fear. And, as we know with Van Gaal, it is all about the team. Aron Winter also weighed in with four goals, as did the Swede Stefan Pettersson. Wim Jonk netted three.

The following season (1992-93) PSV were finally knocked off their perch, but not by Van Gaal's Ajax. No, *Feyenoord* finally got their act together and won the Eredivisie title, pushing Ajax even further off the pace. They finished third, the first time they'd finished outside the top two in the top division of Dutch football since 1984. Football writer David Winner described their form as "maddening". One week they'd beat Feyenoord, the next, lose to "minnows like MVV Maastricht".

But what carried Van Gaal through this sticky patch was the brand of football the team were beginning to play. Ajax, it seemed, had their style back. They were beginning to play that same free-flowing attacking stuff which had made the Amsterdam public fall in love with them in the first place, back in the 1970s. This new style would reach its apex in the final of the KNVB Cup in Rotterdam, where Ajax blew away SC Heerenveen 6-2. Indeed, Ajax enjoyed a wonderfully swashbuckling tournament: they'd already thrashed eventual league champions Feyenoord, 5-0 in the semi-final; FC Twente 4-2 in the quarter-final; MVV 3-0 in the round of 16 and VVV-Venlo 7-3 in the third round.

And, more importantly than that, Van Gaal was beginning to blood the rich crop of youngsters from the Ajax academy. "Golden generation" has become a hackneyed phrase these days. A shambling cliché: when even England's non-achieving footballers Gerrard, Lampard, Rooney *et al* can be called a 'Golden Generation' then you know something's wrong. But Van Gaal's Ajax were no fool's gold. Like Sir Alex Ferguson's 'Class of '92' and Barcelona's astounding teams of the mid- to late-noughties, these guys were the real deal.

The sticky patch was exactly that. A patch. An obvious result of the inconsistency of youth.

And what youth!

Ajax's Golden Generation came in three waves. Just when the rest of Dutch football thought they'd survived the latest crashing wave and come to terms with the current, another white-horse tipped wave would smash in, leaving them reeling. And each new wave was more powerful than the last.

This was some production line.

The Ajax side which won the 1992 UEFA Cup had an average age of 25.5. Youngsters, in the form of the aforementioned Dennis Bergkamp (who was 22), Frank de

Boer (22), Michel Kreek (21) and Brian Roy (22) had forced their way into the side. Goalkeeper Edwin van der Sar (21) made the bench.

Dennis Bergkamp is one of the all-time Ajax greats. We know him as a stylish number 10, but he actually started out as a wide midfielder, before it was decided he would affect the game more if he played in a more central role.

Frank de Boer is, at the time of writing, manager of Ajax. He played a total of 418 games in 11 seasons at Ajax and is amongst the most decorated players in the club's history (he is also the most capped outfield player for the Dutch national team). De Boer began his career as a left-back and it is thought Louis van Gaal was instrumental in the player's switch to centre-back which saw him realise his potential and become one of the very best in the world.

Michel Kreek was less of a hit, though he did go on to make 83 appearances for the Amsterdam club before moving to Italy with Padova and then Perugia. Brian Roy also moved to Italy before he could become a hero to match the likes of Bergkamp and de Boer. After a short spell at Foggia, he pitched up at Nottingham Forest, where for a season he formed a decent striking partnership with Stan Collymore. Roy is now back at Ajax, where he works as Reserve Team coach.

Kreek and Roy both left, as many Dutch stars had before them, to the 'bigger' leagues of Italy, or Spain. But the difference here was they weren't missed. For waiting in the wings at Ajax was an ever richer crop of youth team players who were champing at the bit to be afforded first-team opportunities.

Van Gaal had the stones to provide them with exactly that.

In the KNVB Cup final of 1993, the Ajax team-sheet read: Edwin van der Sar, Danny Blind, Marciano Vink, Sonny Silooy, Frank de Boer, Wim Jonk, Dan Petersen, Edgar Davids, Stefan Pettersson, Marc Overmars,

Dennis Bergkamp.

The average age of the side had now dropped a year and a half, to 24, largely thanks to Van Gaal's introduction of the 22-year-olds Edwin van der Sar (who played in goal), and Marciano Vink (a central defender), and the 20-year-olds Dan Petersen, Edgar Davids and Marc Overmars.

Of that famous five, Van der Sar, Davids, and Overmars would go on to become some of the leading lights of European football over the following two decades. Their list of clubs played for reads like the G-14 organisation of Europe's biggest teams: Barcelona, Juventus, Milan, Manchester United, Internazionale, Arsenal.

Van der Sar, a beanpole of a 'keeper who resembled Shaggy from *Scooby-Doo,* was some player. He would go on to win the most caps of any player for the Dutch national side and would also win the Champions League with two different sides (Ajax and Manchester United).

Edgar Davids was similarly noticeable on the playing field, instantly recognizable due to his dread-locked hair and, later in his career, the goggles he wore to protect his eyes because of a glaucoma complaint. Louis van Gaal called him "the Pitbull" and the nickname stuck. He won 74 caps for the Netherlands, and might have won more had he not carried over his "Pitbull" persona into the dressing room (during Euro '96 he was sent home from England for advising the Dutch boss Guus Hiddink to pull his head out of certain players "asses"). Davids moved to Milan in 1997, and then quickly on to Juventus after he failed to establish himself in the team there. At Juventus, he was simply magnificent.

Marc Overmars was also a cartoon of a player. So quick, many dubbed him "Speedy Gonzalez". Though not strictly an Ajax youth team product, Van Gaal was crucial in the player's ongoing development. LVG described Overmars as the ultimate "multi-functional player" and he was ideal for the Dutchman's system. Overmars scored two goals in the KNVB final and would go on to sign for Arsenal in 1997 and then Barcelona in 2000.

By the time Ajax played Milan in the Champions League final of 1995, the average age of the team would be 23.

What made it easier for these young tyros to make the step-up in grade was the fact that at the Ajax Academy every age group played *exactly* the same system (it would be the same at Barcelona's La Masia *cantera* later, and at Bayern Munich too). Watching Ajax (then Barca and Bayern) youth teams play was scary: you could narrow your eyes and those six-, seven-year-olds were set up in exactly the way as the first team. They moved in the same way, passed in the same way, attacked and defended in the same way. The old Jesuit boast, 'Give me the child for his first seven years, and I'll give you the man,' was never more true than for clubs influenced by this 'Dutch way'.

Players were interchangeable. The system was not.

If a first team player got injured, or demanded a transfer, there was always a hungry youngster waiting to fill in. And what was more, that youngster *already knew* how he was expected to fit in. There would be no square pegs in round holes here.

The 'Dutch way' therefore brings about a continuity which would otherwise be lacking in modern football (with Bosman contracts and diminished club loyalty). It is one way of breeding success. The other, of course, is to spend megabucks. Break the bank and bring in star after star. But this is no guarantee of success. You can have all the great players in the world but fitting them into a coherent unit is something else.

And winning with kids who've been at the club since they were nippers *always* brings more joy than simply *buying* titles. Thus 1995 for Ajax was the pinnacle, the ultimate.

But first, 1994. In an interview with Fifa.com, Louis van Gaal claims his fondest memory of a coach is still that "first league title I won with Ajax in 1994. My wife passed away that year. She died in the January and we won the championship in May. It was a very emotional period."

The season got off to a flier. In the traditional curtain-raiser, Ajax beat champions Feyenoord 4-0 to win the Dutch super cup and in terms of performances, *and* goalscoring, they never looked back. They went on to score 86 goals in 34 Eredivisie games: a full 25 more than Feyenoord, who finished in second spot.

Jari Litmanen was the top-scorer with 26 goals. The Finn had joined Ajax in 1992, when he was twenty-one. Young, but a veteran of three Finnish clubs already and the recipient of a Finnish cup final winner's medal. In Amsterdam though, the starlet found competition for places much tougher than back home and in his first season, his appearances were mainly limited to reserve team football.

It was an injury to Dennis Bergkamp which saw Litmanen called up to the first-team for the first time: Ajax's physiotherapist petitioned Van Gaal to utilise the Finn as a replacement for Bergkamp and Van Gaal, never one to shy away from a risky decision, decided to blood the youngster.

Standing in for Bergkamp, even for one game, was no mean feat: the (non-flying) Dutchman was the Eredivisie's top-scorer in each of the seasons between 1991 and 1993 and was also voted Dutch footballer of the Year in both 1992 and 1993. Standing in for Bergkamp *permanently* was something else.

And yet, Litmanen stepped up to the plate.

The tricky issue was laid on the line for Van Gaal – how do you solve a problem like Bergkamp? And more precisely, how do you fill the gaping hole the ice-cool Dutchman left behind when he jumped ship for Internazionale in 1993? By way of an answer, Van Gaal decided that instead of splashing the £7.1 million transfer fee on a top name replacement, the answer should instead come from within the ranks.

And it should be Litmanen.

Litmanen took on Bergkamp's number 10 shirt for the 1993-94 season. He also took on Dennis Bergkamp's mantle as the league's top scorer, and was voted the league's best player. Playing as a deep-lying second striker, the Finn seemed to float above the turf. He had a splendid touch and extraordinary vision. He looked like a world-beater. And whilst he was at Ajax, he was. Later he'd move on, to Barcelona and then Liverpool. But injuries spoiled his every season. Paul Simpson, editor of *FourFourTwo* claimed later that "his (Litmanen's) career has not been worthy of his talent."

Only Ajax fans who got to see him at his pomp would disagree with that.

And Litmanen wasn't the only new entry into the top of the pops which was this all-singing all-dancing Ajax team. Following in the footsteps of Van der Sar, de Boer, Davids, and Overmars came Clarence Seedorf. On 29th November 1992, the right-midfielder became the youngest professional debutant in the history of Ajax when he took the field against Groningen. He would go on to become the first player to win the Champions League with three different clubs (Ajax in 1995; Real Madrid in 1998; and Milan in 2003 and 2007).

Though Seedorf's debut had come in 1992, it took some time for him to cement his place in Louis van Gaal's preferred starting x11 (he didn't make the KNVB Cup final team in 1993 for example). But in 1993-94 he truly came into his own. Diligent and hard-running, but with no little skill, Seedorf was one of the chief playmakers of this great

Ajax side. He was also one of its unsung heroes, as he would be throughout his career. Upon leaving Milan, the Italian club's CEO Adriano Gallini said: "When Milan played well, which happened often, each and every time it occurred Seedorf played an amazing match. He is a world class player."

Seedorf kept Van Gaal's system ticking along. Tick-tick-ticking along, allowing others – Litmanen and Overmars to name just two – to hog the limelight.

But if the season 1993-94 - in which Ajax won their 24th Dutch league title – was good, 1994-95 was scarcely believable. This was the year Van Gaal's young team touched the sky. This was the year they were invincible: unbeaten in both league and Champions League, they went on to secure both trophies. This was the year they scored over 100 goals in Eredivisie (106), outgunning rivals PSV who could call upon the services of *Ronaldo,* by a full 21 goals (the Brazilian Ronaldo had a wonderful season, scoring 30 league goals, but there was no comparison to the *team ethic* at Ajax). This was the year Ajax beat the famous Milan defence including Baresi and Maldini twice in the group stages and then, like Cruyff, they went back and beat them again in the final because they enjoyed it so much.

There were several other new additions to the first-team squad for this season to end all seasons at Ajax. Van Gaal upgraded youngsters Winston Bogarde, Michael Reizeger and Patrick Kluivert to become regular starters. He also brought in the Nigerians Finidi George and Nwankwo Kanu, the latter whom he'd witnessed starring in the Under-17 World Championships for his national side. George would go on to start in the Champions League final in Vienna. Kanu would come on off the bench.

Of Patrick Kluivert, great things were expected. Kluivert's own biography on his website it states: "During his younger years, he played several different positions, even as a defender. He was strong in technique, football intelligence, and speed." Tall, and with an imposing physique, he possessed perhaps the best heading ability in Dutch football. This, allied with a silky touch when the ball was on the ground, and an ability to turn in enclosed spaces led to comparisons between him and PSV's young Brazilian star Ronaldo.

Kluivert would go on to score the winner in the Champions League final in Vienna, in the 85th minute. Critics might say it was the high water-mark of his career. They might say he never lived up to his burgeoning promise. Others might point to his goalscoring prowess for the Dutch national side as evidence that he *did:* until Robin van Persie overtook him in 2014, he was the Netherlands all-time leading goalscorer.

Winston Bogarde *definitely* did not live up to his early promise. He is best remembered in England for sitting out nearly four seasons at Chelsea – during which he played only 9 matches – as he became embroiled in a contract dispute with the *nouveau riche* club. But at Ajax, in his youth, he was some player: immensely powerful and a strong runner, he was, for a spell, the embodiment of a new breed of mobile central defender.

And it is Bogarde who can help us understand just what it was Van Gaal was doing behind the scenes which forged this Ajax team into one of the strongest units in world football over the past thirty years. "Van Gaal is," he says, "one of the best coaches, he likes to play football. And he enjoys coaching players, getting the best from players. He likes to play with young players, he likes to play with young talent and developing it."

And it is all about the team; the system. "He is not scared of the big decision. If for a certain match he has to bring in one player and leave out another player, he is able to take the big decisions when needed. He plans a lot and you will know exactly as a player what you should do during a game and your opponent, how he plays. In his mind he likes to play 4-3-3 but he can also play in other formations, he can adapt. He will look at the players that he has and then he will adapt to that. But whatever he has it will always be an attacking play."

In an interview with the *Manchester Evening News,* Maarten Meijer, who studied Van Gaal's career for his book: *Louis van Gaal – De Biografie,* talked in more depth about the particulars of Van Gaal's methods. "Van Gaal's insistence is," he says, "on fluid, interchangeable football in which players are comfortable operating in a number of positions."

At Ajax "he used a simple formula known as TIPS to assess his players. They would be evaluated on four basic criteria – technique, insight, personality and speed."

In essence "what Van Gaal was looking for was, as he put it, 'multi-functional players.' Players who could play with both legs, had both defensive and offensive capabilities, were physically strong, were quick starters, had the necessary tactical acumen to function smoothly in rotation football, and, above all, put their skills in service of the team effort. He found them in people like Michael Reiziger, Ronald de Boer, Winston Bogarde, and Edgar Davids."

"I took out players of the old mould and even in the defence replaced them with others who could take initiative. Every single Ajax player is creative," explains Van Gaal.

Creative, but disciplined. Van Gaal staunchly believes that the first principle is discipline. "First of all, you have to do your job, be on time, and be polite. We respect each other, we trust each other, and we are honest to each other. Within such a framework, you can fully develop your identity and creativity. Discipline is the basis for creativity. Players like Kanu, Davids, and Kluivert understood that."

Of course, not everyone likes such discipline. When quizzed by Sports Illustrated about his memories of

Van Gaal – their paths crossed briefly when Van Gaal returned to Ajax as technical director in 2004 – Zlatan Ibrahimovic talked of LVG in militaristic terms: "He's the old tradition. The old general. He's the boss and everybody else can, how do you say—they're soldiers. I mean, you have to have a little bit of feeling in the whole thing. Many big stars have problems with him because of the way he is. I understand if you're 15 to 20 years old, you put the discipline there. Which is normal, because I was in Holland, I was in that school where he built up Ajax. And I understand it, but when you come to a team with 22 big stars, that's what you treat them like? Like small boys?"

"We were in a dining room and sitting there until he says, 'Ok, go ahead, now you can eat.' Then suddenly we could eat. So we could not eat before he says. And he was acting –we had a situation where he was the Director in Ajax and he was, yeah, he was the boss then. No problem. You're the boss. And he was saying to me ... We had a situation with teammate Rafael van der Vaart."

"Van der Vaart got injured and he was blaming me that I did it on purpose. I said to him I didn't do it on purpose. And so it went on, and at the end I said I will not play if Van der Vaart is to play because my own captain is attacking me and blaming me for injuring him. Instead of protecting your team as a captain outside the team and also inside the team, he is doing totally the opposite. He is trying now to attack me and get everybody against me. And we had a meeting with Van Gaal and he says, 'Listen. I'm the boss. If I tell you to play, you play.' And I was like, 'You're the boss but if I tell you I will not play as long as Van der Vaart is playing, I'm not playing. If you can't understand nothing just sit and wait and you will see me that I will not play.'"

Zlatan might not have wanted to be treated like a "small boy", but he certainly sounded like one with all of his *I was like, and then he was like schtick.*

But in the main, the Ajax players of 1995 were *on board*. They bought in to Van Gaal and his philosophy, his blueprint. And they worked like soldiers in order to ensure his instructions were carried out to the letter.

And it paid off.

And it inspired the rest of the world.

In Patrick Barclay's *Football – Bloody Hell*, a biography of Sir Alex Ferguson, he talks of how Van Gaal's Ajax inspired Ferguson to blood *the kids* for Manchester United: "Fabio Capello's Milan had won the previous year's final, beating Barcelona 4-0 with a performance hailed as one of the greatest ever given by a club side. But they could not overcome this young Ajax team of Louis van Gaal's.

"In goal was Edwin van der Sar (later to win the Champions League with United too). He was twenty-four. Among those in front of him were Michael Reizeger, Edgar Davids, and Marc Overmars (all twenty-two) and Clarence Seedorf (nineteen). By the end of the final there were significant performances as substitutes from eighteen-year-olds Kanu and Patrick Kluivert, who scored the only goal against a defence featuring Paolo Maldini. Vienna hailed the new champions of Europe and never again, you might have though, would we hear the words: 'You win nothing with kids.'

Yet that was what Alan Hansen said on the very first day of the next season."

On the first day of the 1995-96 season in England United lost 3-1 at Aston Villa with their (apparently mis-firing) young guns. Later Scholes, Beckham, the Nevilles, Butt and Giggs would fire United to the league and cup double, leaving Hansen's face dripping with egg.

On the first day of the 1995-96 season in the Netherlands, Louis van Gaal and his Ajax squad could have been forgiven for thinking they couldn't do any better than the previous year, let alone better it. And yet, they so nearly did. For 1995 still had trophies in it for Ajax: first a 5-1 aggregate win against UEFA Cup winners Real Zaragoza in the UEFA Super Cup; then victory over Brazil's Gremio in the Toyota Cup (Intercontinental Cup) which brought about Van Gaal's famous barbaric yawp: "We are the best! And not just of Amsterdam. But also of Rotterdam. And Eindhoven. And Europe… And now we are the best of the…. *world*."

In the end, Ajax came *so close* to emulating their feats of the previous season that they could almost taste the polish on the Champions League trophy. Defeat to Juventus on penalties in the final saw to that dream, but throughout the tournament the level of football played by the Amsterdam club was time and again on a different plain to the opposition. They beat Real Madrid home and away in the group stages (eliciting Valdano's awestruck response regarding footballing utopia), devastated Dortmund in the quarter-finals, and then palmed off Panathinaikos in the semi-final. *En route* to Rome, where they'd face Juventus at the Stadio Olimpico, Ajax had conceded just one goal in ten matches, and they'd exit the tournament unbeaten in normal time (having remained unbeaten in 1994-95 also). Ultimately though, Davids and Silooy were denied from the penalty spot and a Juventus team featuring the stellar talents of Alessandro del Piero, Paulo Sousa, Didier Deschamps, Antonio Conte and Gianluca Vialli were victorious.

By way of consolation, Ajax retained the Eredivisie title for the third consecutive year, finishing six points ahead of PSV.

Louis van Gaal's Ajax team had worked miracles. His garlanded players went on to dominate the national team for years to come. Van Gaal himself was awarded a knighthood (in the Order of Orange-Nassau). They hadn't reached their peak. But once the cracks began to appear in Van Gaal's all-important team, they would never recover.

Bigger clubs from bigger leagues began to dangle big carrots in the paths of some of Ajax's biggest stars, and, unable to resist the temptation, they left. And once one left, they all did. In 1996, Seedorf left for Sampdoria; Davids and Reizeger for Milan; and Kanu for Inter. In 1997, Milan poached both Kluivert and Bogarde, and Overmars sped to Arsenal. Van der Sar and Frank de Boer would stay longer – until 1999 – but both would succumb eventually.

And by then, the boss, the general had gone. LVG departed in 1997 after seeing out his contract. For him it was full speed ahead Barcelona. He'd been head-hunted as a replacement for Bobby Robson (whilst Robson was still in the job). In him, Barcelona saw the ideal candidate to lay down a footballing blueprint. A Dutch footballing blueprint.

They couldn't have Cruyff, but they could have the next best thing.

II – WELCOME TO "VIETNAM"

BARCELONA (1997-2000)

Louis van Gaal and Barcelona should have been a match made in heaven. It wasn't. And the Dutchman was left needing every inch of his famously thick skin in order to protect him from the constant slings and arrows of abuse which were fired in his direction by the Barcelona board, by its fans, by the media, and, most damagingly, by his own players.

Zlatan Ibrahimovic described Van Gaal as "a general", and at Barcelona he required all of his martinet persona in order to protect himself. For behind the scenes at the Catalan giants was a mess of political intrigue, back-biting, back-*stabbing*, and sometimes, outright guerilla warfare. He jetted in to replace Bobby Robson (who'd had no little success at Barca) and, as the journalist Enric Baneres put it: "if Bobby Robson had been sitting on a hornet's nest, his successor touched down in Vietnam."

They say that if you take on a lover who is already

attached, and if that lover leaves their previous *beau* for you, that you're only preparing yourself for them doing exactly the same to you farther down the line, and that's exactly how it was for LVG and Barcelona. Only with added special effects. Even now, if Van Gaal gets a slight twitch in the corner of his eye, you wonder if, like the scarred Vietnam vet he can hear the choppers coming, if he's recalling the war-like atmosphere at Barcelona, if he's bristling for another fight.

Barcelona was his *Apocalypse Now,* and Van Gaal was occasionally to play its Colonel Kurtz, driven half-mad by those twin needles poking his brain: power and paranoia. Giovanni, a Brazilian who worked under Van Gaal at Barca went one step further, plucking another demonic figure out of the air and tarring Louis with his brush: "Van Gaal is the Hitler of the Brazilian players, is arrogant, proud and has a problem. He has no idea of football. His type is sick, he's crazy."

But into this heart of darkness Van Gaal plunged, and plunged, and plunged again. Because he knew that in Barcelona was a club full of sweetness and light, just crying to be set free. Because he knew that his blueprint *would work there*. Because he was arrogant. Because he was Dutch, and he played the Dutch way.

Which was also the Barcelona way.

As Sid Lowe would have it: "Louis van Gaal touched down in Catalonia on 29 June 1997, the day Robson was standing on the balcony with his players, trophy in hand. 'I felt like Gary Cooper in *High Noon,'* the Englishman told Jeff King. 'Sometimes I ask myself "why has everyone got it in for me?" If I was coach of a team in England challenging for three trophies I'd be a bloody hero.'" But something was missing. Or perhaps *someone* was missing. Robson's style was not their style, not Cruyff's way. Van Gaal's, on the other hand, was."

"Van Gaal represented a return to Barcelona's

Dutch connection, a chance to re-encounter and re-establish an identity inspired by Total Football."

Cruyff, Van Gaal's old nemesis, was a legend at Barcelona, both as a player and manager. In 1973, Barcelona procured his services (from Ajax) for a then world record transfer fee of around £1.4 million. He helped Barca win their first title since 1960, helped the *blaugrana* defeat arch-rivals Real Madrid 5-0 in their own back yard, named his own son *Jordi*, after the patron saint of Catalonia. Above all else he helped define the 'Barcelona way' which looked a lot like the Dutch way, which looked a lot like the Ajax way. He exported Total Football, and the Catalan crowds loved it.

Wikipedia defines Total Football as: "a system where a player who moves out of his position is replaced by another from his team, thus allowing the team to retain their intended organizational structure. In this fluid system, no footballer is fixed in their intended outfield role; anyone can be successively an attacker, a midfielder and a defender. The style was honed by Ajax coach Rinus Michels, with Cruyff the on-field 'conductor'."

As manager, Cruyff again made the small step/ giant leap between Ajax and Barcelona. He brought Total Football back (thanks in no small part to his on-field conductor Pep Guardiola) and he helped secure Barca's first ever European Cup (in 1992, at Wembley).

Van Gaal told Lowe: "The reason they (Barca) wanted me in 1997 was that they identified with the Ajax style. We'd just been World champions and Nunez (the Barca president) liked our ideas. He wanted me to educate the kids, to be involved in youth development, bringing passing, attacking football back... For the Barcelona directors, it was logical to turn to me. I was selected because of the style and because that Ajax team had an average age of nineteen or twenty."

Sir Alex Ferguson would agree. In his

autobiography he describes meeting with LVG in the aftermath of Manchester United's disappointing defeat to Barcelona in the Champions League final in Rome in 2009: "Later I discussed Barcelona's evolution with Louis van Gaal, their former Dutch coach. The basis of their philosophy was laid down by Johan Cruyff, a terrific coach who conceived their ideas about width and ball-circulation, always with an extra man in midfield. After Bobby Robson, they went back to the Dutch way, with Van Gaal and Frank Rijkaard."

In his first spell as Barcelona manager, Van Gaal led the team to two *La Liga* championships (1997-98; 1998-99) and a Copa del Rey. His first season in charge produced a league and cup double. That year they recorded home and away *La Liga* victories over Real Madrid. They had an exciting, star-studded squad, featuring the respective talents of Rivaldo, Hristo Stoichkov, Luis Figo, Sonny Anderson, Luis Enrique, and Giovanni. In his second season in charge, Barcelona walked the league by 11 points.

And yet, as Sid Lowe notes: "His (Van Gaal's) spell is not regarded with particular fondness; rather, it is often forgotten... Critics had accused Robson of being too soft; now they accused Van Gaal of being too hard."

"Discipline," he notes, "was intense and on his terms... it could feel authoritarian."

Suicidally, Van Gaal clashed with players, particularly senior ones such as Stoichkov and Rivaldo. This he could do at Ajax, where his place at the head of the pecking order was well-established, but at Barcelona? No.

"Rivaldo in particular," writes Lowe, "was a problem and he was also Barcelona's best player (and top scorer). His relationship with Van Gaal would become increasingly fraught. Increasingly public, too. 'He doesn't want to think for the team, he wants to think for himself,' Van Gaal says. 'For the first two years he was not a big problem. I invested a lot of time in him, but he thinks he is bigger than the coach.'"

Jonathan Liew, writing for *The Telegraph* adds: "At Barcelona in 1999, he (LVG) insisted on playing Rivaldo on the left. Naturally, Rivaldo wanted to play in the centre. Rivaldo was temporarily dropped, but despite losing the battle he won the war: Van Gaal was sacked at the end of the season. Two years later, Van Gaal was back. Within three weeks, and before a ball had even been kicked, Rivaldo saw what was coming, and left. 'Van Gaal is the main cause of my departure,' he said. 'I don't like Van Gaal, and I am sure that he doesn't like me, either.'"

Even before 1999 though, the media knives were being sharpened for the Dutchman. Sid Lowe notes: "Van Gaal's tough exterior did not sit well with the media, who are often protective of the players who confide in journalists... (like Rivaldo) 'The media put the players on a pedestal,' Van Gaal says now. 'They adore the players far too much and most players cannot handle that because it's another world; everything is too easy for them.'"

Still, all would have been well had things been progressing on the playing field. And, crucially, they were not. Not on the biggest stage of them all. And whilst one Dutchman – Cruyff – had delivered Barcelona's first European Cup, another – Van Gaal – when tasked with delivering a second, was struggling to even get them out of the *group stages*. LVG's Barcelona flopped in the Champions League. First, in 1997-98, when – ludicrously – they finished bottom of a group containing Dinamo Kiev, LVG's old rivals PSV Eindhoven, and Newcastle United.

Barcelona won only one match in the group, and were famously defeated by Newcastle United (3-2) at St. James' thanks to a fabulous 22-minute Faustino Asprilla hat-trick.

Then in 1998-99, when Barcelona *really* wanted to win it – the final was due to be played at their home stadium, Camp Nou – they yet again couldn't make it out of the group. Admittedly *this* group was more difficult: they faced two former European Cup winners in Manchester United and Bayern Munich. But still. They came up short. (Though the home and away ties against United will both live long in the memory. Both games finished as 3-3 draws and both would surely make the top ten in any 'greatest Champions League games ever' lists.)

In 1999-2000, Barcelona fared better. They walked through a group containing Fiorentina, Arsenal and Swedes AIK unbeaten, scoring nineteen goals in 6 games. The most notable game in the group was Barcelona's 4-2 hammering of Arsenal at Wembley (where Arsenal had elected to play their Champions League ties that year due to Highbury's low capacity).

In his book, *The Professor: Arsene Wenger,* Myles Palmer says: "Tactically, the game was the most interesting contest Wenger ever lost in England. It looked as if Louis van Gaal had learned more from the Nou Camp encounter (where it finished 1-1, earlier in the group) than Wenger had, so Barca had a superior game plan and would probably have won without the penalty gift (Tony Adams was very unlucky to concede an early penalty when Cocu dived)."

He continues: "The way Barcelona played was cool, shrewd and relaxed. They did not support their attacks, did not use overlappers, did not flood the box, and only won one corner against Arsenal's thirteen. Their style was mathematical, geometrical and economical. Very little energy was wasted, very few passes were wasted, and they seemed to have thirteen players to smother every Arsenal move. There was an element of Muhammad Ali rope-a-dope about the night – Arsenal wore themselves out and never saw the punches coming. The pitch seemed to be full of spaces that the Barcelona players decided not to run into because they wanted to save them for later. The game would make for a superb instructional video."

As Louis van Gaal says: "Running is for animals.

You need a brain and a ball for football."

Yet in that year's Champions League competition a whole lot of running would be required, animals or not. The laborious nature of the tournament at this time meant that for the first time in the competition's history teams would have to compete in not *one* group stage, but *two*. Which meant teams would have to negotiate a full twelve group stage matches before they even had a sniff of knockout football.

It was too much. The second group stage was scrapped for the 2003-04 season, in favour of a 16-team knockout round. It will not be missed.

Still, a second group stage seemed to suit Van Gaal's Barcelona in 1999-2000. This time they were drawn in a pot containing Porto, Sparta Prague and Hertha Berlin. Again they breezed it. Again they were unbeaten. Again they scored a lot of goals (17).

In the quarter-finals, they met Chelsea, and, after losing the first leg 3-1 at Stamford Bridge (Zola, and Flo at the double had the Londoners 3-0 up on 38 minutes before Figo pulled one back in the second half), they forged a miraculous comeback at Camp Nou to win 6-4 on aggregate (5-1 on the night).

That meant there were three Spanish clubs in the semi-final of the competition. It also meant that all Barcelona had to do was beat Valencia over two legs and they'd set up the biggest *El Classico* in history. Real Madrid did their part, seeing off Bayern Munich, but Louis van Gaal's Barcelona couldn't do *their* bit. Valencia beat Barcelona 4-1 at Mestalla, and, despite *threatening* a comeback of Chelsea magnitude, it never quite happened. And it was their dreaded rivals Real Madrid who won the famous trophy instead, at Stade de France, in Paris, where they ran out 3-0 winners on 24th May.

By that time, Louis van Gaal had already resigned (on 20th May).

This time there was no consolation of a league title. Deportivo la Coruna had won *La Liga*. And although Barcelona had yet again finished well clear of Real Madrid (that traditional barometer of their form) the fact Madrid had won *yet another* Champions League trophy and Barcelona had only one to their name was becoming an embarrassment.

There we have it. The Louis van Gaal blueprint had failed.

The Dutch way had failed.

And, when it came to the crunch, Van Gaal had failed to be Johan Cruyff.

Again, Sid Lowe: "Barcelona had sought to embrace the Dutch-Barca model but some did not see a reincarnation of the Dream Team in the side that won the league in 1988, still less the reincarnation of Johan Cruyff in Louis van Gaal. He was, says one former player, *theoretically* a continuation of Cruyff's methods; another adds that he was, in fact, a better coach and certainly a more dedicated one, but without the charisma or stardust."

And yet, these days Van Gaal's reign at Barcelona is undergoing a certain degree of revisionism. This is because of the blueprint he introduced at Barcelona's famous *cantera*, La Masia.

Indeed, Lowe notes that it was Van Gaal who re-established the "blueprint for youth development at La Masia" and "gave debuts to Xavi Hernandez, Carles Puyol and Gabri, and later, when he returned for a brief second spell in charge in 2002, to Victor Valdes and Andres Iniesta, as well as Pepe Reina and Thiago Motta."

These are the guys who went on to sweep all before them as one of the most successful club sides ever to play the game, winning La Liga 6 times between 2005 and 2013 and the Champions League 3 times in the same spell. They were also Fifa Club World Cup winners twice, in 2009 and 2011. More: the *blaugrana* provided the overwhelming majority of the players who comprised Spain's all-conquering teams which won *every* major international tournament between 2008 and 2014 (before they were dumped out of the World Cup in Brazil at the group stages, thrashed by hitherto unfancied Van Gaal's Netherlands team). In winning UEFA 2012, Wikipedia declared: "Spain became the first national side ever to win three consecutive tournaments of either the applicable continental championship or the World Cup."

Just like Van Gaal's Ajax team had – via the Ajax academy - fed the Dutch national side, so Barcelona's La Masia complex had fed the Spanish national team.

Van Gaal being the common denominator.

Xavi declares: "People see him as arrogant and aloof but he's really not."

" 'Victor, Xavi, Puyi, me... our generation is very grateful to him," Iniesta says.

And Van Gaal returns the favour: he names Iniesta as his 'ideal' player. "He sees the game so well, he can play in different positions," Van Gaal says. "Xavi has that too but Xavi is more static. Iniesta has that sparkle in his game. Xavi is more like I was. Technically perfect. Tactically strong, but too slow. Like myself. Iniesta is the player I wanted to be, but wasn't."

It wasn't all sweetness and light at La Masia. Not by any means. He wouldn't be Van Gaal if he didn't ruffle a few feathers. There's an amusing aside regarding Van Gaal's introduction to a 14-year-old Gerard Pique, for instance. Pique is *Mr. Barcelona*. A *culé* (hardcore fan) and official member since birth, he had *blaugrana* blood: his grandfather was a director at the club. Pique's grandfather brought Pique to meet Van Gaal, expecting the old arm-round-the-shoulder treatment, expecting at the very least a handshake, or a friendly comment. But instead, Van Gaal went *Colonel Kurtz*. Shoulder-barged the young Pique to the floor. Then stood over him in the manner of Roy Keane standing over

Alf-Inge Haaland, bellowing: "You're too weak to be a Barca defender!"

And this in front of one of the club's most distinguished directors.

Even Xavi (one of the few who denied Van Gaal had an arrogant streak) felt the wrath of the Dutchman on occasion. Alexandra Jonson, a freelance journalist working in Barcelona, appraised me on the (now infamous even in England) Pique anecdote and told me this story about Van Gaal and Xavi:

"The day after Barcelona had played Real Betis in a *La Liga* clash, LVG called Xavi into his office. He took the daily edition of the Spanish newspaper *Sport*, threw it on the floor and screamed at the (then) youngster: "Look what they have written in the paper".

Xavi was taken aback.

In the game against Betis they had played three in midfield. Xavi had been the central midfielder, flanked by Figo and Luis Enrique on the wings. Xavi had been swamped. After the game, a journalist remarked to the young Xavi that he had looked lonely in the middle. Xavi's response: "What do you ask from me, when they came on a counterattack I stood there in the middle against three players."

Sport's headline the next day was, of course: "Figo and Xavi question the tactical system." (They had also asked Figo the same question and he had fallen into the trap just like Xavi.)

Van Gaal pointed on the floor at the newspaper, red with fury and demanded of Xavi :"What is this? What does this look like?".

A cowering Xavi answered: "But mister (Spanish term for manager) I haven't said anything".

However Van Gaal didn't believe him "You haven't said anything?" he screamed. "Get out!"

Instead of an arm round the shoulder of the young

man, it was a furious dressing-down; all of which Figo could hear from outside the door. And even Figo, the experienced, cocksure Figo, quivered. Because after Xavi it would be him. Neither had heard such screams, such fury, as they had from their coach that day.

Unlike a coach like Guardiola, Van Gaal didn't become friends with the players. It didn't matter if it was a youngster like Xavi or the team's biggest star like Figo, no one dared to question Van Gaal. And if they did, there was hell to pay."

But in the most part, Van Gaal is very well remembered by the key members of that Barcelona team.

By young coaches learning their trade who gorged themselves on the LVG Barca style too. A surprising example of this is the Liverpool manager Brendan Rodgers, who, in a 2012 interview with *The Blizzard* (when he was still Swansea supremo) claimed: "I've been a follower of their (Barcelona's) model for many, many years. I was so enthused by it. Louis Van Gaal ... I just loved their way of playing."

And now, loved by Barcelona fans too.

Alexandra Jonson wrote for totalBarca.com on all things Barcelona (particularly the *club identity,* so important for the *blaugrana* faithful) and now writes for InsideSpanishFootball.com, as well as for Sweden's biggest football site fotbollskanalen.se. But by far her biggest qualification is the fact she is a massive Barca fan (she's Swedish, and when Barcelona signed Henrik Larsson that was *it).*

In 2012, she posted an article on totalBarca.com - *The Louis van Gaal dream fulfilled* – which celebrated an achievement which Barcelona fans are immensely proud of. Early in his Barcelona career, Van Gaal announced that "his dream was to win the European Cup with a team of Catalans." At the time it seemed a pipedream, or, to the more sinisterly-minded *culé* a fob-off, an excuse to give himself more time in the job. And though Barcelona didn't win the European Cup with eleven Catalans, the impossible dream *was realised* almost exactly a decade after Van Gaal had made that announcement, on Sunday 25th November 2012. For, in a 4-0 win over Levante, FC Barcelona featured 11 homegrown players for the first time in the modern era.

Liverpool fans used to sing: "We all dream of a team of Carraghers". Not because he was the best player they had, but because he was a born and bred Liverpudlian.

When Glasgow Celtic won the European Cup in 1967, every member of their 'Lisbon Lions' team had been born within a 30-mile radius of Celtic Park.

Barcelona fans – and Louis van Gaal - dreamed of an all Catalan/ all La Masia team, and this had finally been achieved.

Alexandra writes: "Johan Cruyff and Josep Guardiola might be the coach names we mostly symbolize with La Masia. While a coach like Louis van Gaal can easily lead one's thoughts to a Dutch influenced Barça that failed to impress. But the fact is that Louis van Gaal has more to do with the success of La Masia than many may believe. The Dutchman coached the club on two occasions between 1997-2000 and during the 2002-03 season.

"Van Gaal didn't coach in the same way as we have been used to as of late with Rijkaard, Guardiola and Vilanova," she explains. "No, Van Gaal was tough and he would almost intentionally make his players afraid of him. But during his time as coach at Barça, he would also show his trust in the youth players, starting what now is an obvious thing at FC Barcelona in promoting players from the B-team to the first team. Even though it wasn't as close to as many B-team players we see play with the first team today, it was the start of a strategic trend that coaches afterwards would follow."

"What's interesting to keep in mind is that when Louis van Gaal took the risk of putting youth players onto the first team, FC Barcelona was in a horrible position. Barça was losing an embarrassing amount of league matches and had been knocked out of Champions League competition. It wasn't much better for the B-team who were near the bottom of their division. Despite the chaos, Van Gaal kept on insisting to take the younger players up and play them in the first team. Something that today makes it possible for him to feel a part of the present day success. Van Gaal only won two league titles and one Copa del Rey during his four seasons at the club, but he did set one of the standards for what would come to be the best team in the history of FCB when he gave Xavi, Puyol, Valdés and Iniesta their first team debuts. (He also gave Motta, Gabri and Pepe Reina, among others, their debut)."

"Tito Vilanova, a La Masia man himself, put out a starting 11 consisting of 10 players from La Masia with only Dani Alvés coming from the outside. Just that would have been unthinkable during Van Gaal's days at the club, but has become something rather normal during the last season with Guardiola. However, when Alvés hit an injury, Tito was forced to a substitution and took the best man for the position, Martin Montoya. As the youngster entered the pitch, history was written and for the first time in history FC Barcelona featured 11 'homegrown' players. Of these players, four got their debut under Louis van Gaal (Victor Valdés, Carles Puyol, Xavi Hérnandez, Andrés Iniesta), four under Josep Guardiola (Gerard Piqué, Martin Montoya, Cesc Fábregas, Sergio Busquets), two under Frank Rijkaard (Lionel Messi, Pedro Rodriguez), and Jordi Alba got his this season under Tito Vilanova."

Alexandra adds: "The fact that Barça featured 11 players who all got parts of their football education at the club was incredible but what was even more fascinating was that Tito didn't play 11 homegrown players *because* they were all homegrown but because they were his best option to play. If Barça wanted to play a starting eleven with only

La Masia players because the sake of it being only La Masia players they could have done it a long time ago. The first team have, for quite a while now, had homegrown players in the first team for every position. But both Guardiola and Tito are professional and regardless of the opponent decide to play the 11 they think is the best for the team. Last Sunday, that 11 happened to contain players that grew up at the club. What many believe being the best club team in the world, maybe the best in history, the team's best 11 last Sunday contained 11 players from its own youth academy. Of them, eight not only grew up in the club, but are Catalan-born in or near the city of Barcelona. That is the most incredible thing with this whole scenario. To add to that, during the 65 minutes Tito played with this group of 11, fans got to see four goals and an amazing show of football."

It is interesting to note that the 2014 incarnation of FC Barcelona are no longer top of the tree. Last season Barcelona did not win anything. And instead of cooking up ready-made replacements at La Masia, now for the first time in a decade Barcelona are looking elsewhere for new players. They splashed the cash on the Brazilian, Neymar, in a highly controversial transfer before the start of the 2013-14 season, and, despite his heroics in the Confederations Cup and the World Cup in Brazil, that signing has not quite paid off.

And now, some of that La Masia team are beginning to leave. Fabregas, once as big a hope as Messi – he'd become Spain's youngest player for 70 years when he made his debut for the national team - was sold all over again, once more to a London club. Earlier in his career, he'd moved to Arsenal. Now he'd signed for Chelsea.

Xavi is rumoured to be leaving for a big payday in the Middle East.

Puyol has retired from football.

I wondered how much idealism Barcelona fans

would have sacrificed in order to see a victorious side again?

I caught up with Alexandra during the compilation of this book and quizzed her further about this. She told me: "In Barcelona they always lost: both civil wars and league titles. They were Spain's punching-bag. They were always in the shadow of the team from the capital. Desperate to turn around this state of affairs the club tried to figure out how they could become better than Madrid. The answer was art."

"The Barcelona supporters are a discerning lot," said Alexandra. "They appreciate football as an art form. And Barcelona art - with Dali and Gaudi – had always been better than Madrid's equivalents. And so an ethos was born: if the *blaugrana* couldn't win, at least they could always say their games were both more beautiful and more entertaining to watch than those at the Bernabeu. To go to Camp Nou became like going to the theatre to watch a subtle piece of performance art which stated – quite clearly – *this is what we are, and what you are not*. A title won't be accepted nor celebrated in the same way if it's not won in the right way: if the team has not entertained, the supporters become critics: they wave their white handkerchiefs and whistle."

"Playing with homegrown-players and playing the 'Barca way' is more important for the Barça supporters than winning," said Alexandra. "And in this regard the Van Gaal period is a great example."

The club won titles under the Dutchman – in his first spell as boss – and yet the Iron Tulip's reign is still a divisive topic amongst *culé*. Hell, even a brief scan of the comments section of Alexandra's piece provides ample evidence of that. Although most write about how delighted they are with Barcelona's achievement, and are gushing in their praise for LVG, one comment states: "I understand that despite his foresight, Van Gaal's reign at Barcelona is regarded as the Dark Ages and one of the worst periods in the club history."

Alexandra agreed. To a point. "I think one of the biggest reasons to why many regarded Van Gaal's time at Barcelona as the 'Dark Ages' was because the club came from a very successful time during the Dream Team days and under Van Gaal they didn't win as much, or as often, as they had done previously. The football wasn't as entertaining either. What's more, the team was very Dutch-influenced. In Barcelona it's very important for the supporters that they can identify themselves as much as possible with the team, and I guess the Dutch influence didn't help with that."

"People always say that football and politics shouldn't mix, but in Spain and especially in Barcelona it's impossible to come away from that," said Alexandra. "Here politics and football has *and always will* mix. And when Barcelona no longer was a team of Catalans – as Van Gaal had promised - but of Dutch 'mercenaries', it didn't sit well with the Catalans. Van Gaal tried to take the politics out of it and that also made him somehow a villain. Even the Catalan president at the time Jordi Pujol contacted him but Van Gaal didn't understand why the fans were so angry at him for not playing enough Catalans. And that made people in Barcelona think he didn't understand Barcelona well enough he didn't understand their battle nor what Catalonia meant for them."

Van Gaal's personality did not help matters. "I think people had a hard time liking him because of his quite harsh personality," said Alexandra. "In Spain in general and in Catalonia in particular people are extremely passionate but also quite sensitive. They care a lot for their club and they want their coaches and players to do the same: to show their affection openly. All Catalans will forever remember Van Gaal's very strange way of barking "Barca Barca" from the balcony at Plaza de Jaume (where Barça used to celebrate their titles). Instead of roar of joy he barked it like he was some kind of mad-dog military general. Later, when he was asked about his strange way of barking the clubs nickname like it was *an order*, Van Gaal didn't even understand the question."

"He was very tough and rough in his way of being and that never really won over the Catalans nor the Barcelona supporters," Alexandra added.

Leaving aside the negative stuff, Alexandra and I talked a great deal about our (almost maternal/ paternal) pride when homegrown dreams come true. Alexandra's pride in Barca's *La Masia* x11 matched my own when Manchester United had its own rich crop of youngsters – the class of '92 which contained Beckham, Giggs, Neville (x2) and Butt – which swept all before it domestically before winning the Champions League (at Camp Nou). We discussed exactly what it is about (quality) homegrown teams (or the spine of the team being made up by homegrown players) which makes them so wonderful.

Alexandra said: "I think the thing that makes a homegrown team so beautiful is that you have players in the team who love the club more than anything else. Especially in today's world of football where most players go where they get paid most handsomely, homegrown players often keep the love for the game and their club higher than other players: they give more on the pitch and they bleed the colors on their shirt. I don't think a player like Carles Puyol would have made it as one of the best defenders in the world if he didn't play for his dream club, the club he cried for when they lost when he was a kid. Puyol would offer his life on the pitch in a way I think is impossible for a player to do for a club they haven't grown up loving."

And the Barcelona youth system is a gift which will keep on giving, at least as far as Alexandra is concerned. "I watch the Barcelona B team quite regularly at the MiniEstadi and also try to follow the other youth teams at the club as well as I can, and for sure there are huge talents there," she admitted. "If the club do things right there is no doubt that they will keep on producing top-class players. Last season the B-team ended third in the Spanish second division (which would have meant if they weren't a B-team that they'd play in the play-offs for *La Liga*). They did that without their two best players: Deulofeu and Rafinha having left on loan to Everton and Celta respectively before the season began. And they did that with a team of players who were on average over 10 years younger than their opponents. In one game they even had a player *20 years younger* than one of the opponents. For me, 19-year old Sergi Samper - who is the Sergio Busquets of the B-team - is the best player I have ever seen at that age: he already reads the game better than most top-players."

Investing in a blueprint which would run right through the club was a legitimate way of challenging the hegemony of Real Madrid. "When Barcelona started to create their own players in a way Real Madrid never had done, and then *won* with those players, it became a bigger victory for the club," said Alexandra. "Barcelona president Joan Laporta loved to tell the media that while 'Real Madrid buy Ballon d'Or winners', Barcelona 'create them'."

In this book, I'm exploring Louis van Gaal as a man, but I am also trying to give Manchester United fans new hope after a dismal 2013-14 season. Van Gaal's project will be a long-term one at United, but I think it is important to realise he has a vision, a blueprint, and this is what I really want to write about, exploring the Dutchman's methods across the continent, from the Ajax academy to La Masia in Barcelona; and from the giants of 'FC Hollywood' Bayern Munich to minnows AZ Alkmaar. Throughout his career Louis van Gaal's 'blueprint' has allowed young players to come to the fore, and it has allowed older players to "discover surprising and previously hidden gifts". It is now hoped that Van Gaal will transfer this to Carrington.

Bringing through young players and playing quick, attacking football is built into the DNA of Manchester

United, going right back to the Busby Babes, who died so tragically in a plane crash in 1958 in Munich. Therefore, to me at least, LVG *feels right* as the new boss. Certainly he feels righter than David Moyes did.

Witnessing *that* youth team featuring Fabregas, Pique and *Messi* must have been wonderful. I asked Alexandra: was it *known* they were going to be so good? At United, I went to see Beckham, Giggs *et al* when they were 16/17 in the FA Youth Cup, and with some of them you could just tell they would be amazing. Giggs was willo' the wisp: so slight, so fragile, but so quick, so skilful too. Sir Alex Ferguson described him like so: "I remember the first time I saw him. He was 13 and just floated over the ground like a cocker spaniel *chasing* a piece of silver paper in the wind."

Manchester United have their 'Class of '92', which swept all before it. Barcelona's own even more stellar version was the 'generation of '87' (Barcelona youth sides are named for the year most of the players were born). They were the team of Messi, Fabregas, and Pique.

Alexandra replied: "Of course people realized quite early that this was a special team as they broke record after record. They barely lost a single game. Indeed there is some very famous footage of Gerard Pique in tears after losing a tournament final against Real Madrid as a ten year old (before Messi came to the team). Pique's mother recalls it as the only time her little boy couldn't be comforted. The reason: he'd simply never lost before and didn't know how to handle it."

"But it wasn't just Messi, Cesc and Pique who stood out in the team. The captain, Marc Valiente, was tipped by many observers as the one who'd go on to be the team's biggest star. But he never really realised his potential. He did make it to the Barcelona B-team, where he played under Guardiola in 2008, but was soon moved on to Sevilla, where he struggled for a place in the reserves. Today he plays for Real Valladolid. Another of the most shiny stars of that team was Victor Vazquez. He was the real goalscorer of the team. He made his debut for Barcelona's first team as early as 2008, but that soon proved a false dawn. After five seasons with Barcelona's B-team he left for Club Brugge in 2011."

Which just goes to show how difficult it is to pick which young stars will make it.

Unless they're named Lionel Messi.

"Messi," said Alexandra, "arrived in 2002 and it took awhile before he could play because of some troublesome paperwork issues. Then he got injured in training and missed a few months. And so, when Tito Vilanova took over as coach in 2003 Messi was a reserve. Vilanova soon promoted him on the recommendation of Charly Rexach, the then youth director of the club."

Rexach had an eye for young talent and he knew, from the moment he laid eyes on the tiny, young Leo in a trial game, that it was love at first sight. Rexach had arrived at the trial game five minutes late, but all it took was the short walk from one side of the pitch to the other to convince him that he'd seen "something out of the ordinary. No matter what, this little boy would stay at Barca."

Off the pitch, "Leo didn't talk much: it took months before his teammates knew he even could talk." On the pitch, Messi was wonderful. "Extraordinary." An artist. From the very off, Fabregas and Pique knew they had to protect him as they would a precious stone: a precious *touchstone* to the identity of FC Barcelona.

The identity of a football club is not *wholly* shaped by the things they are – historical winners, producers of great young players, purveyors of a fine brand of attacking football – they are also developed as part of an ongoing conversation with *what they are not*. Another of the comments under Alexandra's piece states that the glory of that *La Masia* x11 is: "also a direct contrast to their

(Barcelona's) counterparts in Madrid, where there's only one regularly starting *cantera* player (Casillas). They fancy themselves as the 'club of Spain' yet they only field four Spaniards regularly in their starting XI. Barcelona: the "anti Spain Catalan Nationalist" club fields ten Spaniards as part of the regular XI (Dani Alves and Lionel Messi being the lone exceptions)."

I wonder whether Manchester United, are deliberately setting themselves up as the polar opposite of Manchester City and Chelsea, with all of their new money. I wonder whether United are banking on Van Gaal being able to produce young players (and develop the ones we already have, such as Adnan Januzaj, James Wilson, and Tom Lawrence), rather than breaking the bank to wrest control of the Premier League back from the new-money clubs.

Certainly it will be a long-term project, and United fans will need to call upon vast reserves of patience.

The fans stuck with David Moyes for as long as they could, and provided him with unbelievable support even during the bleakest of days. Until his position became simply untenable.

But under Moyes, there did not appear to be a direction, a blueprint.

Under Van Gaal, there will be.

At Barcelona, Van Gaal most definitely had a long-term plan. It was just a shame he was not there to see it come into fruition.

And there was a certain irony at play there too. Because the team which put the final nail in the coffin of the *tika-taka* Spanish team of Xavi, Iniesta, Fabregas, Pique *et al,* was the Netherlands in the 2014 World Cup. The Dutch beat the Spanish 5-1, and all but put them out of the competition.

Their manager?

Louis van Gaal.

III – "I'VE SIGNED A CONTRACT WITH THE DUTCH NATIONAL TEAM UNTIL 2006, SO I CAN WIN THE WORLD CUP NOT ONCE BUT TWICE."

NETHERLANDS NATIONAL TEAM (2000-2002)

L ouis van Gaal was typically humble when presented to the press in 2000, upon his appointment as manager of the Netherlands national team. He said, with barely a hint of a smile: "I've signed a contract with the Dutch national team until 2006, so I can win the World Cup not once but twice."

Two years later, he was to quit, having failed to even qualify for the 2002 World Cup in South Korea and Japan.

Eight years after his apocryphal statement, when the dust had settled – somewhat – on a qualifying campaign of near-apocalyptic failure, Van Gaal talked to Fifa.com regarding any regrets he might have had about his time as *Oranje* coach. He sniffed: "I always look to the present and the future, not the past. I never had the chance to take part in a major tournament with the Netherlands and that's a real shame, but I resigned because some of the players refused to accept my methods. I am who I am and I have my own ways. I'm not going to change and I have no desire to."

At Barcelona, according to Jon Reeves in his book *The Managers* Van Gaal "often struggled to implement his footballing philosophy on a group of big-name players that had equally large egos and hadn't been schooled in the Ajax traditions. The manager's response was to bring in Dutch players that had worked with him before…"

But it didn't work. The same was true of Louis van Gaal's time as Netherlands boss. He inherited a team packed full of the players he'd had as youngsters at Ajax: Overmars, Seedorf, Kluivert, the de Boer brothers, Davids, Reiziger, van der Sar. Only they were now more worldly-wise and wouldn't take orders and submit to his rigid discipline as they once did.

He was no longer their "general".

And they certainly no longer wanted to be treated like his "soldiers".

Ego clashes have been – sadly – par for the course within the Dutch national team. Abhishek Iyer, writing for BigFourza.com describes how, too often, the Netherlands remain "fused to their larger footballing image; a bunch of artistic, moody individuals with ego-balloons the size of Kirov airships." He describes the players as "temperamental typhoons of self-worth".

When the clash of egos produces good football, rich in the "characteristic elegance and panache of Dutch teams past", Iyer says, this is all very well: "the flowing brush-strokes which somehow ran across a rough canvas" have "constituted a flawed but entertaining football team".

But sometimes the clash of egos becomes too much, and the team ceases to function as a team.

In that Dutch side of 2000-02, there were a lot of egos. Edgar Davids already had form as a disruptive influence, having been sent home in disgrace by Guus Hiddink from Euro '96 in England. He would also go on to have a well-publicised dressing-room bust-up with Mark van Bommel in 2003. Van Bommel himself was a well-known hothead. Ruud van Nistelrooy, Roy Makaay, and Jimmy Floyd Hasselbaink bickered over who should partner Patrick Kluivert up front. Pierre van Hooijdonk was on the scene: this was the same van Hooijdonk who fell out with the Celtic owner Fergus McCann during his stint with the Glasgow club, and who left in a huff after Celtic's *derisory* wage-hike offer, which he described as "good enough for the homeless to live on, but not enough for an international striker." Yes, the same van Hooijdonk who went on strike at Nottingham Forest in 1998.

In 2001, during qualifying, Frank de Boer, Edgar Davids and Jaap Stam would be suspended for allegedly getting all 'roided-up on nandrolon. And we all know what stable, happy people steroids allegedly make us, don't we?

It was a powder-keg, waiting to blow.

The Dutch were drawn in qualifying group 2, alongside Portugal, the Republic of Ireland, Estonia, Cyprus, and Andorra. The opening game was on 2nd September 2000: a home tie against a very good Ireland team – containing such luminaries as the Keanes, Roy and Robbie; Damien Duff; Steve Staunton; Jason McAteer; and Niall Quinn - who were thought to be amongst the Netherlands' main rivals for top spots in the group. This was, according to the Football Association of Ireland (FAI)'s own website, a "well-balanced" Ireland team with a "recognisable and proven pattern of play".

The Dutch were *supposed* to be the same, playing *their* proven brand of Total Football, under a leader who would ensure they were well-balanced.

Only it didn't quite work out like that at the Amsterdam ArenA.

The game was to end in a 2-2 draw, but it could have been so much worse for Van Gaal's team: with 20 minutes to go they found themselves 2-0 down (thanks to goals from Robbie Keane and Jason McAteer) and staring down the barrel of a gun. Jeffrey Talan pulled one back on 71 minutes, and then, with just 6 minutes remaining on the clock, Giovanni van Bronckhorst spared Dutch blushes with an equaliser.

Cue widespread relief in the stadium.

Cue disappointment amongst the massed hoards of Irish fans who'd travelled over for the game: the FAI called the equaliser "lucky".

Cue also, once the dust had settled, an inquest in the Dutch media into how things in the group had gone wrong so quickly: one game gone and they'd already handed the advantage to one of their major rivals in the group.

Still, it would be okay, wouldn't it? All the Netherlands would have to do was beat the Republic of Ireland *in* Ireland - in what would eventually come to be seen as the group's decisive game - and things would be back on track. As it happened Jason McAteer – 'Trigger' to his friends on account of his sharing with the *Only Fools and Horses* character a bad case of cotton wool between his ears - again struck for Ireland on the return, almost exactly a year later on 1st September 2001, at Lansdowne Road, in a 1-0 win for an Irish side who'd only ever qualified for the World Cup on two prior occasions.

This is how the FAI's website describes the crucial encounter:

"So the highly-rated Dutch rode into town, basking in their achievement of finishing third in the European

Championship in Belgium/Holland a little over twelve months previously. Ireland were top of the qualifying table but Portugal had the easier run in and looked certain to finish top to take the one automatic qualifying spot for the World Cup finals of 2002 in South Korea/Japan.

The contest at Lansdowne Road, before a full house of close to 40,000, was virtually certain to decide second place and Ireland were determined they would not fail. They were focused and driven from kick-off but met strong and capable opponents who showed they were just as determined as a classic contest unfolded.

It quickly became apparent that Netherlands' left-winger, Marc Overmars, was set to provide problems for Ireland. His elusive running tempted full-back Gary Kelly into two ill-timed tackles that earned yellow cards and the second, in the 58th minute, meant that Ireland were down to ten men with more than 30 minutes left to play.

The Dutch were outstanding but Ireland were even better and magnificent defensive work by goalkeeper Shay Given and, especially, centre-backs Richard Dunne and Stephen Staunton was critically important. Roy Keane offered them great protection and Ireland maintained their composure in face of sustained pressure.

One particular incident, as Ireland defiantly manned an overcrowded penalty area in the closing half-hour spoke volumes – Van Bronckhurst hammered a powerful shot at goal from 30 yards, Dunne stepped into the path of the ball and simply volleyed it over half-way.

Such flamboyant defiance served Ireland well after Jason McAteer had volleyed the only goal of the game from Steve Finnan's cross in the 68th minute. McAteer was totally unmarked outside the left-hand post as Finnan found time to measure a cross from the right that was despatched from 20 yards with impressive confidence.

The Dutch cause was not helped when they made an extraordinary substitution by withdrawing the brilliant

Overmars in the second half. They sought to break down Ireland's defence by employing four tall strikers in Kluivert, van Nistelrooy, Van Hooijdonk and Hasselbaink and feeding them high balls from a withdrawn position through Cocu.

This played into Ireland's hands with Dunne and Staunton dominating in the air and revelling in the aerial bombardment. Netherlands grew increasingly more desperate as the clock ticked down and with Overmars off the pitch they lacked penetration.

Ireland's win meant they were now sure of at least a play-off and manager McCarthy commented: 'We were fifteen seconds from qualifying for the European Championship (last time out) when we lost a goal to Macedonia and that hurt ... this is no more than we deserve."

Clive White, writing for *The Telegraph,* was slightly less biased but was still in congratulatory mood as he celebrated Ireland's: "famous win against their old nemesis", the Dutch. He wrote: "With half an hour to go yesterday they looked about as far away from a play-off against one of the Asian countries as that continent is from Dublin when Gary Kelly was needlessly sent off for a second bookable offence."

And yet: "It was probably even to the disbelief of their adoring audience when they took the lead within seven minutes of Kelly's departure. Roy Keane, inevitably, was at the heart of the game's critical moment when his former club-mate, Jaap Stam, attempted to halt his run with an illegal challenge. Helmut Krug, the German referee, played advantage and the ball ran fortuitously to Steve Finnan, who had replaced Kelly on the right. He looked up to see McAteer unmarked and he picked him out. If the unsettled Blackburn player ever needed to keep his nerve it was then and he did so admirably, driving the ball past Edwin van der Sar."

Keane was also responsible for an early "reducer" on Marc Overmars which seemed to put the wind up the Netherlands winger.

And yet still the Dutch came.

In the end, White felt the Irish worked their way back into the game through "luck and grit". They "stuck to their task of trying to live with a very good Dutch side and eventually forced them back on their heels, thanks primarily to the trickery and blistering pace of Duff." And, in the second half when Irish legs began to tire after having been reduced to ten men, it was "courageous defending" which carried them over the line.

The history books do not place an asterisk next to the result of the match. They do not acknowledge that Van Gaal's Netherlands team *played well*. Came up against a brick wall but kept going. Instead the narrative of the game was already written: it was the plucky Irish against the "temperamental typhoons of self-worth".

Van Gaal could not rewrite the story.

But he tried, manfully.

Between those two Republic of Ireland games, the Netherlands put together a series of decent away results, dispatching Cyprus 4-0 (Seedorf netting two, and Overmars and Kluivert with the others); smashing Andorra 5-0 (Kluivert, Hasselbaink, Van Hooijdonk (two) and Van Bommel with the goals); securing a creditable 2-2 draw away in Portugal (with Hasselbaink and Kluivert netting); and hammering Estonia 4-2 (thanks to an own goal, Van Nistelrooy (two) and Kluivert).

And Van Gaal's essential arrogance didn't seem to have taken a knock at all. Ian Herbert in *The Independent* describes Van Gaal's reaction to a routine win against Andorra. Louis talked up his own credentials, referring to the badly-kept secret that he'd been on the short-list to replace Sir Alex Ferguson as Manchester United manager the previous year, before Fergie performed a U-turn and declared there was no way he could retire. Van Gaal said: "I knew I was first on the list to succeed (Ferguson) last year," he said. "I don't have any contact with them now because I am coach of the national team but I can imagine that a club like Manchester United are still interested in Louis van Gaal."

And of course they would be, but not for another twelve years.

And Van Gaal might have had cause to regret having to stay on as manager for the national team as they stuttered again in their qualification campaign in *another* home game – this time at De Kuip stadium in Rotterdam - in which the damage to their World Cup dreams was done. On 11th October 2000, the Netherlands were beaten 2-0 by Portugal, their *other* key rivals for qualification. (This game would prove the catalyst for the rivalry between Portugal and Holland to turn ugly: the next time they met was in the semi-final of Euro 2004, when an Arjen Robben dive caused an ugly on-pitch set to. And after that, it was in the World Cup proper, in 2006, in a game which has been christened "the Battle of Nuremburg". There were four sendings-off and *sixteen* bookings – a World Cup record – and somehow one goal, as the Portuguese won through to the quarter-finals.)

And though Van Gaal's team followed the Portugal defeat up with an easy win against Cyprus in Eindhoven (with Hasselbaink, Overmars, Kluivert and Van Nistelrooy on the scoresheet), they now stood little chance of qualification. And despite scoring nine goals in their final two games – with none conceded – they were still short of second spot by a point.

But this, remember, was the Netherlands. They'd been semi-finalists in their last major competition proper - the European Championships of 2000 – and were brimming with world class talent.

And yet, instead Portugal and Republic of Ireland were bound for South Korea and Japan and all that was left was the blame game, the bitter acrimony, the finger-pointing.

And, of course, as manager, Van Gaal was the fall-guy.

Elko Born wrote in *The Telegraph:* "Dutch fans and pundits alike blamed this debacle on Van Gaal, of course. It was the manager who had been at fault, people said. It was Van Gaal who had failed to motivate his players to perform. Unsurprisingly, Van Gaal was (…) replaced by Dick Advocaat."

Ian Herbert noted in *The Independent* that "Van Gaal flopped badly".

And of course, there were extenuating circumstances. The group really had been a tight one: Portugal – containing Rui Costa and Luis Figo – were a very good side; the Republic of Ireland were tough to beat (in that season's qualifying campaign they had *eleven* Roy Keanes). And only two could qualify.

And of course, the Netherlands have a history of failure in World Cups. They have a 100% record in finals: all defeats. But these failures were *glorious*. Cliched, but glorious. Luca Gunby, of *Forza Italian Football* claims: "The clichés portray the Oranje as a team capable of beautiful, innovative football that ultimately counts for nothing as splits in the camp or bad luck contrive to crush Dutch dreams at the World Cup and send them home trophy-less."

And yet.

And yet *this* failure was in *qualifying*. Not in the finals.

And yet Van Gaal departed, tail between his legs, muttering about the "disruption" he'd experienced throughout the campaign by key players in the squad. He talked of how he'd given so much time to improve "the relations between myself and the players" only to see it thrown back in his face.

Auke Kok, writing for the Dutch website NRC, describes how Van Gaal went further in his criticism of his Netherlands team than ever before in the 2009 book *Biography & Vision:* "the manager attributes the debacle to the unprofessional lifestyle of the international players."

"When he resigned in November of 2001," says Kok, "Van Gaal alluded to the idea that his players weren't willing to make the sacrifices necessary to be successful. But he didn't go into the kind of details that are in his new book. For instance, Van Gaal suggests that behind the fatal defeat against Ireland was a clear culture divide between the coach and his players."

' "My assistant, Andries Jonker, thought I was more quiet after Ireland. Timid. I can still hear him asking: 'Louis, you're not ill, are you?' A month later: 'Louis, are you sure you are alright?' This meant I was done with the group and that attitude."

" 'That attitude' refers to the preference players had for leisure over training, a call-girl over a good night sleep. 'Nothing actually happened as far as partying and girls are concerned, but the fact that that's what they were focused on is too crazy for words,' Van Gaal writes. He reveals he hired a security guard to make sure the attempted nightly revelries remained fruitless."

"Of course much of the blame for the biggest flop in the recent history of the Dutch team can be assigned to injuries and the 'nandrolon affair' - captain Frank de Boer, Edgar David and Jaap Stam were suspended for using the steroid in 2001 - but personal conflicts were also at play. The players had become self-assured celebrities over the years; they were no longer the compliant youngsters Van Gaal's Ajax had earned the Champions League with in 1995. Everybody seemed to realise that, except for Van Gaal."

"The biography quotes Frank de Boer who compares Van Gaal to his anti-pole, fellow Dutch coach Guus Hiddink, who had reached the World Cup semi-finals with the same generation of players in 1998. Hiddink wasn't dead set on training hard or special practices, according to De Boer. 'But he made sure the atmosphere and the chemistry were right.' Van Gaal's successor Dick Advocaat made it to the European Cup semi-finals in 2004 with the same crew of then 'sedated' players.

" 'It was the biggest disappointment of my career, mainly because these were the guys I had educated myself. It was hard to handle,' Van Gaal now writes in his biography."

"Indeed, if anyone should have known the players, it was Van Gaal. He had taken many of the Dutch stars with him when he became Barcelona's coach in 1997. It was under his watch that they became the celebrities who drank more and stayed up later than their teammates in Barcelona. Van Gaal's wife even warned him about the behaviour of the players there, but Van Gaal didn't know how to handle it."

After this "debacle", after his "flop", it was clear Louis van Gaal's next career choice would be a crucial one. He needed to go somewhere quiet, stable. Somewhere he could work a long-term project. Somewhere the players would submit to his system and his blueprint.

So, knowing the man as you might do now, where do you reckon he pitched up?

Some footballing backwater? Some fair-to-middling club with no superstars, no celebrities, no boardroom shenanigans? Somewhere he could take the time to work on his relations with the players?

No, of course not.

Van Gaal picked Barcelona.

Again.

After all, he'd enjoyed such a lovely time in "Vietnam" during his previous spell, hadn't he?

Van Gaal went back to Camp Nou bristling with intent. He wanted to right some wrongs. He wanted to prove *his doubters* wrong. He wanted to see the rich crop of *his* La Masia finally bearing fruit.

Barcelona was like a red rag to his bullish personality. It simultaneously attracted and repulsed him.

He had to go.

IV: "I SHOULD HAVE KNOWN THAT SEQUELS ARE NEVER ANY GOOD... IT WAS LIKE THE DEVIL HIMSELF WAS RETURNING."

RETURN TO BARCELONA (2002 – 03)

AND RETURN TO AJAX (2004)

L ouis van Gaal bears a striking resemblance to the boxing promoter Frank Warren. Though if Van Gaal *was* playing Warren – in, say, some movie biopic of his life – the Dutchman's version of him wouldn't have stopped at the ropes. No, LVG's Frank Warren would have entered the ring. Would have taken a few punches too, and worn their scars (and broken bones) with pride.

In Van Gaal's 'wilderness years' of 2002 to 2004, he began to resemble Al Pacino in *The Godfather Part III*. His catchphrase, during those years in which he wandered from European place to place looking for a place he might call home, might well have been: "Just when I thought I was out, they pull me back in." First to Barcelona, where he returned for the 2002-03 season; then to Ajax, where he'd end up for a portion of 2004.

First, to Barcelona, where he'd departed with some acrimony, the Millennium bug well and truly *up his ass,* in 2000. His parting shot being this beauty: "Barcelona is nowhere near as important a club as everybody here thinks it is. You have not won much. *I* won more in six years at Ajax than Barcelona have won in one hundred."

It was all going to end in tears, wasn't it?

(And indeed it would, when as Jon Reeves puts it "the old La Liga demons returned" and Van Gaal "left his position halfway through the campaign", and Joan Gaspart, the Barcelona president said: "I should have known that sequels are never any good... It was like the devil himself was returning.")

Louis van Gaal returned to a Barcelona where the Dutch influence remained strong. Marc Overmars, Patrick Kluivert, Phillip Cocu, Frank de Boer, and Michael Reiziger were still present within the first team squad. Still reeling from the debacle which was the Netherlands qualifying campaign for the 2002 World Cup.

Also present in the squad were a number of players from La Masia who would eventually come to credit Van Gaal in their development: 22-year-old Xavi, a youthful Victor Valdes, and an 18-year-old Andres Iniesta. Iniesta – the man who would go on to score the winner in a World Cup final for Spain - would make his full debut in 2002.

But in the main, it was a squad in the midst of a large-scale upheaval. There had been numerous personnel changes over the past two summers. Amongst the departures were Pep Guardiola, Jari Litmanen, Boudewijn Zenden, and Emmanuel Petit. So, importantly for LVG, was Rivaldo. The Brazilian had proved to be the main trouble-causer from Van Gaal's first spell in charge of

Barcelona, but had now left the scene of his 'crimes'. As had his compatriot Giovanni. Yes, that Giovanni: the one who'd accused Van Gaal of being the "Hitler of the Brazilian players."

In their wake, Van Gaal sanctioned the signings of three players in the close season: the gifted, if rather unpredictable Argentine Juan Roman Riquelme joined for €10 million from Boca Juniors; cultured Spanish midfielder Gaizka Mendieta arrived on loan from Lazio; and German goalkeeper Robert Enke was brought in from Benfica on a free. Robert Enke's story is an incredibly sad one, a devastatingly dark one, told wonderfully by his close friend Ronald Reng in the book *A Life Too Short* - a William Hill Sports Book of the Year winner.

Reng describes Enke's first impressions of Van Gaal during the rather protracted contract negotiations between Barca and Benfica were formed in a brusque telephone call. At the time a desperate Enke – who feared the on-off transfer was finally *off* for good - called Van Gaal "who was on holiday in Aruba. 'Yes, very good of you to call, Mr. Enke. That's good. Because I'm the one who decides who plays for Barca,'" Reng has Van Gaal saying, sounding very much like a Bond villain.

Van Gaal continued: " 'I'm not the one who's going to sign you up. The sporting director wants you. I don't even know you. Each of the three goalkeepers in pre-season gets the same chance to make it as number one, even if you sign.'"

Enke's first impression: Louis was hard, arrogant, but *fair*.

Yet Reng paints Van Gaal – mostly – as a pantomime villain. He does not speak, he "barks" – particularly that phrase "I don't even know you." His manner is "gruff". He "waddles". Everything about him is "enormous – his belly, his neck, his head." Reng seems obsessed by the size of Van Gaal's neck. Later he describes the press conference to announce Enke as only the second German ever to sign for Barcelona after the great Bernd Schuster. "Van Gaal had buttoned up his stiff white shirt under his tie, which made his enormous neck look even more impressive than usual." Enke cowers at his side looking "even younger (and smaller) than usual."

At the press conference, Van Gaal reaffirmed his claim that he was prepared to give all three of his 'keepers equal chance: " 'The three goalkeepers, Enke, Bonano, and Valdes, are starting at nil, even if the chances are better for the first two. (...) But everything can change.' His voice boomed. "Because when I'm in charge no one has a safe place on the team."

At Barca, Van Gaal's coaching team tried to change Enke's playing style. In essence, they tried to make him like Van der Sar, Van Gaal's ideal 'keeper and the ideal 'keeper for Van Gaal's system. They wanted him to be a sweeper-keeper. But he patently wasn't cut out for that, no matter how hard he tried. Nor was the incumbent of the number one jersey, the Argentine Bonano. But young Victor Valdes was, and it was to him that Van Gaal turned. And in his first game, "Victor Valdes was demonstrating his huge talent".

Reng says: "Van Gaal has a thing about young players, like a man possessed he was trying to cement his reputation as a discoverer of new stars, and he favoured reckless young talent."

Enke – who lived in a different postcode to young, and in a different state than reckless - wasn't cut out for Van Gaal's Barcelona. That much is clear. Reserved, highly introspective, he was nothing like the rest of the team with their showmen and stars. With their egos. Egos were everywhere. Enke's wife Teresa describes how: "at Camp Nou the women (the WAGs) behaved as if they themselves were the football team, competing for the starring roles. She was just the substitute goalkeeper's wife."

Because of all the egos, and because of all of the chopping and changing within the squad, many predicted Barcelona would find it hard to hit the ground running. Even so, their start to the La Liga campaign - featuring two wins, two losses, and two draws – was uneven at best, and as it proved, set the tone for the whole miserable five months of Van Gaal's tenure. There were upturns in form - a 6-1 home win against Alaves in October stood out - but they were all-too often found to be flashes in the pan. The first *Classico* of the season saw Barcelona draw 0-0 with Real Madrid at Camp Nou, and this stalemate preceded a run of three defeats on the bounce for the *blaugrana*.

"Barcelona entered the Christmas holidays tenth in the table. Madrid's Galacticos had collected almost twice as many points," says Reng.

Indeed, by the time Van Gaal departed, Barcelona were just three points above the relegation zone. They would eventually finish in sixth place: Barca's worst position in 15 years. They had employed three managers over the course of the season. Van Gaal was gone just after the Christmas decorations, in January.

In the Copa del Rey things got even worse. They drew FC Novelda, "bottom of Segunda Division B – the Spanish third division" (Reng).

It was "Novelda – population twenty-seven thousand" against *more than a club* Barcelona, whose members *(socios)* number over 170,000.

The game was to be played on 11th September 2002. "You can't forget the date," says Reng, "one year after the New York terror attacks and a Catalan holiday."

In its own way, it was to prove an apocalyptic day for FC Barcelona. But prior to the match, Van Gaal talked the match up as one in which "he would use some of his reserve players". To Robert Enke he said: " 'You'll have your chance there.' To Robert it sounded like a threat."

Pre-game Enke decided (somewhat presciently as

we shall see): "He could only lose. Whatever he tried to think about to distract himself, he always ended up with that thought. If everything went as planned, Barca would win 3-0 or 4-0 and no one would mention the goalkeeper. If it went wrong, he would get the blame."

In the dressing room: "Robert tried to listen as the coach dispensed instructions on tactics. Van Gaal's voice was droning about pressing in attack, winning the ball back straight away, being aggressive, passing the ball behind the defence only in the last third of the pitch."

Enke's instructions: play like Van der Sar. Come out quickly.

Lining up for the pre-kick off team photograph on the pitch in Novelda's tiny stadium, Enke's "mouth is open and his eyes wide. His fear is frozen in those photographs for ever."

And yet, in the first half, that rabbit in the headlights was untroubled. Barcelona scored an early goal, made by a piece of magic by Van Gaal's star-signing, his "saviour", Riquelme. Reng says: "Van Gaal had only put up a three-man defence – a risk hardly a coach took these days, but against a Segunda B side it was plainly fine."

At half-time it remained 1-0 Barcelona. Plain-sailing. Everything going exactly as expected. The minnows looked over-awed. Reng says: "Novelda's goalkeeper came up to Robert in the tunnel and asked if they could swap shirts after the game."

On the hour mark however, everything changed. Enke should have come out for a Novelda free-kick which was - in the manner of underdogs everywhere in the footballing world - lumped-into the mixer. But the German remained rooted on his line. A free man finished and suddenly it was one apiece.

And suddenly Barca were nervous. Reng says: "Frank de Boer was starting to criticize everyone and everything."

Novelda took a pot-shot from distance. Enke could only slap it away. And suddenly "everyone could see the state he was in."

Then: "again Novelda slung a free-kick into his penalty area", and this time Enke tried the opposite tack. This time "Robert was stranded in no-man's land" as it became 2-1 to Novelda.

"Three minutes later," Reng says, "Riquelme equalised with a penalty. (…) The underdog had put up a great fight, but now the big favourite, the twenty-five-time Copa del Rey winners from Barcelona, would dash the hopes of the upstarts."

But, Reng notes: "the game had long since come apart at the seams. Now the hearts, not the brains, of both teams were driving them back and forth."

Enke's heart wasn't in it. He missed *another* cross. So did Frank de Boer (who was perhaps still under the mistaken impression it was van der Sar behind him – hell, he'd heard the Dutchman's name mentioned enough; certainly more than Enke's had been). Unbelievably, against the odds, Novelda scored *again*.

Aurelio Borginio, the Novelda 'keeper, recalls looking out from the scrum of celebrating underdog players and seeing: "De Boer (…) standing in the penalty box. He was railing at Enke, A professional doesn't do something like that, humiliating a team-mate on the pitch. Robert Enke stood there, his face pale, eyes lowered, and didn't say a word."

Reng says, sadly: "There were twelve minutes left, but the game had already found its concluding image."

Its concluding score-line too. In the post-match interviews De Boer was still raging. Once more he was highly critical of Enke's performance.

For LVG, this was too much. "Coach Van Gaal roared at his fellow Dutchman: a professional didn't behave like that, certainly not one with his experience."

And yet, Van Gaal "didn't talk to" Enke. Instead, "he was thrown to the lions," as Victor Valdes said.

In the aftermath of the game, as the black dog of depression reared its ugly head, Enke found a German psychologist in Barcelona to help him deal with the trauma of the Novelda game. "The doctor," Reng says, "diagnosed alienation, a deep melancholy of a kind many people experience after a bereavement, after being fired from a job, or after being bullied."

Robert Enke tragically committed suicide on 10th November 2009. He was 32. By then he'd found a way out of Barcelona, and had almost made it all the way to the German squad for the 2010 World Cup. But he'd never found a way to shake off that black dog of depression.

Louis van Gaal should in no way shoulder the blame for driving Enke into the depths of depression at Barcelona. Depression was in him anyway. And besides, football at this level is a high-pressure environment: livelihoods are at stake. At Barcelona, where every game – hell every *training session* – is put under the microscope by any number of daily sports newspapers, magazines and blogs, TV shows and radio, where the board have famously itchy trigger fingers, where the supporters are apt to draw out the white handkerchiefs after a single poor game, the temperature of the pressure cooker is ratcheted up a few more notches.

Football becomes like war. Barcelona can seem like Vietnam. The players – the "soldiers" – have to have skins as thick as that of a rhino. If they don't, if they're too sensitive – as Enke was – then it can become too much. That description of Enke frozen in fear in the team photo before the Novelda match strikes me as very much like those of the foot-soldiers in the First World War, before they were made to climb out of the trenches and be mown down by machine gun fire.

Of course, some players – some managers too -

become inured to the tension of it all. They create caricatures of themselves. They become great, stonking *stereotypes*. Van Gaal must have created his own thick-skin, his huge neck, his arrogant persona in order to deal with the slings and arrows. Enke couldn't do this.

This is not Van Gaal's fault.

And it was not purely the Dutchman's responsibility to remove Enke from the firing line. Fellow players might have helped. Enke's captain, de Boer, might not have criticised him so publicly, and might have instead chosen to lend his support.

This is football at its darkest.

And nobody shone a light for him.

Van Gaal was simply one of many who might have.

So, I'll stress again, he shoulders none of the blame.

But he did not help foster the kind of atmosphere *within* the club in which someone *like* Enke could have felt *okay* to seek help for his problems.

Instead, the atmosphere around the club was one of paranoia.

And poison.

The team was falling apart.

There was no team.

Reng says: "For this team with too many problems Van Gaal's ruthless approach was exactly what they didn't need."

Bonano, Enke's rival for the number one jersey at Barcelona – or, as it would turn out, his rival for the *unlucky 13* jersey after Valdes exploded onto the scene – talked to Reng about how "things got ugly".

"The atmosphere was crazy," he says. "There was something different every day. Sometimes the coach was furious and he would insult a player, or else a member of the board would tear into us."

Enke himself recalled how after one defeat: "Van

Gaal got up on a massage bench in front of the whole team and yelled at us from above."

Like an angry, and vengeful God.

Like a God who was losing his grip. Whose powers were waning.

In Europe, Barcelona fared better. They still had that *aura,* that *prestige.* Van Gaal was still someone approaching the Divine. *En route* to the Champions League quarter-finals they set a tournament record of 11 consecutive wins. They beat Legia Warsaw home and away in the Third qualifying round before winning all six of their first group stage matches (against Club Brugge, Galatasaray, and Lokomotiv Moscow, home and away). In the second group stage, they continued their streak by beating Bayer Leverkusen away and Newcastle United and Internazionale at home, before a draw away at Inter stopped them at 11. Still, they completed the second group stage with two more wins, and there were high hopes their form would continue past the quarter-final.

As it was they came up against a brick wall which was disguised as 'the Old Lady': Juventus. Both games finished 1-1 at the end of normal time, but in the second leg at Camp Nou on 22 April, Juve won it in extra time with a goal from Zayaleta.

By which time, of course, Van Gaal was long-gone. He was manager for ten of the eleven of the winning streak, but missed the eleventh, a 3-0 home win against Internazionale.

One quick note about Barca's European campaign, and a redemption – of sorts – for Robert Enke. Having already qualified from the first group stage, Barcelona faced Club Brugge in Bruges in what was effectively a dead-rubber. Again Van Gaal blooded the reserves. They were dubbed "Baby Barcelona", and they counted in their number one Andres Iniesta, who was just 18-years-old. They also counted Enke, as 'keeper.

Barcelona won 1-0. Riquelme scored the winner. Enke protected the lead like a demon, pulling off one of the best saves the Champions League has seen to deny a Brugge forward.

Reng recalls: "Francisco Carrasco (…) wrote in *Mundo Deportivo* 'Enke's performance was a message to Louis van Gaal. I'm here if you need me.' And the trainer who was constantly barking, revealed a compassionate side. No one is emotionally one-dimensional, even Van Gaal can be sympathetic; it just isn't always so easy to spot it. He never talked in public about individual players, the trainer said at the press conference 'but a goalkeeper is a lonely player, which is why today he deserves a special mention. Enke was very good; in the end he saved our victory for us."

Enke left Barca eventually. He moved to Fenerbache in Turkey.

He outlasted Van Gaal.

Louis van Gaal's contract was terminated in the week following a 2-0 defeat against Celta Vigo at Estadio Balaidos, Vigo, on Sunday 26th January. The reverse saw them fall a full twenty points behind the surprise La Liga pace-setters, Real Sociedad.

"After reflecting on the recent performances of the club and speaking with Barcelona president Joan Gaspart we have decided that it is in the best interests of the club that we go our separate ways," said a strangely reserved LVG. "I am really upset that as a coach I haven't lived up to the expectations of the Barcelona fans."

Van Gaal, whose contract was due to run until June 2005, received €4 million in a severance deal with Barca. Carlos 'Charlie' Rexach, from whom Van Gaal took over at the start of the season, found himself back in the hot-seat, albeit in a caretaker capacity.

Speaking more recently (in an interview with Fifa.com in 2008) about his two spells at Barcelona, however, Van Gaal seemed to have rediscovered his Sinatra-esque *My Way* groove. Regrets, he'd had a few, but none he'd like to expand upon. Gone was the slumped shouldered "I am really upset I have not lived up to the expectations of the fans" *schtick*. Instead, he insisted, it was all about the *context*.

"You always have to look at the context. I don't regret any of my decisions since my philosophy today is no different from what it was then. I don't want to act out a role. As I've already mentioned, I want to be myself, and I'm not going to change my personality. I'm happy as a coach, even if it's not easy at times. And I still won two titles, a Copa del Rey and a Supercup, and there aren't many coaches who can say that. When Nunez was in charge, the club spent a lot less on transfers. We never broke the bank to get a player."

Indeed they didn't. But replacing Rivaldo with the just-as-temperamental Riquelme was *not* one of Van Gaal's masterstrokes.

Nor, it seemed, was Van Gaal's next career move.

They say you should never go back. That things are never as good second time around. Hell, Barcelona had provided him with indisputable evidence of this. And yet, Louis van Gaal's next step was to follow in his own footsteps, all the way back to Ajax, this time as technical director. He was appointed in 2004 and lasted less than a year in the job: inevitable clashes with head coach Ronald Koeman left Van Gaal's position untenable.

Van Gaal had replaced Leo Beenhakker as technical director. Beenhakker was the guy who'd given Louis the big break at Ajax when he made him his assistant back in 1988. Beenhakker had been very much a *hands-off* technical director, and his relationship with Ronald Koeman had been fine: Ajax had won the double with the pair of them steering the ship. But Van Gaal was never going to *not* stick his oar in, and when Koeman and Louis began paddling in different directions, the Ajax boat began to swing round in circles.

Van Gaal wanted more involvement with the players. He wanted to oversee their development from close quarters. He wanted to move away from the 'superstar' model Ajax had begun to adopt, and opt for a more parsimonious route – such as the one he'd taken in his first spell at Ajax when he'd brought through *the kids*.

Koeman wanted guaranteed performances from bonafide stars.

The main beef between Koeman and Van Gaal centred around one man who had an ego to match the pair of them: Zlatan Ibrahimovic. Zlatan had joined Ajax as a 20-year-old, from Malmo in his homeland of Sweden for the rather hefty price-tag of €8.7 million. Even at an early age, he trod a thin line between genius and madness. His goals had fired Ajax to a Dutch title in Zlatan's first year, and he'd followed this up with some devastating performances in the Champions League the following season. However, he was also accused of intentionally injuring *his own team-mate*, Rafael van der Vaart. He scored goals of the season, but was also, in Van Gaal's eyes, untrustworthy.

In Ibrahimovic's book *I am Zlatan*, the Swede describes just one of their clashes (and sheds some light on the turbulent relationship between the two stewards at the helm of the good ship Ajax):

"We headed to a training camp in Portugal and, by that time Beenhakker had resigned as director and was replaced by Louis van Gaal. Van Gaal was a pompous ass. He was a little like Co Adriaanse. He wanted to be a dictator, without a hint of a gleam in his eye. As a player, he'd never stood out, but he was revered in the Netherlands because, as a manager, he'd won the Champions League with Ajax and received some medal from the government.

Van Gaal liked to talk about playing systems. He was one of those in the club who referred to the players as numbers. There was a lot of Five goes here and Six goes there, and I was glad when I could avoid him.

In Portugal, I couldn't escape. I had to go in for a meeting with van Gaal and Koeman and listen to how they viewed my contribution in the first half of the season. It was like a performance review with grades, the kind of thing they loved at Ajax. I went into an office there and sat down in front of van Gaal and Ronald Koeman. Koeman smiled. Van Gaal looked sullen.

'Zlatan,' said Koeman, 'you've played brilliantly, but you're only getting an eight. You haven't worked hard enough at the back.'

'Okay, fine,' I said, wanting to leave.

I liked Koeman, but couldn't cope with Van Gaal, and I thought, Great, an eight will do me. Can I have a break now?

'Do you know how to play in defense?' Van Gaal was sticking his oar in, and I could see that Koeman was getting annoyed too.

'I hope so,' I replied.

Then Van Gaal started to explain, and, believe me, I'd heard it all before. It was the same old stuff about how Nine—that is, me— defends to the right, while Ten goes to the left, and vice versa, and he drew a bunch of arrows and finished with a really harsh 'Do you understand? Do you get all this?' and I took it as an attack.

'You can wake up any of the players at three in the morning,' I said, 'and ask them how to defend and they'll rattle it off in their sleep: Nine goes here and Ten goes there. We know that stuff, and we know you're the one who came up with it. But I've trained with Van Basten, and he thinks otherwise.'

'Excuse me?'

'Van Basten says Number Nine should save his strength for attacking and scoring goals, and, to tell the truth, now I don't know who I should listen to, Van Basten—who's a legend—or Van Gaal?' I said, putting special emphasis on the name Van Gaal, as if he were some completely insignificant figure.

And what do you reckon? Was he happy?

He was fuming. Who should I listen to, a legend or Van Gaal? 'I've gotta go now,' I said, and got out of there."

Zlatan would become the straw which broke the camel's back.

Van Gaal's fingerprints were all over the sale of the Swedish striker in the August transfer window, when he left for Juventus. And, though it was blamed on the Van der Vaart injury row, LVG had marked Ibrahimovic's card ever since the incident in Portugal.

And the *real problem* came when Ajax sold Zlatan so late in the transfer window they didn't have enough time to replace him with a player of comparable quality. The mooted replacement - Roda Kerkrade's Arouna Kone (who'd later end up at Wigan Athletic) - failed his medical.

Sans Zlatan, Ajax struggled. By October, they were fourth in Eredivisie, puffing and panting behind PSV and Feyenoord, and even FC Utrecht. The official announcement of Van Gaal's resignation came on Wednesday 20th October 2004, after Ajax beat the Israeli side Maccabi Tel Aviv FC 3-0 in a Champions League group stage tie. Van Gaal had tendered his resignation earlier than that, on the preceding Sunday, after a humbling 3-1 home defeat to Heerenveen, but since two other defeats – they lost 1-0 to Juventus and 4-0 to Bayern Munich – most observers had felt it was only a matter of time before either Koeman or Van Gaal left the club. The pair had a very public spat after the Bayern reverse, with Van Gaal claiming Ajax's "expectations for his young and inexperienced squad were unrealistic" (CNN) and Koeman claiming the composition of the squad was wrong (leaving the ball firmly in the technical director's court).

"My resignation is in Ajax's best interests and has nothing to do with the poor results this season," Van Gaal said in the press conference to announce his resignation.

Meanwhile, the Ajax players he left were breathing a sigh of relief. The win over Maccabi Tel Aviv meant that although Ajax wouldn't qualify for the knockout stages of the Champions League, they would at least be sure of European football in 2005, in the UEFA Cup. "This was super. There was so much tension for this match and when it works out like this it feels great," said Van der Vaart: he of the Ibrahimovic row. "We are going through a tough period but today we stood up as a team."

Van Gaal, the manager who stressed *team* above everything else, had been proved detrimental to the team.

The question was: where would he go now? Where *could* he go now?

Who would have him?

V – "OMSCHAKELING"

AZ ALKMAAR (2005 – 2009)

After his traumatic spell at Barcelona, his underwhelming time in charge of the Dutch national team, and his troubles at Ajax when he was briefly made technical director, Van Gaal's reputation had taken a severe beating. He needed to re-group, rediscover his *mojo*. Remember the rolling-shouldered, barrel-chested, boxer's-nosed man he'd once been. And so he went back to his roots, to AZ Alkmaar where he'd been given his start in coaching back in 1986.

It could have been a massive mistake; the equivalent of a punch-drunk fighter taking one final payday at the end of his career. Though LGV's eternal nemesis Johan Cruyff was no longer in management, other Dutch managerial heavyweights were now stealing all of *Louis's* headlines, winning bouts across the world while Van Gaal – apparently – was ready to put his feet up.

When Van Gaal took charge of AZ, 'Golden Guus'

Hiddink was enjoying a very successful spell in charge of the Australian national team. He took them to the World Cup in Germany, and there defied all expectations by guiding the Socceroos through the group stages and into a second round game against Italy, which they would eventually lose in highly controversial circumstances as the Italians won and converted a late, late penalty.

Van Gaal had never managed a single game in the World Cup proper.

Hiddink's reward for his Australian 'miracle' was to secure the job as boss of the Russian national team. He would eventually guide them to the semi-finals of Euro 2008.

Van Gaal had never managed a single game in the European Championships proper.

By 2009, Hiddink had been installed as caretaker manager at Chelsea, charged with stabilizing that rather turbulent club after the singularly unsuccessful reign of 'Big Phil' Scolari. Guus would only lose one game as Chelsea manager, and would deliver an FA Cup trophy after a final win against Everton at Wembley.

Another heavyweight managerial contemporary, Dick 'the Devil's' Advocaat, was also enjoying international success. Advocaat had also been present in Germany in 2006, as manager of South Korea. And though Advocaat's team didn't make it through the group stage, still, he'd been there, flying the flag for 'the Dutch way' on the biggest of stages.

Advocaat resigned from his role with South Korea after the World Cup and took up a lucrative job with Zenit, with whom he won nearly everything in a golden spell between 2007 and 2008. Zenit won the UEFA Cup, the UEFA Super Cup, the Russian Premier League and the Russian Super Cup. Advocaat himself was awarded the status of an Honorary Citizen of Saint Petersburg, thereby becoming the first foreigner to win such a prize since 1866.

Saint Petersburg is one of the grandest cities in the world.

So is London.

And yet, while his rivals were winning hearts and minds in such metropolises (this was exactly true in the case of Hiddink, who was begged to stay at Chelsea by senior players such as John Terry, and Michael Ballack),Van Gaal had pitched up at Alkmaar.

Alkmaar is a city of just under 100,000 in northern Holland. In terms of population it is around the size of a Kettering, a Lincoln, or a Falkirk. Numbers are boosted somewhat during the tourist season (April – September) when its famous cheese market makes it a relatively popular port of call. And visitors can also pay a visit to Alkmaar's very own museum dedicated to the music of The Beatles: apparently John Lennon's first guitar was made in Alkmaar.

Eventually, this sleepy backwater made all of Holland sit up and take notice when Van Gaal led their football team, AZ, to an unlikely Eredivisie title in 2009. For a spell, Louis was as famous as The Beatles, and Jesus, all rolled into one. And though Advocaat had won Honorary Citizen status for his feats at Zenit, Van Gaal could probably have demanded free cheese for the rest of his life for what he managed to pull off with the equivalent of Lincoln City.

Winning the title in 2009 was some feat. Alkmaar, in terms of population, is nearly ten times smaller than Amsterdam. And though the city's football team AZ moved into a new stadium in 2006, its capacity is just 17,000. Ajax Amsterdam had moved into their own new stadium ten years earlier: the 52,000 capacity Amsterdam ArenA. In 2008, Ajax paid €16.25 million to Heerenveen – a record between two Dutch clubs – to secure the services of Serbian winger Miralem Sulejmani. The only time AZ appear on such lists is as the selling club.

Louis van Gaal succeeded Co Adriaanse as

manager of AZ. Adriaanse is another interesting character from the Dutch football hall of fame. Though he doesn't quite occupy the same vaunted space as – say – an Advocaat or a Hiddink or a Van Gaal, he was another with Ajax connections. In his final season in the hot-seat, he guided AZ to an enviable third-place finish in Eredivisie before he departed for Porto (where he won the double). He was fondly remembered by AZ fans, whom he dubbed "the cheese viewers".

Those same fans might have been forgiven for viewing the appointment of Van Gaal with some trepidation. For theirs was a stable club, and if Louis was famous for anything, it was his ability to start a fight in an empty room. Still, it was the club's stability which persuaded Van Gaal to sign-up.

In the press conference to announce his arrival, Van Gaal explained his reasoning: "My decision to work for AZ is based on three criteria. They have a stable organization, where I believe that I can do my work in the right way and the quality of the squad shows lots of opportunities. The ambition of the club fits in with my own ambition."

In a later interview, Van Gaal was rather less modest. "When I signed at AZ it changed the environment surrounding the club. We are technically still a sub-top club, even though the media attention is rapidly increasing. The product – soccer - is a cooperation between the players, the technical staff and the medical staff. First of all there is the quality of the players, quickly followed by the quality of the coach. I think the coach is very influential in a team."

Speaking with Fifa.com in 2008, Van Gaal expanded even further, explaining the giant leap the club took under his management. "When I got here, they were still playing in an 8,000 capacity stadium which hardly ever sold out. Now we have a new ground with room for more than 20,000 fans, and last season we sold out almost every match. That's already an important step. The aim is for AZ to become a big club domestically and recognised throughout Europe on the same level as the big three over here: Ajax, PSV and Feyenoord. The president wants to work in stages so that every aspect is covered, not just the results on the pitch. Having said that, the fact that we are ahead of the big three in the UEFA rankings thanks to what we achieved last season is an essential element in the progress we are making."

Eventually his immodesty was borne out in the team's results over his time at the helm: within the space of two seasons, he helped bring AZ back to the forefront of Dutch football, and won their first Dutch league title since the heady days of 1981.

But first, LVG had to work his magic upon the club. Impose his blueprint.

That blueprint had to be altered slightly at Alkmaar, mainly as a result of the quality of the players at Louis' disposal. James Robson, writing for the *Manchester Evening News* notes: "He (LVG) began focusing on the instant when a team loses the ball. It's the moment – *omschakeling* – when the opposition's defence might be out of position. Built on the foundation of total football, AZ's game is to sit back and wait for its opponents to overstretch themselves and then break out."

No longer was the Van Gaal system about all-out offensive play and domination of the ball. Van Gaal, talking in hindsight about his time at Alkmaar, says: "Everyone said we played so offensive, but we really didn't. We were quick on the break once we had the ball, sure, but we always created our space first.....I believe in bypassing the nearest stations and finding the goal more directly. You need to provoke the space first, so to speak. And then you can utilise space for swift, deep actions. I think it's more entertaining and more effective."

In that first season at AZ LVG worked hard on

inspiring the players' trust and confidence in him. He won their trust by convincing players he *saw something in them* and that *what* he saw might transform careers.

The Guardian's Manchester United correspondent Jamie Jackson spoke to Simon Poulsen, a player under Van Gaal at Alkmaar. Poulsen said: "He can get an extra five or 10% from players. He made me better. I changed my position under him. I was a left-winger, now I'm a left-back and I made a lot of international games in that position. The first time he told me I thought he was crazy but it turned out to be my best position."

"It doesn't make a difference to him players who are not in the team," Poulsen continued. "For instance with myself, in the beginning I wasn't playing so much but even if I had an argument with one of the players who play every game he didn't take their side. He was always honest. When you're not on the field he will come and ask you: "How are you?""

Under Van Gaal's tutelage, AZ finished second in the 2005-06 Eredivisie season. PSV won the league by some margin, but Alkmaar finished a full 14 points above Ajax, in fourth, and boasted a goal difference of +46.

They almost went one better the following year, but in the end, 2006-07 would end *so near, yet so far.*

Still, it was an enjoyable season. AZ recorded the highest-scoring home win by any team that year in defeating NAC 8-1, and, though PSV Eindhoven had made a rip-roaring start to the campaign, AZ gradually clawed back the points gap. Jon Reeves, writing in the book *The Managers: Football's Greatest Managers,* says: "Working under less pressure and with less high-profile players (than at Barca and with the Dutch national side), the Dutchman successfully implemented his coaching techniques, as he guided AZ to third-place in the Eredivisie and the final of the Dutch Cup in 2007, narrowly missing out on a place in the Champions League."

Indeed, going into the final game of the season, it was still mathematically possible for AZ to win Eredivisie. Going in to that last game, AZ were top on goal difference from both Ajax and PSV. Yet Alkmaar – who were down to ten men after just a quarter of an hour - slumped to defeat against unfancied Excelsior Rotterdam (who finished third from bottom in the table), allowing PSV to clinch the title on goal difference from Ajax (and by three points over AZ) after they beat Vitesse 5-1.

Speaking to Fifa.com in 2008, Van Gaal recalls the frustration of finishing third. "It's always a real disappointment to lose out on a championship in the final match. The club needs a title to confirm the progress it has made. It's the next step that we have to take if we want recognition in the Netherlands. We only have a budget of 16 million euros, compared with 65 million for Ajax and 60 million for PSV, but we have been in the top three the last two seasons and we got to the final of the cup, which we only lost on penalties. The president is a wealthy man but he doesn't want to bump up the budget for the sake of just spending more. Money isn't the be all and end all. Ajax, PSV and Feyenoord all pay two to three times the wages that we do, but the gap is closing."

Closing, sure. But not closing quickly enough. The hangover from the disappointment of losing out on the title in 2007 led to a "less impressive 2007-08 season" (Reeves). They finished in 11th place – a decline of seemingly Moyesian standards – missing out on European qualification entirely and recording a goal difference of -5. PSV won the title – their 21st – and concluded the season nearly 30 points above AZ.

Jon Reeves writes that the rapid decline in AZ's fortunes "was the catalyst for Louis to announce his intention to leave AZ, but after the players campaigned for him to stay, he pledged to remain with Alkmaar. The manager promptly guided his team to an unlikely Dutch league title in 2009, as the team went unbeaten for the majority of the season."

That unbeaten run was something else: it lasted 28 games.

And 28 was an important number in 2008-09. For Alkmaar's title win meant they were the first club outside the Ajax, PSV Eindhoven, Feyenoord triumvirate to take the Eredivisie crown in 28 years.

Eventually AZ finished with "the best defensive record and the second-highest rate of goalscoring. AZ's title was sealed by an 11-point margin" (Reeves) and they leaked just 22 goals all season.

Poulsen said: "We maybe didn't have the best team but he does the best for each player and we had 24 games where we kept a zero, and we were playing good football."

James Robson said: "if Van Gaal's success at AZ proved anything, it is that he does not have to be blessed with the greatest individuals to fashion a successful team."

Following the success, Van Gaal became the toast of Dutch football all over again. Once more he was *the* undisputed Dutch heavyweight manager. It was football fairytale stuff.

LVG the HGV carried off the peer-voted and much-vaunted Rinus Michels Award as best Dutch coach at a glittering end of season awards ceremony. (The runners-up were Mario Been of NEC Nijmegen and former Manchester United assistant manager Steve McClaren – who actually *did play* for Lincoln City - of FC Twente Enschede.)

Six weeks later, Van Gaal left. On 1st July 2009 he was announced as manager of German giants Bayern Munich. He'd gone from unfashionable AZ to the *ultra*-fashionable FC Hollywood of European football in just a few small steps. "FC Bayern," he announced at his unveiling, "is a dream club for me."

And fitting reward for four years' hard work at AZ.

A more cynical explanation for his departure to Munich might be this: our Louis needed the money.

For although Van Gaal may be a "visionary" football manager, he was decidedly less so when it came to his financial affairs. Or so it appears if we judge him by his ill-advised investment in Bernard L. Madoff Securities; a scheme in which he ultimately lost €6 million of his personal fortune according to Dutch newspaper *De Telegraaf*. A textbook Ponzi scheme (in which the organisation pays returns to its investors from funds accrued from new investors rather than from any profits… until the money runs out) the scandal broke in 2008, and the investors who lost out were made public in 2009. Van Gaal's was one of the most famous names on the list.

Perhaps he'd been caught up in the moment – *omschakeling* – and had taken his eye off the ball.

At Bayern, he wouldn't make the same mistake.

Indeed, everyone in the Munich dressing-room would get a full, unadulterated look at their boss's balls during an infamous team-talk.

After a four-year-spell in a relative footballing backwater, "volcanic" Van Gaal had exploded back in the limelight. And how.

VI: "DEATH OR GLADIOLI"

BAYERN MUNICH (2009 – 2011)

The Dutch have a saying: "Death or Gladioli". Apparently it dates back to Roman times. It roughly means all or nothing. Louis van Gaal famously issued the phrase during a press conference at Bayern Munich, prompting widespread confusion, much shrugging of shoulders, and many quick Google searches from the assembled ladies and gentlemen of the German sportswriting fraternity.

At Bayern Munich, Van Gaal went hell-for-leather. All guns blazing. He was a "fundamentalist" in his desire to see his football philosophy made flesh once more at one of Europe's largest football clubs.

And for a while it worked. But then it didn't.

Indeed there is a case to be made for the fact that Van Gaal's career has been all or nothing. The players he has managed have either wholeheartedly embraced the Dutchman's system. Submitted themselves to it. Allowed themselves to develop as players within it. Or else they haven't. Or else they've bought into it for a while – for as long as it takes them to become successful, wanted by other clubs, offered large sponsorship deals – and then they've thought themselves too *stellar* for it. They've become the big I AM. And there is no I in team.

You either take *all* of Van Gaal's blueprint. Or you take none of it.

Daniel Cossai of Bayernforum.com claims: "The problem lies in the fact that although Van Gaal has remarkable beginnings, his endings are an entirely different story."

The beginnings, when Van Gaal brings his great vision to bear on a club and its players are glorious. But the endings, tinged as they are with bitterness, with acrimony, with wild accusations, are almost always diabolical.

So it was for Louis van Gaal at Bayern Munich.

At Bayern, the Dutchman was at loggerheads with the board for almost the entire second season. Uli Hesse noted in *Four Four Two* magazine: "In early October (2010), Bayern were in 12th. Rummenigge was livid. 'It can't be that we are 13 points behind first place with the squad that we have,' he said. Van Gaal was unmoved, probably because he knew that the main reason for the bad start was a string of injuries and the fact that his players were tired after the World Cup (a situation which was closely mirrored by his slow start at Manchester United in 2014, when a surfeit of injuries saw the Reds fail to win any of their opening four games under Van Gaal's charge). A few days after Rummenigge's censure, he presented his autobiography to the public. Waving a copy in the general direction of Hoeness and Rummenigge, who were in attendance as invited guests, he lectured them: 'It's important for you, too, to read this.' It may have been the straw that broke the camel's back. (…) Hoeness called Van Gaal 'advice-resistant', adding 'A modern football club mustn't be a one-man show."'"

Yet that was exactly how it had started. Van Gaal rode into Germany's third biggest city flushed with pride and a renewed vigour after of his unlikely success at AZ Alkmaar, who he'd guided to the Dutch league title. He signed a two-year contract, starting 1st July 2009. He would succeed Jurgen Klinsmann, who was sacked by Bayern in April when the German giants qualification for the next season's Champions League was in some doubt (as it was, with caretaker boss Jupp Heyneckes at the helm, they finished second).

"We are happy to have gained an experienced and successful coach," said Karl-Heinz Rummenigge, the Bayern chairman, upon unveiling Van Gaal as new supremo.

He also said: "If we had wanted to sign everybody's darling, we'd have gone for George Clooney."

Though he wasn't everyone's favourite *dream-boat*, Van Gaal labelled Bayern his "dream club".

However, according to Jon Reeves, "the first few months were more like a nightmare, as Bayern claimed just one win in his first four games and came close to an early exit from the Champions League. Speculation surrounded the manager's future as he struggled to implement his tactical beliefs."

Daniel Cossai of Bayernforum.com concurs: "Bayern under Van Gaal did not start off well at all. In the Bundesliga, we took just two points from our first three games. After the third game we signed Robben, who scored two goals on his debut, and won the next three games."

Van Gaal's capture of his compatriot Arjen Robben would prove a masterstroke. Like Van Gaal, Robben had struggled to find a 'home' which would appreciate his talents. He'd wandered from club to club, from Groningen and PSV in his native Holland, to Chelsea in England, and to Real Madrid, never once completing more than seventy games for his team. Though it was obvious he was talented, he was also incredibly selfish, and not exactly a team-player. So not the ideal Van Gaal player, you might think. But in his first few games at Bayern he was something else. His form would fade, eventually. But more recently, in the World Cup of 2014, Robben seems to have discovered a previously unseen level of performance. He'd delivered the same at Bayern over the previous two seasons. Unfortunately, Van Gaal hadn't been at the helm to enjoy them.

So masterstroke yes, but Van Gaal would not reap the full benefits, at least not in club terms.

And splashing €25 million on a player – especially a frustratingly inconsistent one like Robben - was hardly typical Van Gaal behaviour.

He'd rung other changes in the Bayern squad too: Mario Gómez, Alexander Baumjohann, Edson Braafheid, Ivica Olic, Danijel Pranjic, and Anatoliy Tymoshchuk all came in. Brazilians, in the form of Ze Roberto and Lucio, left the club. Then again, Van Gaal had always counted Brazilians amongst his 'favourites' wherever he'd managed.

And building a coherent team from so many fresh faces began to cause another downturn in form. After the initial explosion after Robben signed, "Bayern started dropping points again" (Cossai).

They were made mincemeat of in an away loss to Hamburg, and then, more embarrassingly, stunk out the place in a home draw with Cologne. By the end of September, they were languishing in eighth place in Bundesliga and statistics – apparently the one thing with which Van Gaal could not argue – made it Bayern's worst start in decades.

The Cologne draw was as bad as it got in terms of domestic form, and from there, things began to get better. That draw was the catalyst for a run of 19-straight unbeaten league games. However, worse was yet to come in the

Champions League. Between September and November they lost twice to Bordeaux in the group stage, meaning their progress from the group was very much in doubt.

In the end, the group came down to a crucial game against Juventus. It was practically a straight knock-out tie. Whoever won would finish second in the group (behind surprise winners Bordeaux). Whoever lost was out.

And Juventus had home advantage.

8th December 2009 would be "death or gladioli" for Van Gaal and his Bayern charges. They would have to take the Stadio Olimpico di Torino by storm...

Daniel Cossai calls it "the most memorable of Van Gaal's games for me. Ribery and Robben both missed the game, and Bayern ended up with Muller and Pranjic on the wings. Despite missing its two most important players, the team managed a memorable comeback, winning 4-1 after going a goal down (to a Trezeguet strike) in the first half."

The scorers for Bayern on the night deserve some note. The equaliser was scored from the spot by goalkeeper – yes, *goalkeeper* – Hans-Jorg Butt. (Actually this was not so much of a rarity: the German scored 26 penalties in the Bundesliga during his career, and *twice* from spot-kicks against Juventus in European ties. In a feature for *Four Four Two* magazine, Uli Hesse notes: "It was the first penalty the club had been awarded all season and the players looked at each other to see who had the nerve to take the most important kick in Bayern's recent history. The man who stepped up was none other than Hans-Jorg Butt (who) coolly sent his fellow No. 1 Gianluigi Buffon the wrong way and made it 1-1.") The others were netted by Olic, Gomez, and Tymoshchuk, Van Gaal signings all (although technically Tymoshchuk was already a Bayern player: Louis van Gaal had simply recalled him from a two-year loan spell).

Van Gaal, and Bayern, had their gladioli.

And they could go into the winter break warmed by those memories of a famous night in Turin.

They returned from the break even better: winning on all fronts now. Five in a row in the league (nine if you included pre-winter break games); a 6-2 rout of Greuther Furth in the Cup; an away goals victory against Fiorentina in the Champions League's first knockout round.

Things were beginning to click, and in a big way.

Van Gaal's system, his tactics, were beginning to take effect and a new style of play was in evidence on the field.

Christian Nerlinger, the then sporting director at Bayern Munich says: "In terms of tactics Van Gaal is not fixated on one particular formation. He develops the system in relation to the players at his disposal. When he came to Bayern, he identified Franck Ribery as his key player. He played him as No. 10 at the tip of a midfield diamond, then realised it did not work. We changed to a 4-3-3 and Arjen Robben was brought in for the right-hand side. But much more important and totally necessary at the time was his introduction of some basic structures and order. We had no left-footed players in the team. Van Gaal promoted Holger Badstuber because he wanted a left-footer on that side of the defence. It doesn't sound like a big deal but these changes had a huge positive impact in terms of balance and stability."

Balance and stability: these were two terms which wouldn't have readily been associated with Van Gaal during his tenure at Barca, nor when he was manager of the Dutch national side. But apparently his methods were working.

Nerlinger says: "It took some time for the team to settle and for the results to become consistent but I defended him in front of a doubtful board as I was totally convinced by him. I had never seen such a high level of coaching, it was totally different from what I had experienced as an active professional. In those days coaches moved you around. They had you training in shots, dead-ball situations and stamina. But I had never seen someone who came equipped with a whole, meticulously thought-out concept for practice sessions."

Nerlinger drills down into the details: "His work with the team was very impressive. There were two basic elements: firstly the individual work with the players – on a technical, tactical and physical level; secondly the physical conditioning of the whole team. All sessions were done with the ball. Van Gaal had players playing four against four with incredible intensity – much more fun than running through the woods. He drilled a passing and possession game into them and they developed a kind of passion for performing. There was an incredibly competitive spirit on the training ground."

Competition and details. It was all about the detail. Nerlinger says: "Some of his sessions looked quite banal but each one was performed with maximum intensity."

But then Van Gaal would change it up. "Two or three days before a game he would have the 'A' team play against the "B" team," says Nerlinger. "The latter had to fill in for the opposition. It was a bit difficult at the beginning for the guys in the 'B' team because they had to play roles that were sometimes alien to them. He had to coach them a lot, talk a lot, to ensure the exercise was done at a proper level. The match preparation focused on four elements: possession, opposition possession, transition to defence and transition to attack. He gave the players very clear instructions of the sort that you can use on the pitch."

Finally: "Everybody knew what was expected of them. He improved everyone individually. Bastian Schweinsteiger, for example, became a world-class central midfielder under his tutelage. Collectively the team went up another notch in the space of six months." High-praise indeed from Nerlinger.

As the season approached its business end, Bayern

were in fine fettle. Despite suffering a reverse at Eintracht Frankfurt in March, they held on to first place in the Bundesliga. And there were bigger things on the horizon. First, a DFP Pokal Cup semi-final against rivals Schalke 04. Then a *league* encounter with the same team (closely followed by a tie against challengers Leverkusen). And finally, and most glamorously, a Champions League quarter-final against Manchester United.

The United game was surely the tie of the round, drawing together as it did two perennial continental rivals who'd clashed regularly in the Champions League, most notably in the final in 1999 at Camp Nou, when two injury time goals had won the trophy for Sir Alex Ferguson's team, breaking Bayern Munich hearts in the process. And whilst the German club had gained some manner of revenge in the 2001 Champions League quarter-final, 1999 *still hurt.*

The first leg was played on the night of Tuesday, 30th March 2010 at the Allianz Arena and it couldn't have started in a worse fashion for a Munich side already robbed of Robben (he was sitting in the stands, injured). Manchester United – through Wayne Rooney – netted a vital away goal after just 66 seconds, volleying home from a Luis Nani free-kick. "It was," Sam Lyon wrote for BBC Sport, "exactly the start United boss Ferguson wanted, especially after he had admitted beforehand that he would take a goal over a clean sheet from the tie in Germany."

But steadily, Bayern played their way back into the game. "Most notably," writes Lyon, "Ribery began to torment right-back Gary Neville. It was he who forced the first save of the tie from Edwin van der Sar with a deflected 18-yard effort, and the Frenchman who then twice caused panic in the home defence in quick succession."

In the second half, Bayern began to dominate: "Olic, Thomas Muller and Mark van Bommel all brought Van der Sar into action with decent efforts, while a mazy dribble from Altintop was almost topped by a cracking finish only for the Dutchman to save."

This prompted Ferguson to make a tactical switch. He "replaced Michael Carrick and the ineffective Ji-Sung Park with Dimitar Berbatov and Antonio Valencia, but still the Bayern chances came – Olic's toe-poke saved at his near post by Van der Sar and then, ultimately, came their equaliser."

With 77 minutes on the clock "Neville gave away the free-kick with a needless handball, and Ribery punished the veteran's lapse in concentration to the full extent when his tame free-kick made its way through the wall and in via a deflection off Rooney."

Lyon writes: "United responded briefly and almost pulled themselves back in front completely against the run of play when Nemanja Vidic rattled the crossbar with a bullet header from Ryan Giggs corner. But still they looked vulnerable at the back and, in a finale reminiscent of that in 1999 when United came from a goal down in injury time to beat Bayern to the Champions League trophy at the Nou Camp, the hosts had saved their most dramatic moment until the last. Evra was the guilty party, dallying on the ball and allowing Olic to steal in, drive into the box, and clip past Van der Sar to send the home fans into raptures."

But it was only half-time in the tie. And on Wednesday, 7th April 2010 at Old Trafford, Bayern Munich would run into a Manchester United side bristling with attacking intent and with a point to prove after their rather toothless display in Munich. Before kick-off United were buoyed still further by the news that Wayne Rooney, who'd limped out of the game at the Allianz Arena, had been passed fit to play. Not only did this galvanise the United team, it also helped give the fans voice, and it was a rip-roaring atmosphere at Old Trafford on what might have been one of their famous European nights.

Rooney himself seemed desperate to re-write the

narrative of the tie. Starting like a Tazmanian devil he was all over the pitch, winning tackles, pinging balls to either wing, and, as Phil McNulty observed on the BBC Sport website: "he was quickly a thorn in Bayern's side, setting up Darron Gibson's opener after just three minutes."

The Manchester club's rip-roaring start continued. "United," McNulty writes, "looked on course for the last four when Nani turned in Antonio Valencia's cross four minutes later to put them ahead in the tie."

Wave after wave of United attacks crashed down upon a decidedly creaky-looking Bayern defence, and the Red Devils, roared on by 74,482 fans ecstatic at what they were seeing. "If Bayern had any plans to contain United," says McNulty, "they were in tatters."

"Bayern," writes McNulty, "were being run ragged and Nani capped United's complete supremacy when he scored his second and their third as half-time approached - but the whole mood and shape of the tie was turned when Ivica Olic took advantage of poor defending to bundle home a crucial goal before the interval."

It was game-on again. "Louis van Gaal's side suddenly discovered hope, and a measure of composure, their cause being helped when Rafael was sent off after 50 minutes following his second yellow card for a foul on Ribery."

From a United perspective, the sending-off was questionable: Ribery made the most of negligible contact to go down, but young Rafael *invited* the Frenchman to go over, and Ribery was never going to decline the opportunity. The only surprise was that it was Ribery and not Robben who'd been fouled for the red card.

Robben had missed the game at the Allianz but had been passed fit to play at Old Trafford. Like Rooney's return for United, it could have been the fillip Bayern needed pre-game. Only, he was non-existent during United's Red rampage in the first-half. Anonymous. Finally though, with the numbers skewed to ten against eleven, the Dutchman began to find space to run into.

Finally Robben decided to write himself into a match which had heretofore been dominated by the other R's: Rooney, Ribery, and Rafael.

His strike was magnificent. I was sitting directly in line with it at Old Trafford and were it not for the net, I think it might have wrecking-balled right through the stands and out onto the forecourt. He caught it that well. "United," says McNulty, "fatally left him unmarked at the far corner of the area, but he provided a classic low left foot volley that gave Van der Sar no chance."

It was the strike Bayern craved and it would prove to be the winner. And even through my red spectacles I could see it was a goal fit to win any game.

As in the previous round, Bayern had drawn 4-4 on aggregate, and again they'd progressed to the next stage – the semi-final – by the skin of their teeth: on away goals. But for the German giants this was a giant leap forward. Though they'd had a great record in the competition at the turn of the millennium – they were finalists in 1999, semi-finalists in 2000, and winners in 2001 – their record in the following years hadn't been great. Though the self-style FC Hollywood had qualified for the Champions League in practically every season (they only missed out in 2008, when they reached the UEFA Cup semi-final), the closest they'd come to the glitz and glamour of a return visit to the final was a spot in the quarter-finals, in 2002, 2007, and 2009. Their other seasons in the Champions League sun had been nothing much to write home about.

Yet suddenly Van Gaal had dragged them back into the big time.

They celebrated the illustrious aggregate win at Old Trafford by returning to home soil and hammering Hanover 7-0 in Bundesliga.

But there was barely time to take a breath for

Bayern as they continued to fight on three fronts: a famous treble looked on. They were helped by a somewhat favourable draw in the semi-finals of the Champions League. They avoided a clash with Van Gaal's 'Vietnam': Barcelona, the pre-tournament favourites and arguably the best team in the world. Barca were instead drawn against another team managed by a disgruntled former employee, Jose Mourinho's Internazionale. Instead Bayern pulled the French club Olympic Lyonnais. And though Lyon were perennial over-achievers in the Champions League at this stage, they were most definitely no *Barcelona*, no *Inter*.

The first leg of the semi-final – at the Allianz Arena - was a tight affair. Franck Ribery's sending off just before half-time incensed Van Gaal, and seemed to have tipped the balance of the game Lyon's way.

"Lyon's numerical advantage was short-lived, however," said Andy James, writing for UEFA.com. "Jeremy Toulalan collected two yellow cards early in second period, and the Bundesliga leader's reward for a dominant display finally arrived as the game moved into its final quarter. Robben – who scored winning goals against ACF Fiorentina and Manchester United FC in previous rounds – fired in from outside the penalty area."

James called it a "frustrating night" for Bayern, and noted: "Lyon still have work to do at the Stade de Gerland."

Bayern had work to do too: they'd denied the French side an away goal, but their advantage going into the second leg was as slender as Arjen Robben's hair. But a week later, at Stade de Gerland, Bayern yet again produced a sparkling away performance which blew away all doubts.

A fantastic treble from the Croatian forward Ivica Olic allowed the German giants to dream of a treble of their own. His hat-trick "capped a majestic performance from FC Bayern Munchen who impressively brushed aside ten-man Olympique Lyonnais to book their place in the

UEFA Champions League final."

Matthew Spiro, writing for UEFA.com, said: "Already leading thanks to Arjen Robben's solitary first-leg goal, the four-time European champions never looked like surrendering their advantage as they picked up where they had left off in Munich with another dominant display. From the moment Olic slotted in his first on 26 minutes Lyon were fighting a desperate battle, and when the French side lost skipper Cris to a red card just before the hour, Bayern merely had to bang nails into OL's coffin. Olic duly obliged, scoring his second midway through the second half before completing his treble on 78 minutes."

Despite all the odds which had been stacked against them at the start of the season, Bayern were through to their eighth Champions League/ European Cup final. Van Gaal himself was through to his third final.

Daniel Cossai, of Bayernforum.com told me: "I would say that the peak of Van Gaal's tenure was definitely reaching the Champions League final in 2010. It was unexpected and it meant a lot to us fans, seeing as the club had not managed to make it past the quarter-finals since winning the trophy in 2001, and had even played in the UEFA Cup two seasons before. It put the club back on the European map and Bayern went on to reach three European finals between 2010 and 2013."

Daniel takes issue with the idea that Van Gaal *always* puts his system above the players however. He says: "I think that the players played a big role in reaching the final in that season. The club was almost eliminated in the group stage, in the last sixteen, and in the quarter-finals. It was the magic of individual players, especially that of Robben and Olic, that saw Bayern all the way through to the final."

The first step towards the dream treble came on 1st May when Bayern wrapped up the Bundesliga title – with four games to spare – by beating Bochum. The second came a week later as they won the DFP Pokal Cup final in Berlin against holders Werder Bremen. Again they won with something to spare, having thrashed Bremen 4-0. Robben scored a first-half penalty, awarded after the referee spotted a handball by Bremen's Per Mertesacker, and Bayern never looked back. Olic, Ribery and Schweinsteiger (magic individuals all) put the gloss on it in the second half. It was Munich's 15th German Cup victory; their eighth domestic Double. But now all thoughts were on that third and final step to heaven.

The final was scheduled for 22nd May, at the Bernabeu in Madrid. There Bayern would face another side gunning for a hat-trick of trophies in Internazionale. The Milan side, guided by Jose Mourinho – who'd worked under Van Gaal as Barcelona in the capacity (Barca fans would have it) of 'interpreter', though he was actually on the coaching staff – had already secured the Serie A title to display alongside their Italian Cup trophy, and had seen off much-fancied Barcelona in the semi-finals (prompting another of Mourinho's famous self-serving displays of triumphalism on the Camp Nou pitch after the final whistle was blown).

On the Wednesday prior to the final, however, Bayern received some bad news. Van Gaal's team had appealed against the three-match Uefa ban which had been dished out to one of their leading lights, Franck Ribery, after his sending-off for a high-tackle in the home leg of the semi-final against Lyon. The Court of Arbitration for Sport upheld the punishment and Bayern would be without one of the key prongs of the attacking trident which had served them so well throughout the competition.

The Champions League final of 2010 was the first in the competition's illustrious history to be played on a Saturday. Over 80,000 fans turned out in Madrid. Van Gaal's Bayern started the better: "only Walter Samuel's timely intervention turning away Ivica Olic's dangerous cross before Bayern's Croatian forward shot wide at the near post after Arjen Robben had skipped away from Cristian Chivu and Walter Samuel down the right," reported Andrew Haslam for UEFA.com.

Indeed, "Bayern enjoyed 60% of the possession in the opening half-hour. However, Inter swiftly proved how quality counts for more than quantity. Julio Cesar's long kick was flicked to Sneijder by Milito, who raced onto the Dutchman's perfectly-weighted return to clip his shot over the advancing Butt."

1-0 after 35 minutes.

But Bayern refused to be beaten. They "continued to push Inter back into their own half, with Robben running at the Nerazzurri defence with increasing regularity. It was the winger's free-kick that led to Müller firing in another goalbound shot which was unwittingly kept out by Esteban Cambiasso, before Robben took matters into his own hands, cutting in from the right again and working space for a shot that Cesar clawed away from the top corner."

However, "though the German side continued to dominate territory and possession, there was no way back when Milito again broke through with 20 minutes left to secure Inter's first European Champion Clubs Cup victory since their consecutive triumphs of 1964 and 1965 and, with it, a special treble."

The dream was over for Van Gaal and his Bayern charges.

And yet, when the dust settled, the German giants could look back on their season with no little satisfaction. They'd made significant progress as a club: the appearance in the final in Madrid once again showcasing them amongst the continent's best. Fans were pleased with the new style of play. The board too were happy. So much so that they extended the Van Gaal's initial two-year contract well beyond June 2011. "We are delighted with the work of Van

Gaal and we have absolute confidence in him," said Karl-Heinz Rummenigge.

And yet, from this apparent position of strength, and authority, the Dutchman somehow managed to spoil it. The problem, as ever with Van Gaal, appears to be the fact that although *his way or the highway* worked when they were successful, when they weren't, all those people Big Louis had crossed were only too happy to come out of the woodwork and kick him while he was down.

Christian Nerlinger says: "Things took a turn for the worse in the off-season (...) There were clashes with the board and he proved very stubborn. The club wanted to strengthen but he insisted on keeping the squad lean and bringing through young players, like David Alaba. His rationale was to give everyone a realistic opportunity to play; too many unhappy players would have a negative effect on team spirit, he argued."

Nerlinger continues: "But a club like Bayern always has to add quality. He underestimated the need for depth in the squad and we paid a heavy price when a number of key players were injured. I was in the crossfire between him and the board but I continued to argue his corner – until he suddenly promoted the inexperienced keeper Thomas Kraft to the starting XI after the winter break, at a time when there was already a lot of disquiet in the team. At Bayern reaching targets is more important than developing a young keeper. His decision added to what was already a fraught relationship with the board. It was obvious to me that it was only a question of time before everything fell apart."

When things fall apart under Van Gaal, he, the centre, can no longer hold. Disaster ensues. Daniel Cossai says: "His second season with Bayern was disastrous, with the club ending trophyless, eliminated in the last 16 of the Champions League and barely qualifying for the same competition for the following season. In his second spell at

Barcelona he was fired after just six months, with the club not far above the relegation zone."

"The problem," Daniel tells me, "lies in the fact that although he has remarkable beginnings, his endings are an entirely different story."

His endings are car-crash stuff. Egos collide to the soundtrack of rending metal and screeching tyres, to the percussion beat of behind-the-scenes whining and back-biting. Van Gaal begins *barking*, as he did at Barca. Ahead of a match to defend their DFP Pokal Cup crown, Van Gaal *gruffed*: "I hope the desire to win is greater than the tiredness. But the body is less strong than the mind. And we've got a few wimps in this team."

Van Gaal was beginning to show his stubborn side. Daniel tells me: "He always wanted things his way. After his first season he refused Bayern's offer to make transfers, despite the obvious need for reinforcements. He wanted to be clear that he is bigger than anyone at the club, and this is what led to the incident of him pulling down his trousers in front of the team. He told them that he had the balls to take anyone off the pitch regardless of how big a name they were, and they would have to simply deal with it. He dropped his trousers to show them that he did, indeed, have balls."

"This authoritarian attitude led to trouble with some players. Luca Toni allegedly nodded off in a team meeting and Van Gaal wanted to get rid of him. Players like Ribery have said they were unhappy with Van Gaal as coach. It is no coincidence that Ribery's form exploded (resulting in the European Player of the Year award) once Heynckes, a warmer, friendlier person, became coach. Van Gaal's coaching method is not necessarily a bad thing, because a coach must not be overruled by his players, but he had taken it to such a level that it harmed the team."

The team, in fact, was one of the things that was missing.

As was one of the major stars. Arjen Robben had been injured during the World Cup. He'd spend over two months on the sidelines. During which time Bayern's title defence got off to a terrible start. A meagre eight points from their opening seven games fell well below expectations of both board and supporters. And the poor form continued all the way up to the winter break, with Bayern unable to pull away from their position of mid-table obscurity.

The problem, as Daniel Cossai would have it, was Van Gaal's utter disregard for the more defensive aspects of the game. "He insisted that he must have a left-footed and a right-footed centre-back on the field, but it seems that under Van Gaal it was more important that the centre-backs could pass well rather than actually defend. The team played a high defensive line despite Van Buyten and Demichelis being quite slow. The system exposed Bayern's weaknesses and made the team more vulnerable to them. This is evident if one compares Daniel Van Buyten's performances under Van Gaal with those under Heynckes. He played much better when the latter was coach."

In summary, Daniel tells me: "Van Gaal created a defensive system that allowed opponents to score easily, and he could not (or would not) deviate from it. And this is exactly why I believe that Van Gaal was merely the beginning of success, and for that success to be maintained it was inevitable that someone else must be brought in."

It got so bad that when I asked Daniel to give me an example of the Dutchman's *low points* during his spell at the helm at Bayern, Daniel told me, unequivocally, that the low point "would be *his entire second season.*"

When I pressed Daniel to explore those painful memories even further, he told me the very worst. "The very lowest, in my opinion, was the second leg against Inter in the Champions League. Bayern were at home on the back of a 1-0 away win. I think that game showed exactly what Bayern under Van Gaal were really like. Bayern's attacking power was evident in the first half. The team could have easily scored four or five. But it also exposed Bayern's weakness: the attacking was covering up the defensive weaknesses. Bayern failed to score despite creating lots of dangerous chances, and eventually were punished as Inter capitalized on the mistakes of the much-neglected defence."

Tactically, once again, Van Gaal was outmanouvred by an Inter Milan coach, just as he had been in the Champions League final of 2010. This time, Jose Mourinho was no longer in charge – he'd departed in the wake of the treble win, for Real Madrid: actually he hadn't had to go far, seeing as though the final was *played* at the Bernabeu. Instead it was the Brazilian, Leonardo.

Leonardo led Inter to victory against Van Gaal's Bayern in the Champions League Round of 16. As Daniel says, Bayern had done the hard part: they'd won at San Siro – and bagged an all-important away goal - thanks to a last-minute strike from Mario Gomez on 23rd February 2011. But on 15th March they were shown up. Samuel Eto'o wiped out Bayern's away-goal advantage as early as the fourth minute, and though Bayern swung the tie their way before half-time through goals from Muller and Gomez, in the second-half Bayern continued to press and were caught twice. Goran Pandev scored the decisive away goal to seal the tie with two minutes to spare.

Prior to the Inter defeat, the Champions League had seemed the season's saving grace. Bayern had walked through a group containing Roma, Basel, and Cluj losing only once at Roma's Stadio Olimpico in the penultimate game of the group, when they'd already qualified. They'd progressed to the knockout stages boasting a plus 10 goal difference and had secured handsome wins against Roma (at home) and Cluj (away).

But once Bayern had been knocked out of the Champions League, Van Gaal was on thin ice. And in April, as the Munich club flirted with *not qualifying* for the next year's competition, the board had had had enough. He was fired.

"The dismissal hurt him", claims Nerlinger.

What would no doubt have hurt him more was the fact that *after* he was replaced – eventually, on a permanent basis by Jupp Heynckes – Bayern would go from strength-to-strength. Eventually the German giants would come to be seen as – arguably – Europe's premier club, succeeding Barcelona, another club at which Van Gaal had arguably laid the foundations for success.

Van Gaal would never be there to enjoy what he'd built.

As early as December 2011, Daniel Cossai spotted the fact that Bayern were attempting to build their club based on the Barcelona model. In an article on Bayernforum.com entitled 'How Bayern Munich has followed in Barcelona's footsteps in the chase for European domination' he discussed the reasons why.

"Last month," he noted, "Philipp Lahm said that there are similarities between Barcelona, and the current FC Bayern team. This statement was not without basis, and we can see how Bayern are currently developing in the same way as Barcelona did a decade ago. (…) Unsurprisingly, the situation in both clubs began thanks to the same man. This is, of course, Louis van Gaal." The Dutchman "laid the foundations of the offensive, possession-minded football at the heart of both teams' style. His contribution in the promotion of young talents was also very important, and Barcelona have kept this up even after his departure."

"What has allowed Barcelona to be so successful," said Daniel, "and what Bayern seem to be trying to achieve, is the continuity in the squad. This was helped a lot by giving importance to players from their own youth academy, who know the system inside out and can be introduced at the right pace."

"It is about time that Bayern stop rebuilding the team every two years (…) But if Bayern keep faith in this project they have undertaken… they have so far developed in a similar way to Barcelona, why shouldn't a similar end be possible? Barcelona's era of domination is nearing an end, and it seems to me that Bayern is the club which is closest to replacing them at present."

After reading the article I contacted Daniel to ask him where he kept his crystal ball. Not only did he predict back in 2011 Bayern's recent success, he also identified the man who would perfect their "system" for them: Pep Guardiola.

Daniel Cossai told me Van Gaal "was a great visionary, and was very important in putting Bayern on the European radar again after an absence of nine years. If we look at humans as divided into thinkers and doers, Van Gaal would definitely fall under the former category. Success undeniably requires both thinkers and doers, and I think that this is what explains Van Gaal's shortcomings as a coach. It is the reason why the club needed Jupp Heynckes to develop Van Gaal's philosophy and bring success. Although Van Gaal's ideas were at the heart of Heynckes's team and, although perhaps to a lesser extent, still are with Guardiola at the helm, I firmly believe that the club would not have won a treble had it persisted with Van Gaal as coach."

He continued: "For this reason one needs to be careful as to how much praise and recognition Van Gaal should be given for Bayern's present success. It is easy to fall into the trap of saying that he is the mastermind behind it all because he devised the system. However, one must not underestimate the influence of subsequent coaches. The fact is that with Van Gaal as coach the team was very unbalanced. I would say that he introduced Bayern to possession football, and also the attacking system. To this day Bayern's attack still focuses on the wings, while taking advantage of space in the centre as defenders are drawn towards the wings. Bayern began doing this under Van Gaal with Ribery and the newly-transferred Robben on the wings, and Muller and Olic (and later Gomez) in the centre."

Van Gaal announced that Bayern were his "dream club" upon his appointment in 2009, but he was not the club's dream manager. "That," according to Daniel Cossai, "was Jupp Heynckes (his successor), who actually *won* the treble (although that would not have been possible had Van Gaal not preceded him)."

Guardiola is in charge at Bayern now, having played under Van Gaal at Barca, and having then perfected Van Gaal's system whilst managing the same club. It has been a three-tiered process, through Van Gaal, through Heynckes to, finally, that zealot of the possession game, Guardiola. And Daniel Cossai said: "Van Gaal was a very important *element* in Bayern's present success; Heynckes was the stepping stone that eliminated Van Gaal's weaknesses (such as the defensive side of the game), and then comes the man to perfect it all. And although Guardiola continues to tinker and experiment to make the system better, the possession-based *total football* that Van Gaal introduced remains at the heart of it all. If we compare Guardiola's and Van Gaal's first seasons, they more or less had the same success. I would consider Guardiola to have been superior because he relied much less on individual quality and more on the system. With Guardiola as coach I felt, for the first time ever, as though Bayern could truly win regardless of who the eleven starting players were."

Christian Nerlinger agreed: "He (Van Gaal) gave Bayern a strong football identity that subsequent coaches – Jupp Heynckes, Pep Guardiola – have successfully built upon."

Daniel told me that Van Gaal's other big contribution, other than the style of play, was *shaping the squad* and *developing the players*. Alaba and Muller, who are still very important for Bayern today, were promoted by Van Gaal. So was Badstuber, who was also a regular until December 2012 when he was sidelined with an injury and still has not featured again for Bayern. Contento and Kraft also got their opportunities with the first team thanks to Van Gaal, although neither ever really succeeded."

"In this regard," said Daniel, "Van Gaal is again seen to be a great visionary. Not only did he identify these players and give them their chance, but he also made decisions which may have been shocking at the time, but have in the long run been seen to be genius."

"Van Gaal famously said 'Alaba is a left-back, even he doesn't know it himself yet.' The player had always been a midfielder and Van Gaal had been widely criticized for putting him at left-back for a handful of games, where he committed a number of mistakes."

"Today, Alaba is arguably the best left-back in the world and is almost untouchable for Bayern in that position."

"A similar case is that of Thomas Muller. Having always played as a striker for Bayern's youth teams, Van Gaal utilized him in a number of positions. He played on both wings and as a central attacking midfielder. This clearly worked out, as Muller went on to win the Golden Boot at the 2010 World Cup playing as a right attacking midfielder. It worked to such an extent that in the past season several fans criticized Guardiola for playing Muller as a striker."

"Van Gaal was also the first one to play Schweinsteiger as a central midfielder. Schweinsteiger went on to have his best season ever, at least up until that point, and has never really looked back. It was under Van Gaal's guidance that Schweinsteiger lived up to his potential and became a consistent player."

I asked Daniel to take another look into his crystal ball and tell me what he thought Van Gaal might achieve at Manchester United.

He said: "I would expect Manchester United to have a much better season than the past one, but I also think his first season will be trophyless. With Manchester United, Van Gaal must not only introduce a visionary kind of football like he did with Bayern, but he must also rebuild a squad from scratch and fill in the void left by Sir Alex Ferguson. I think that Manchester United under Van Gaal will look very different from the one we are used to, both in terms of players and playing style. I am convinced that the move is a good one for the club, but based on what I have seen of Van Gaal at Bayern, I would say that Manchester United too must see him as a stepping stone, one who revolutionizes the club and prepares the tools which a later manager can use to restore the club to its glory."

But first, before Manchester, Van Gaal had one huge stepping stone of his own to cross over: a return to the helm of the Netherlands national side, and one more shot at managing in a major international tournament.

VII: "GOLDEN WILLY"

NETHERLANDS NATIONAL TEAM (2012 – 2014)

Arjen Robben's comments about Louis van Gaal in Brazil 2014 gave a whole new meaning to 'World Cup Willy'. Recalling Victoria Beckham's famous phrase about her "Goldenballs" husband, Robben, when asked whether he thought Van Gaal was a lucky coach, said that Louis must have "a golden willy".

Perhaps he does. Certainly Robben will know one way or the other, having been present in that Bayern dressing room in which Van Gaal lowered his pants and flashed his genitals.

During the World Cup 2014 there was plenty of discussion about whether Van Gaal was a lucky coach or just a very, very good one. There were a number of stand-out examples of his tactical switches altering the conclusions of matches involving his Netherlands team. Amongst the headline moments of tactical 'genius': the formation change he made during a short, regulation drinks-break against Mexico in the Round of 16, which brought about a late, comeback win; the dramatic late introduction of goalkeeper Tim Krul as substitute for Jasper Cillessen, and Krul's amazing antagonizing of the Costa Rican penalty-takers before he saved two and secured the Netherlands place in the semi-finals; the utilization of Dirk Kuyt, a man who started out as a striker in his native Holland, as both left- and right-full-back during the competition.

Hell, in Brazil Van Gaal was such a bonafide miracle worker that Rob Bleaney, with his tongue firmly implanted in his cheek, noted in *The Guardian*: "After reinventing Dutch football with a 3-5-2 system stolen from Martin O'Neill's Leicester City side of the late 1990s, he (Van Gaal) has managed to get Robin van Persie scoring headers from outside the box and transformed Dirk Kuyt into a hard-running tactically astute left-back. The stone-faced Dutchman has even got Arjen Robben admitting he dives after a decade of feigned injuries and faux innocence."

That is some Midas-touch for a gold-member.

The Dutch went into the 2014 World Cup as 33/1 outsiders. Much longer odds than they'd been in any previous major international tournaments. And yet, under the tutelage of Van Gaal, the Netherlands came close enough to touch the World Cup final. They were only penalty-kicks away from reaching a fourth final. That was some going.

And it could so easily have been England who were the recipients of Van Gaal's good fortune/ tactical genius. Back when the Dutchman was in charge at Alkmaar, he told an interviewer from Fifa.com that he had a clause in his contract which enabled him to leave earlier "but only to coach a national team. (…)England were on the list."

But England chose Fabio Capello instead (and then Roy Hodgson).

Still, clearly Van Gaal had international-scale ambitions. He told Fifa.com that his goal was "to take part in a major international tournament with a country and to win it. I've won almost everything there is to win at club level. What I feel is missing is the experience of a EURO or a World Cup at the head of a national team."

Back in 2008 (when the Fifa.com interview took place) Van Gaal would have scarcely credited that chance would come with his own national team.

Back in 2012, when Louis van Gaal succeeded Bert van Marwijk as Netherlands coach nobody would have credited the Dutch would have been going for gold in Brazil.

For one, Van Gaal's first spell as national team coach had ended in ignominious failure: his charges had flopped, badly, and hadn't even made it through qualification. For two, the Netherlands were struggling somewhat with their global image, having gone wildly against type and played the epitome of destructive football – sometimes literally, as with De Jong's kung-fu kicks – in the 2010 World Cup final against Spain. This had been followed by a winless, row-full group stage exit from Euro 2012 in Poland and Ukraine.

After that, new players had been brought in but they weren't thought to be of the same quality as those they'd replaced and they had nothing like the stellar names Van Gaal's squad had boasted when he'd singularly failed to steer them through a group containing Portugal and Republic of Ireland in 2000-01. Back then, the overwhelming majority of Dutch players had played for a veritable *Who's Who* of major European club sides: Barcelona and Real Madrid, Milan and Juventus. Van Gaal's squad would feature players from – meaning no disrespect – lesser clubs such as Norwich and Swansea City, Aston Villa and FC Augsburg.

"This is the challenge I've been waiting for," said

Van Gaal, upon his appointment. It was rather less provocative than what he'd said upon his *first* unveiling as Dutch master, when he'd claimed: "I've signed a contract with the Dutch national team until 2006, so I can win the World Cup not once but twice."

They say hubris can do that to a man.

They say experience can do that to a man, also. And finally, Van Gaal appeared *restrained, on the leash, far from the maddened barking dog* he'd been characterised as at Barcelona, and then Bayern.

And things went swimmingly in qualification: the Dutch, in transition though they were, were the first European side to qualify for the 2014 finals, boasting an exemplary record of nine wins out of ten group games (they drew the other one). They scored 34 goals and conceded just five. However, Daniel Cossai was just one sounding a note of caution: "it must be pointed out that the quality of the opposition was questionable," the Dutch "having played against Romania, Andorra, Hungary, Estonia, and Turkey."

During qualifying (and friendlies) Van Gaal experimented: he used a whole host of new players (45 across one 17 game stretch). *FourFourTwo* magazine noted: "He handed debuts to 19 players, of which 12 were under the age of 23".

Of the 23-man squad eventually Van Gaal took to Brazil, *ten* had won under ten caps.

However, despite the nay-sayers, Van Gaal (and he was seemingly alone in this) was confident he had the requisite quality players to adhere to the Dutch style 'guidelines'. He said: "The KNVB gave me a clear mission to play 'Dutch School' football, and with the quality of this squad that must be possible."

Yet even he must have had misgivings when the draw for the group stages was made. For the Netherlands were drawn in Group B, alongside holders Spain (who'd defeated them in the 2010 final), the dark horses Chile, and Australia. And though USA made claims that *theirs* was the tournament's group of death (they faced Portugal, Ghana, and Germany), the Dutch could have been forgiven for thinking that luck was against them.

And then Kevin Strootman, the crucial pivot in the Van Gaal system got injured in April 2014 whilst playing for Roma and was ruled out of the World Cup. "Strootman," wrote Jonathan Liew in *The Telegraph,* "was the key to the system. A strong, quick runner with exceptional vision, Strootman's ability to carry the ball out of midfield at speed and set defences on the back foot gave Holland a wealth of angles going forward. Just 24 years old and at Roma, he has invited comparisons with Roy Keane and Yaya Toure."

Van Gaal was inclined to agree: "Strootman is a player who brings a balance to the entire team," he said. "I will have players like Rafael van der Vaart and Sneijder, of course, but no one will be able to replace Kevin."

Tactics expert Jonathan Wilson witnessed a Strootman-less friendly for the Dutch, in which central defender Bruno Martins Indi was "tormented by Karim Benzema."

"Troubled by his defenders' ability to handle one-on-one situations, Van Gaal went to watch three of them play for Feyenoord against PSV Eindhoven. They lined up in a 3-5-2, the extra man in the middle at the back meaning one-on-one situations were minimised, and that, he realised, was the answer."

But there were other potential problems. Van Gaal made the intriguing – some might say crackpot – decision to select two notoriously temperamental players (and for that read Iyer's "artistic, moody individuals with ego-balloons the size of Kirov airships" remark from the chapter on Van Gaal's *first* spell as Dutch boss - as his captain and vice-captain: Robin Van Persie and Arjen Robben respectively.

Whatever could go wrong?

Well, as it turned out, nothing.

Amy Lawrence, in *The Guardian,* noted: "both players have responded brilliantly to the enhanced sense of responsibility."

Van Persie in particular seemed enamoured with Van Gaal throughout the tournament: indeed, one of the most memorable images of the 2014 World Cup was Van Persie celebrating his famous goal against Spain with a (slightly-botched) high-five with his boss. Not only was tight relationship a bonus for the Netherlands during the World Cup, it is also one huge plus point for Manchester United fans after Van Persie's rather less than happy 2013-14 season at Old Trafford.

It is a relationship built on mutual respect. In Leo Verheul's excellent book on Robin van Persie, he writes: "Van Persie is now the captain of Holland and in October 2013 he became his country's all-time leading scorer, surpassing Patrick Kluivert's record with a hat-trick against Hungary. 'It was a fantastic moment,' Van Persie said, 'especially because my two kids were there. Normally matches are too late for them, but that time the two of them were there. Maybe they don't realise exactly what happened, but it'll be wonderful to be able to talk about that memory in the future.'"

After sealing his hat-trick Van Persie was substituted by Van Gaal, allowing the crowd to show their appreciation. "The public," said Van Persie, "stood up and gave me a hell of an ovation. That's Van Gaal. I was injured in the days before, my little toe. Ridiculous, but very painful. A couple of days before the game it was still hurting. The house-rule within the Dutch team is that you if you're in pain, you have to go home. But the coach made an exception for me. And that paid off. Sometimes every piece of the puzzle falls together. This was such a night."

Van Persie went on: "Van Gaal gave me all the confidence I can ask for. He made me the main striker, my favourite position. At last. He made me captain. I owe him something. So I will be as sharp as a knife in Brazil. I will walk on fire for him if I have to. Like the rest of the team. We have a lot of options. Our coach has a lot of choices over there. I think we are going to do something special: like in 2010 but hopefully this time winning the final."

Some confidence there, from our boy Robin. But then again, like Van Gaal, he's never been short of a touch of the old confidence.

Still, amongst the rhetoric, there are some important points here. Suddenly, the unbreakable Van Gaal had been talked of as having "made exceptions for players".

Shorn of Strootman, Van Gaal's system would not work as effectively as it was supposed to: there was no adequate stand-in. And so, in the World Cup, Van Gaal made what seemed like an extraordinary about-turn. For so long it had all been about the system, the system, and nothing but the system. Then, in Brazil, it became about *the players*. And in particular the three stellar names: Arjen Robben, Robin van Persie, and Wesley Sneijder (none of which particularly fit the LVG mould – hungry young players – all three were 30 at the World Cup).

There is a case to be made that the Netherlands would never have made it out of the group stage had Van Gaal not changed his thinking on this: had he not trusted to the temperament of *players* rather than the workings of the system.

Not that Van Gaal would have it that way.

Still, backs to the wall, the Netherlands – very much outsiders in the betting stakes – came out fighting in the group and, thanks to luck, judgement or individual skill, they exceeded all expectation.

In their first game, against Spain, they were given little chance, and yet produced the performance of the World Cup to send shockwaves around the globe, running out *5-1* winners (in the old days of the vidiprinters, that 5 would probably have had to be followed by a *five* in brackets, just to make sure the viewers could appreciate the veracity of what they'd seen.)

It was magnificent.

"On BBC television," wrote Jonathan Liew, "Thierry Henry evoked Johan Cruyff, saying that he and coach Louis van Gaal 'brought Total Football to Barcelona and the Spanish squad; I think tonight, the Dutch got their style back'."

"In one sense," said Liew, "this was true. Holland played with a verve, a swagger and a purpose that we have not seen from them since at least the late 1980s, when a team containing Ruud Gullit, Frank Rijkaard and Marco van Basten swept to the European Championship under Rinus Michels, himself the architect of Total Football at Ajax in the late 1960s. The sight of blue shirts (not orange, unfortunately; thank the sages at Fifa for that) swarming all over the world champions was a sight to stir all football fans of a certain age. The Dutch were masters of their craft once more."

The game was a feast for the eyes. Not least Robin van Persie's worldie: a header from outside the box which sailed over the stranded Iker Casillas and into the net. This equaliser was scored at the ideal time – just before both teams trooped off for the half-time break – and imbued the Dutch with the impetus and belief to go on and blitz Spain in the second half. *Arjen Robben* knew this. You just had to witness him as he left the field at half-time, dancing around as though the Dutch had already won. This reaction came in for some criticism from the BBC pundits, but it was what it was: an act of supreme confidence from a man who'd play a vital role in the second half.

And yet, there was more to the game than met the eye. Jonathan Liew observed that "three of the goals came from long diagonal balls over the Spanish defence. Another,

Stefan de Vrij's oh-god-I'm-about-to-crash-into-the-post header, came from a set-piece from the left. And one more came from the leaden boot of Iker Casillas, allowing the ball to squirm away so Robin van Persie could win it. Then there are the statistics. In a resounding victory, Holland had just 43 per cent of possession, and committed 18 fouls to Spain's five. So was this the return of Total Football? Or have Holland and Louis van Gaal managed to create something completely new?"

"The 3-4-3 that Van Gaal played on Friday night was essentially a reactive formation designed to combat Spain's dominant midfield," said Liew. "The wing-backs did not venture too far forward, and with midfielders Nigel De Jong and Jonathan de Guzman essentially screening the back three, Holland reverted to a 5-2-3, or even a 7-3, without the ball. And seeing as this was Spain, they were quite often without the ball."

But when the Netherlands *did* get the ball, they moved quickly. They moved it "not with short passes and intricate triangles, but with long diagonal balls, unleashing the pace of Robben and the movement of Van Persie, exposing Spain's high line and creaky defence."

"Perhaps," said Liew, "the greatest irony of all was that Spain, as ever, were playing a very similar style of 4-3-3 to the one that Cruyff and later Van Gaal had pioneered at Barcelona. Van Gaal's fingerprints are all over Spain's recent successes: he gave Xavi, Andres Iniesta, Carles Puyol and Victor Valdes their Barcelona debuts, oversaw the progress of Gerard Pique and Cesc Fabregas at La Masia."

"It was Bayern Munich who offered the blueprint for overcoming tiki-taka, when they demolished Barcelona 7-0 in the Champions League semi-final last year. Van Gaal's protégés Schweinsteiger, Alaba and Robben were all in that side. Now, with Holland, he has done it again, and in so doing may well have struck another nail in the coffin of modern possession football, a doctrine he helped to create.

If that sounds fanciful, then at the very least he has played a leading role in its two greatest catastrophes."

Not that Van Gaal was thinking in terms of catastrophes. No, the Dutchman was in a boisterously cheery mood in the aftermath of the game. "I did not expect that it would go this way," he said, "it could have been 6-1 or even more, and we had a very happy feeling."

Suddenly he was a stand-up guy: everyone's friend. He was all high-fives and winks. Nudges and laughs. *Smiles.*

Still, before the second group stage game, Van Gaal had found *something* to rage against. In a pre-game press conference, he railed against the positioning of the *cameramen* in the Estadio Beira-Rio, where the Netherlands would take on Australia. "In the middle of the pitch there is a cameraman who deprives me of the view, and with me all the coaches and managers sitting in the ground, because we are dug under rather than dug out," he barked. "That obliges us to stand up. I'm a sitting-down coach, not a standing-up coach." Still, he did manage a weak joke (which the assembled media latched upon as though it was the quip of the ages: much as they'd reacted to a jovial remark from Sir Alex Ferguson). Van Gaal then joked that he may have to get himself a barstool so he could see the pitch.

After the game – a 3-2 win for Holland in which they had to come from behind - some bar-room commentators might have been forgiven for observing that perhaps Australia might have even *won the game* had they had Dutch stars Arjen Robben and Robin van Persie playing for them. In *The Guardian,* Pete Smith thought that was most definitely the case: "A feature of this World Cup already has been the pivotal intervention of the world's best players in front of goal. Robben and Van Persie (…) have found an extra level of quality to turn tight games into wins."

Yet again we come back to that shift in Van Gaal's thinking: from team above all else to *players, special players.*

"Holland," Smith wrote, "were on the back foot and turned over possession more times than they usually do over multiple matches. Louis van Gaal changed from a nominally 3-5-2 formation to their well-known 4-3-3 at the interval, and with it the momentum of the game started to shift."

"Fortunately it turned out OK, but it could just as well have turned out differently," said Van Gaal. "In the second half we created more opportunities. I really have to congratulate the team, compliments to them, because the way we came from behind was incredible. I never want to put any individual in the limelight, but the way in which Nigel de Jong took the lead was impressive."

Quick off the blocks in qualifying, the Netherlands were now amongst the first teams to qualify for the knock-out stages of the World Cup. This gave Van Gaal the chance to tinker with the starting line-up. With Robin van Persie suspended, he picked the first Dutch starting x11 *without* a 'van' for nearly twenty years. But even more notable than that was the fact LVG selected the ex-Liverpool striker Dirk Kuyt as an auxiliary *left-back* in what was a very defensive line-up.

In the game against Chile, the South Americans enjoyed 64% possession – which is Dutch/ Spanish-style stats – and yet Van Gaal's makeshift Holland side went on to win 2-0, thereby securing top spot in the group (and avoiding Brazil in the first knockout round). When asked about his controversial 5-3-2 formation, Van Gaal said: "I believe you have to create a strategy to win. The proof is in the pudding. If it had not worked you would have chopped off my head. I know that."

Which is some backtracking from the man who once said: "I believe you should always entertain the fans and the fans are, in my opinion, entertained when you play offensive soccer."

Van Gaal was in imperious form as he "deadbatted

questions over whether this was the best moment of his career. 'If you look at my CV, you'll see that I win a lot of matches. That's not new.'" (Owen Gibson, *The Guardian*). He "put his match-winning double substitution down to luck but his smile betrayed the fact he thought otherwise. A second-half header from Norwich City's Leroy Fer two minutes after coming on ensured Holland topped the group with maximum points in front of Chile."

The Dutch nation didn't care if it was luck or judgement. Before the Round of 16 game against Mexico a Forza Football poll of 100,000 Oranje army supporters showed the approval rating for Van Gaal had jumped from a pre-tournament 67% to a near-perfect 93%.

And while we're playing this numbers game, the Mexico match in Fortaleza was played in temperatures sometimes exceeding 38C. This meant that a drinks-break had to be scheduled into proceedings. In *The Guardian*, Michael Cox spotted how Van Gaal used this break to good effect: "At 1-0 down, Louis van Gaal switched from 3-4-1-2 to more of a 4-2-1-3, with two natural wingers, and Holland built pressure down the Mexico flanks." After that, the Netherlands found their way back into the game, and two late goals carried them through to the quarter-final.

Before it, the Netherlands had been *out of it*. It had started as "3-5-2 against 3-5-2, with predictable consequences – both teams had a spare man at the back, the midfield battle was even and the wing-backs spent the duration of the game chasing one another up and down the touchlines," said Cox. "Neither had an advantage in a particular zone and none of the attacking players could find space."

"Mexico were the dominant side," he continued. "Their strategy was simple – they know the Holland defenders concentrate on man-marking very tightly, so Giovani dos Santos and Oribe Peralta made decoy runs into deep positions, opening up space for midfield runners.

Hector Herrera and Andres Guardado obliged – sporadically, considering the heat. Holland defended in numbers, and always had someone sweeping, sometimes the goalkeeper, Jasper Cillessen, who started very high up the pitch. He looked nervous throughout, and seemed slow to get down to Dos Santos' long-range opener."

Then the drinks break, and then "we saw Louis van Gaal's tactical genius, switching from a three-man defence to a back four, as he had done against Australia in the group stage. Soon after Holland went 1-0 down he summoned another attacker, Memphis Depay, with the right wing-back Paul Verhaegh sacrificed and Dirk Kuyt switching flanks. Holland were now 4-2-3-1, with width on both flanks and Arjen Robben pushed to the right. Immediately the situation was different. The Mexico wing-backs, who had concentrated on tracking their opposite numbers, were now forced back against out-and-out wingers, and formed a five-man defence. This opened up space for the Holland full-backs to bring the ball forward and, while Kuyt and Bruno Martins Indi are hardly the most dangerous full-back pairing, they helped increase the pressure on the Mexico backline."

"The key, however," concluded Cox, "was Robben's new position on the right. He was involved in everything – dribbling with the ball at speed, crossing for a fine Wesley Sneijder headed chance and forcing Guillermo Ochoa into an excellent one-on-one save as Holland mounted their fightback. Following Sneijder's late equaliser from a corner, it was again Robben who wreaked havoc in the Mexico defence, forcing Rafael Marquez into a clumsy challenge for his third penalty appeal of the game – this time successful. On this form Holland's tactics should be obvious – get the ball to Robben."

But, in the quarter-final against Costa Rica, Van Gaal had an even better trick up his sleeve.

Costa Rica were the surprise package of the 2014

World Cup. They'd been drawn in a group with three former winners – Italy, England, and Uruguay – and most observers thought they'd be the whipping boys. When, on the eve of the tournament, the Costa Rica manager was interviewed on BBC Radio Five Live and he claimed his team stood a chance of progressing through the group, his claim was met with widespread hilarity. His further claim that he fancied his boys would pick up three points against England had many rolling in the aisles.

As it was, Costa Rica could only draw against England, but before that they'd taken both Uruguay and Italy by surprise, leaving England (miserably) and Italy (limply) as the sides who missed the cut.

Costa Rica had played a fast, incisive brand of hard-running attacking football over the three group stage games, but against Greece in the last 16, they'd adopted a far more defensive game-plan and had taken the match all the way to penalties, where they'd won out. And it was clear from the off the Costa Ricans were attempting the same trick against the Netherlands. They stifled and frustrated Van Gaal's team over 90 minutes, restricting the Dutch to half- and quarter- chances until right at the last, Robin van Persie slipped free of his marker – you would have bet your house on him scoring – only to miss the ball with an embarrassing fresh-air shot.

In his match report *The Guardian's* Owen Gibson said: "the Dutch laboured at times against opponents determined to use all means at their disposal to stop them and who were superbly marshalled by Navas and Giancarlo Gonzalez. Having switched from 5-3-2 to 3-4-3 in the absence of Nigel de Jong, the *Oranje* were disjointed. Memphis Depay, brought in on the left of a front three, disappointed. The forwards thrown on by Van Gaal to break the deadlock, first Jeremain Lens and then Klaas-Jan Huntelaar, were largely anonymous."

They weren't the only ones. Of that much-vaunted triumvirate – Van Persie, Sneijder, and Robben – only Robben looked in any kind of form. "Van Persie," wrote Gibson, "having invested so much in recovering from injury to captain his side in Brazil, looked heavy-legged. He missed several chances he might ordinarily have gobbled up and was frequently caught offside."

Sneijder, "aside from a free-kick that smacked a post and a dipping shot in extra time that came back off the crossbar (...) also found it hard to impose himself."

"That left the imperious Robben. Dripping in sweat and with at least two Costa Rica defenders in close attendance at all times, he kept going and going. Riding tackles and apparently determined to stay on his feet this time, he was," said Gibson, "his side's relentless heartbeat."

But, when the whistle was blown to signal the 90 minutes was up, the Costa Rica fans celebrated wildly. It was as though they'd already won. It was as though reaching extra-time (with the promise of spot-kicks on the horizon) they'd already won. After all, only England have a more miserable record than the Netherlands when it comes to penalty shootouts, and the Costa Ricans had already shown their dead-eyed prowess in the previous round against Greece.

Costa Rica stifled and frustrated the Dutch in extra-time too. Time dripped by, hotly. Everyone was simply sweating on the penalties now. Penalties and then the inevitable Dutch exit. But, just before the referee signalled the end of 120 sun-beaten minutes, Van Gaal pulled his rabbit out of the hat. Or rather, he pulled his substitute goalkeeper off the bench. Sending on Tim Krul for Jasper Cillessen in order that the Newcastle United stopper, Krul, the taller and larger-framed of the two, would face the penalties was a huge gamble. One which, had it failed, would have left Van Gaal's face dripping with egg.

But it did not fail.

Owen Gibson wrote that throughout the competition, Van Gaal's "every gamble has paid off as Holland have found a way to clear each hurdle. Yet, as any departure lounge self-help book will tell you, the harder you work the luckier you get. (…)" But, he noted, "Van Gaal's bold gamble (…) had been seven weeks in the making. That is how long the imposing Newcastle United goalkeeper (Krul) had been studying the penalty takers of the other teams in the competition. The scheme, cooked up by Van Gaal with the goalkeeping coach, Frans Hoek, was based on cold, hard logic."

"With the plan kept secret from the other players, Krul was taken aside shortly before kick-off to explain that he would be called on if the match went to penalties," wrote Gibson. "Krul had saved two penalties of his last 20. The 25-year-old Cillessen had saved none of the 16 faced in his career."

"As Costa Rica's exhausted players lined up on the halfway line on their knees and Holland's put their arms round one another, Krul began psyching out each opponent by telling them he knew where they would put the ball. And he did, going the right way every time."

Krul "defended his behaviour. 'I don't think I did anything wrong. I did nothing crazy. I didn't shout in an aggressive manner. I was trying to get in their heads and it worked,' said Krul, adding that he would do the same against Argentina (in the semi-final) if the situation arose."

And it *worked.* Krul saved two spot-kicks (from Brian Ruiz and Michael Umana) in a shoot-out which was far more gripping than anything the preceding 120 minutes had provided. And Holland's penalty-takers – for once – honoured their part of the bargain. That triumvirate - Robin van Persie, Arjen Robben, Wesley Sneijder – all dispatched their penalties with ease (as did Kuyt, another of the "old guard").

In the wake of the shoot-out win Arjen Robben said: "We have a superb trainer, a coach who works magic like this all the time. Nobody knew about what he was going to do apart from one goalkeeper."

Scott the Red from the Republik of Mancunia Manchester United blog claimed Van Gaal's "brave gamble" was one other managers should have had the "golden willy" to take. Specifically Sir Alex Ferguson. Scott recalled: "The FA Cup final in 2005 should have been the one positive of what was otherwise a hugely depressing time to be a Manchester United fan. Chelsea ran away with the title and United lost out on second place in the league to Arsenal. The Glazer family took control and plunged the most valuable club in the world in to an unthinkable amount of debt. The rain poured down in Cardiff for the final, a week after the takeover, with fans holding protests before the game."

"However," Scott continued, "when United went on to play Arsenal off the park for two hours, our fans were allowed to believe that maybe it wasn't as bad as it could be. After beating the London club home and away that season, ending their 49 game unbeaten run at Old Trafford, then thrashing them 4-2 at Highbury with ten men, an FA Cup final win, for the second consecutive season, would have been the icing on the cake."

"Unfortunately, these were the days when Sir Alex Ferguson couldn't make his mind up between Tim Howard and Roy Carroll, two, admittedly, inadequate goalkeepers. Howard had initially impressed, winning the PFA Goalkeeper of the Year award in his first season, but after a few crucial mistakes, Ferguson opted for Carroll instead. If that isn't going to destroy a goalkeeper's confidence, being dropped for Carroll, then I don't know what would."

"Fergie went with Carroll for the final but when the game finished 0-0 after extra-time, it looked as though Howard was going to come on. Maybe that was never the case, but from my seats, through my desperation, Howard looked to be hovering around and I hoped Fergie would be bringing him on. We had only made two substitutes so bringing on the goalie who was clearly the superior shot-stopper."

"Fergie left Carroll on the pitch though and he didn't get close to any of Arsenal's penalties. Lauren and Freddie Ljungberg sent Carroll the wrong way, whilst Robin van Persie left him with no chance as he rifled it in to the top corner. Then Ashley Cole stepped up and reduced the goalkeeper to just falling on his knees, before Patrick Vieira won Arsenal the FA Cup."

"Louis van Gaal did what Ferguson didn't, and replaced a goalkeeper purely for the penalty shoot-out. Tim Krul saved two of Costa Rica's five penalties and booked Holland's spot in the semi-final of the World Cup."

"Of course, it is Van Gaal who will get the credit, after Krul becomes the latest 'super sub' for the Netherlands in this summer's competition. In their second group stage game, it was substitute Memphis Depay who scored their winning goal against Australia in a 3-2 victory. In the next match, it was substitutes Leroy Fer and Mephis who scored the two goals in their 2-0 win over Chile. In the round of 16, it was substitute Klaas-Jan Huntelaar who scored a 94th minute winning penalty against Mexico."

"The substitution of Krul was win-win for Van Gaal though. If the goalkeeper made no saves, then no one could have given him or the manager a hard time. But if he made saves, as he did? Well then Van Gaal gets hailed as a genius.

That won't stop United fans celebrating the latest success of their new manager though."

As the World Cup hurtled towards its business-end, it seemed *everyone* was celebrating Louis van Gaal. Prior to the Argentina semi-final, Barney Ronay (that reliable barometer of the footballing big picture) wrote in *The*

Guardian: "Depending on how the next five days go Holland's manager has a fair shot at emerging by the end as the most influential single participant at this World Cup. A tournament that had seemed likely to be decided by a shimmy between the lines from some magenta-booted princeling could yet end up being defined by the spectacle of a 62-year-old Dutchman pointing and waving and glowering on the touchline."

Ronay observed: "Van Gaal (...) has just kept on coming at this tournament, his nudges and tactical shifts a tangible feature in Holland's run to this stage – so much so that should Van Gaal uncover the managerial grail and successfully still Messi's influence it is not impossible to imagine him turning up on the touchline at the final in a Mozart wig waving around a conductor's baton."

Stilling Messi's influence, though: easier said than done.

"It (the Argentina game) is a classic club management challenge – stop the opposition's best player (Messi), while also leaving yourself a chance of winning – that shines an interesting light on Van Gaal," said Ronay. "Manchester United's new manager has described himself as a process trainer, a manager with a set of ideas that will of necessity take time to seep through his team and attach to all its working parts. The intention is not to tinker at the edges but to create a style so coherent and well-grooved that what the opposition do in reply is almost irrelevant."

He continued: "Tournament football is of course very different. It is a matter of reacting and adjusting, getting out the string and Sellotape mid-match, a challenge from the Mourinho-esque pragmatist's school. For Van Gaal, this tournament has been a series of miniatures where he would normally aim for the big, sweeping masterpiece. It must be said, however, he has looked throughout like a man enjoying himself to an almost indecent degree, as though this is, in fact, the closest he is ever likely to get to a genuine summer holiday."

"Against Spain that bespoke deep-set, direct-football approach (…) was a stunning success," Ronay judged. "Against Australia Van Gaal had the satisfaction of tweaking his formation in adversity and wrestling the match back Holland's way. Against Chile a counterattacking plan worked well. Even against Costa Rica, a thrilling mess of a match, Van Gaal found a way of standing out, just as Messi has for Argentina. His Tim Krul intervention stole the headlines, even if it was not quite a stroke of instinctive genius but pre-planned logic based on Krul's extra reach."

But Lionel Messi does not play for Costa Rica, Chile, or Spain.

Before the 2014 World Cup began Louis van Gaal had based his whole managerial *credo* on the fact that *he was not* Johan Cruyff - that most messianic, that most Messi-anic of players. As a coach he'd always trusted to *systems* rather than individuals. Players, he'd argued, were interchangeable. The system was king. And yet now Van Gaal would face his ultimate test when his Netherlands side faced a nation, a team, who was – more than any at the World Cup – defined by one player: Lionel Messi.

Which is all kinds of ironic.

As is this: Messi was the most polished diamond ever produced at Barcelona's La Masia. Despite being born in Argentina, he'd honed his skills at Barca, and had learned how to implement them as part of a team-system. Van Gaal was, of course, one of the key men involved in the development of that system.

And now the hopes of all South America rested on his shoulders.

The two previous World Cup finals had been played out in the absence of a South American side. And after Brazil had been humiliated (7-1) by Germany on the night before Argentina's clash with Holland, if Argentina did not make it through to the final that would make it three-in-a-row. Such European dominance had never happened before in World Cups. And certainly not when the tournament was being played *on South American soil.*

Argentina themselves had not reached a semi-final since 1990 – during which time Brazil had rubbed salt in the wounds by winning it twice – but once Argentina *do reach* semi-finals, they were generally pretty reliable: the South Americans had progressed from their three previous last four appearances and had gone on to win the competition twice.

Once, of course, *against* the Netherlands in 1978.

Argentina hadn't shone brightly in the competition thus far. The case *against* their being Messi and ten others wasn't easy to argue. He'd scored two crucial late goals to win games (on his own) in otherwise disappointing performances. But Argentina fans could take comfort from the fact they were not Brazil. After their neighbours' stunning defeat in the other semi-final, they delighted in singing (to the tune of Creedence Clearwater Revival's *Bad Moon Rising)* this little ditty (translated for us via *The Huffington Post):*

"Brazil, Tell Me How It Feels,
To Be Bossed Around In Your Own Home,
I Swear That Even If Years Pass,
We Will Never Forget,
That Diego (Maradona) Out-Skilled You,
That Cani (Claudio Caniggia) Surprised You,
You Are Crying Since Italy (World Cup 1990) Till Today,
You Are Going To See Messi,
The World Cup Will Be Ours,
Maradona Is Greater Than Pele."

Argentina-Holland became a "personal duel" between Louis and Lionel. Miguel Delaney in *The Independent* talked of how Messi "dominated the psychology of this match (…) even before kick-off. (…) The Dutch manager, Louis van Gaal, who has never exactly been a man for airs and graces, stayed lingering around the line-ups in order to catch Messi's eye and shake his hand."

But would Messi be greater than Van Gaal's *team? (Or even his "golden willy"?)*

In the end, they weren't the right questions. As Sam Wallace reported in *The Independent*: "The greatest player of his generation has his place in football's greatest game. Lionel Messi will walk out at the Maracana stadium on Sunday to take on Germany in the World Cup final…" *but* this "was not Messi's finest two hours on a football pitch."

Instead, the 2014 World Cup semi-final "was one for the dogs of war".

Daniel Taylor went further: he called it a "wretched semi-final" - a "stinker" - in his *The Guardian* match report. Miguel Delaney, again in *The Independent,* reached for the dog metaphors again in a comment analysis column: he called it a game full of "dogged tenacity and tension rather than devastating technique."

The Guardian's Owen Gibson said this was: "Attritional Football" rather than Total Football. Van Gaal's "Dutch team (…) showed little or no ambition" (Wallace) and we were left with a game which was "far from a classic".

The Dutch were – if anything – *too* focused on Messi. In this "drab old game in the rain in Sao Paulo" (Wallace's lovely phrase) "De Jong (was) following Messi around like a bad undercover detective".

The players were *all* hunting for a clue to crack the case for the defence but never quite could. "The game's great attacking players – Messi, Robin Van Persie and Arjen Robben – were forced to take bit-parts in a match played out between two cautious defences and two zealous midfields," said Wallace. And: "it went to extra-time without Van Gaal's side mustering a decent shot on goal."

By the time extra-time had been played, Van Gaal's

Netherlands had "failed to score in 240 minutes of football" (Owen Gibson).

Daniel Taylor agreed: "this was not the same, fluid Dutch team that had illuminated the competition with so much rich promise in the earlier stages. Perhaps they had peaked too soon."

It was turgid stuff. "The game started slowly and never really quickened up and, by the second half, it had become riddled with carelessness." (Taylor).

And, as Sam Wallace reported: "It told you all you needed to know that one of the game's few outstanding players was Vlaar, the Netherlands' centre-half who patrolled the defence, and Messi in particular, with a certainty that had not always been evident in his time at Aston Villa. Javier Mascherano, who looked like he might have been briefly knocked out in the first half, was superb, never more so than when he blocked a late run and shot by Robben."

"A pragmatic man, Van Gaal was not too proud to send out a Netherlands teams that was primarily set-up to neutralise the threat of Messi – as much as any team can – rather than try to exploit the explosive attacking force of Robben and Van Persie," said Wallace. "It meant that the first half drifted by with very little of note from the Dutch, and just seven touches of the ball for Robben."

"As for Van Persie, he was substituted halfway through the first period of half-time looking shattered but without having had a sight of goal. The introduction of Klaas-Jan Huntelaar was the last of the Netherlands' three substitutes." (Wallace)

So there would be no grand gamble for the penalties, as there had been against Costa Rica. No LVG magic trick. Though the Dutchman's hand was forced – Van Persie was clearly running on empty – the very fact he'd had to use up his three substitutions before he could call on Krul meant there would be no *psychological shock tactics* with which the Dutch could gain the crucial upper-hand.

Hauling off Van Persie also meant he was unavailable to take the first penalty – the one which sets the tone for the whole shoot-out – and instead that honour went to Ron Vlaar. You just knew he was going to miss. And he did – Romero plunging to save - and from that moment on, the narrative, the *momentum,* was *obvious.*

Lionel Messi's primary contribution to the game was to score his own penalty – Argentina's first. And though Robben nervelessly struck to make it 1-1, Argentina maintained the upper-hand. They scored their next penalty and then it was the turn of another of Van Gaal's "old masters" to step up to the plate. Though Wesley Sneijder's penalty was well-hit, Romero again guessed right (he'd clearly watched where the Dutch players placed their spot-kicks in the Costa Rica shoot-out) and saved outstandingly.

It was left to Van Gaal to lament the fact that he "taught Romero how to stop penalties (at AZ Alkmaar)." He added: "so that hurts." (Van Gaal signed the Argentine in 2007 from Racing Club and spent two years as his coach before leaving for Bayern.)

Daniel Taylor concluded: "Holland should not just reflect on the inability of Ron Vlaar and Wesley Sneijder to beat the Argentina goalkeeper, Sergio Romero, but also the fact their entire team did not manage a single shot on target during the 120 minutes that preceded the shootout."

But once the dust settled on the defeat, the Netherlands could be rightly proud of their young team's performance in the tournament. Dutch football expert Michiel Jongsma, writing on the Republik of Mancunia, noted that this was "their youngest selection to the World Cup in 76 years", and yet they'd done as well as – if not better than – so many of their more celebrated predecessors.

Arjen Robben said: "We must be proud of what this young team has achieved."

In the end, the Dutch went down – and out – as a team. But throughout the tournament it had been their trio of star players who'd carried them through.

The Netherlands finished in third place. Though Louis van Gaal was a staunch advocate for the scrapping of the Third Place play-off, his Dutch side did win it, by three goals to nil, heaping further humiliation upon hosts Brazil. And the game gave him the opportunity to throw *another* goalkeeper into the fray as a late substitute. This time it was Swansea's Michel Vorm, who became the 23rd member of Van Gaal's squad to appear in the tournament. This meant every member of the Netherlands squad was used in Brazil – the first time this had happened at any World Cup.

Of the controversial – in LVG's mind at least – play-off, the Dutchman said: "I think that this match should never be played. I have been saying this for the past 10 years."

"We will just have to play the game but it is unfair," he continued. "The worst thing is, I believe, there is a chance that you lose twice in a row in a tournament in which you've played so marvelously well. You go home as a 'loser' because possibly you've lost the last two matches."

In the end though, the Netherlands went home as winners and Van Gaal in particular had had his reputation very much enhanced by the competition.

And, seemingly, he'd finally laid to one side that argument over whether he is a very, very good coach, or just a lucky one.

Because it is amazing how lucky you get, the harder you work, and, as Jon Reeves claimed in his book *The Managers*: "Van Gaal didn't simply rely on the talents of his players to succeed, he prepared them with obsessive intensity".

The World Cup was a hothouse competition, bristling with intensity. Holland had been long-shots, but through hard work and vision, Van Gaal guided them to the brink of their fourth final. Ryan Giggs, who'd been named as Van Gaal's assistant in the Dutchman's *next* job had witnessed the coach's feats from afar, and he said: "It's excited everyone. He's mixed up his formations, he's juggled around the players. To get to the semi-finals of the World Cup is a great achievement. He'd have liked to have gone further but it wasn't to be. The group they were in – to get out of that was an achievement in itself, so to go so far I'm sure he'll be pleased."

And while Lionel won the "personal duel" against Louis and reached the World Cup final – which he would lose: in the end the best *team* won the competition rather than the team boasting the best individual - there was no doubt that Van Gaal's reputation – which for years had been up and down like the incurable sufferer of OCD who was *sure* he'd left his bathroom taps on – had almost never been higher (Ajax's miracle of Vienna in 1995 notwithstanding) than in the wake of his brazililliant 2014 World Cup campaign.

Certainly in the UK his stock had never been higher.

Indeed the near-deification of him as some kind of Super Coach had reached such ridiculous levels – even the victorious Argentine central defender Martin Demichaelis *who Van Gaal sold off as surplus to requirements at Bayern* described the Dutchman as "the best coach in the world" - was lampooned by Jacob Steinberg in *The Guardian's* The Fiver. Steinberg claimed the World Cup had taught us many things, but the most important one was this: "Louis van Gaal is clever, he's cleverer than you, he's cleverer than Einstein and that there is nothing he didn't think of first. The internet? Van Gaal. Television? Van Gaal. Sliced bread? Van Gaal. Medicine? Van Gaal. Thinking? Van Gaal. Vanishing spray? Van Gaal."

That caricature of him at Barcelona as the brick with hair? Gone. Replaced by - as Steinberg would have it -

a new image (which plenty of us bought into (as though it was a Ponzi scheme): Van Gaal as a mad-scientist/ genius who "spends every match watching from the touchline while simultaneously drawing quadratic equations on a Fifa-erected chalkboard, delivering lectures on Plato to the Dutch bench and coming up with cures for baldness."

And though Van Gaal had not achieved his ambition of winning the World Cup, he would depart on a high, his contract with Manchester United – a club he regards as "the biggest in the world" – already signed, sealed, and delivered.

And with United, he'd face a task as difficult as any he'd ever faced as a coach.

But then, Van Gaal likes a challenge.

VIII: VAN UNITED

PART 1 - THE APPOINTMENT

MANCHESTER UNITED (2014)

When I was a lad my favourite restaurant in Manchester was the Dutch Pancake House. It stood on St. Peter's Square, opposite the Central Library, and boasted big plates which would have pleased even Alan Partridge. It's long-gone now, but every time I hop on the Metrolink to Old Trafford and the tram stops at St. Peter's Square, I remember it like a ghost of birthdays past.

Louis van Gaal – with his boxer's nose and weak chin – has a face as flat as any pancake the Dutch Pancake House might have served up, and when he signed on as the new manager of Manchester United I felt the kind of lurch of heart I *used* to feel on only the most special occasions, like the birthdays we spent at the Pancake House, like when United won the FA Cup in 1990, like when they *finally* won the Premier League in 1993, like when the Reds signed Eric Cantona.

Sir Alex Ferguson left one gaping hole in the dug-out at Old Trafford when he retired in 2013. David Moyes did not adequately fill that hole. Indeed he frequently appeared scared to; instead haunting the touchline like a ghost of present-day inadequacy, some round-eyed Gollum in the possession of something – the manager's hot-seat at Old Trafford – which was greater than all his earthy desires but which was also destroying him, piece-by-piece, wrinkle-by-wrinkle.

Incidentally, on the theme of ghosts past, present and future: I sit in the corner of the Stretford End, where it joins up with the Sir Alex Ferguson Stand. Robin van Persie has the corporate box just behind my seat. And Louis van Gaal was the recipient of Van Persie's hospitality on more than one occasion during the 2013-14 season: primarily to check in with his captain prior to the 2014 World Cup in Brazil. And so, for David Moyes, during those painfully embarrassing Old Trafford defeats of 2013-14, not only was the spirit of 'Christmas' Past present, in Sir Alex Ferguson upon whose crimson-hued cheeks the TV cameras unfailingly flitted, especially after a United concession, but also the spirit of 'Christmas' Future, in Van Gaal, up there amongst the gods, casting his withering gaze over the clueless, luckless shambles over which Moyes presided.

Van Gaal and Ferguson on opposite sides of the pitch, but joined by their vision, their *credo,* the brand of attacking football their teams play. Van Gaal and Ferguson: a bridge joining them, arcing over – editing out – the haunted David Moyes, leaving him forgotten, a troll underneath the bridge.

Van Gaal and Ferguson, two men cut from the same managerial cloth. "Particular personalities," wrote Daniel Harris, in *The Guardian,* "suit particular positions." And both men had the personality to lead Manchester

United. Not just manage it. *Lead* it.

Van Gaal, the obvious choice. Daniel Harris again: "Despite plenty of pontificating and prevaricating, rarely are these notions complex, or even unique; clubs are distinguished far more by history than principle. In the case of Manchester United, the requirements, more or less, are fast, attacking play, fighting spirit, youthfulness, attitude and zest."

"These were values personified by Matt Busby," he continues. And "this explains why Louis van Gaal is the perfect replacement for David Moyes and Sir Alex Ferguson – United all over, even if he fails. And though his pedigree suggests this to be unlikely, it also fortifies him with an important degree of levity, because his career will not be defined by it. Should he succeed, he will still boast finer achievements; should he not, his reputation will get by."

"United," as Barney Ronay noted, "have never had a foreign manager, the Irishman Frank O'Farrell aside. They have never appointed a manager anywhere near Van Gaal's 62 years of age." But *still* Van Gaal was the obvious choice.

He "represents, in outline, the complete opposite of his predecessor. (…) Moyes offered trophyless continuity with the promise of a long stay. And received opinion seems to be that Van Gaal represents the anti-David Moyes, not so much continuity or longevity, but a gold-standard track record and a sense of playing once again with the big boys."

Moyes," argued Ronay, "was a sentimental, oddly literal kind of continuity appointment. United has been managed by Scots for 75 of the past 100 years (…), but Moyes was only ever the most flattering, rootsy Glasgow-centred Ferguson-Busby facsimile. It is Van Gaal, Jose Mourinho and the well-travelled elite of European management who represent continuity. Ferguson broke up, bought in and sold off teams on a similar scale to the itinerant big beasts of European football through his own successive United eras. He just didn't have to move house to do it."

"So," continued Ronay, "to Van Gaal, whose career makes a fairly good case – according to Louis van Gaal at least – for existing in a class of one. In the past few days the word genius has been routinely bandied about. Sir Bobby Robson once called him 'the top of the tree'."

And yet, his "three spells at Europe's established financial giants – Bayern and Barça twice – have ended" badly, as we have seen within these pages. And that, Ronay claims, "is something that could work in United's favour. Van Gaal – who lost up to £4m in the Bernard Madoff scandal in 2009 – remains a hungry-looking managerial genius, a man who clearly feels he has unfinished business, another dynasty in him."

"This is where the Dutchman starts to distinguish himself most favourably from his immediate successor," said Ronay. "With United right now it isn't just about trophies won or clubs managed, but methods, development and attitude. This is a club still in the process of a traumatic succession. Van Gaal has the aura, but more than that the philosophy, the clear and unarguable structures to make a productive break with the old ways. We're not talking Steve Round, Jimmy Lumsden and Phil Neville here. Van Gaal is an enduring intellectual aristocrat of the European game, with a strong personal connection to a distinct footballing philosophy, Ajax's triumphant total football of the 1970s and his own bespoke 90s era. In this light Van Gaal again starts to look less like a stopgap or a three-season stabilising force and more like a more wide-ranging answer to United's current need for a clear-out, a bolt-on set of methods, an answer to the basic question of how this team wants to play."

Manchester United have flirted with the *Dutch way* in the past, but this has mainly been seen in the form of buying Dutch Masters such as Arnold Muhren, Jaap Stam, Ruud van Nistelrooy, Edwin van der Sar and Robin van Persie (and to a much lesser extent Jordi Cruyff, Raimond van Der Gouw and Alex Buttner) to bejewel an already glistening crown. Oranje has been the colour for a number of important United wins: Stam had been the rock-foundation upon which the 1999 treble was built; Van Nistelrooy was the thoroughbred with the dead-eyes of a killer whose goals had kept United in the hunt during the early noughties; Van der Sar's saves in the penalty shoot-out in Moscow had secured United's third European Cup in 2008; and Van Persie had made the difference during United's procession to their twentieth league title in 2013.

But never had United *gone Dutch* to such an extent as they had in appointing Van Gaal. And never had the need for change – for the Dutchman's blueprint for success – been more obvious.

Mind you, United have never been afraid of change. Even in the aftermath of their most successful season. In his piece entitled 'Imagining Louis Van Gaal', by Phil, on Livelifeunited.com, the author argues that as the dust settled on the '99 treble-wining season, "Fergie knew that in order to move the club forward, he had to adopt a more progressive way of playing in response to the changing landscape of modern football. Thus, he brought in Carloz Quieroz as his no.2."

Quieroz, Phil argued: "had a lot of continental exposure to change the tactical approach in order to bring the club forward. This resulted in the birth of the 2008 team which Jonathan Wilson described as the "world leader in tactical innovation in this decade".

However, "since Quieroz left United" and we witnessed the departures of "Ronaldo, Tevez , Hargreaves (due to his injury) and Scholes (retirement) United have slowly regressed tactically." And "United hit rock bottom tactically when Moyes took over: his rigid and outdated tactics were being found out time and time again."

"Hence," Phil stated, "United are in dire need of fresh ideas and a more progressive approach to the game in order to catch up which Van Gaal will able to offer with his right footballing philosophy and the knowledge of the game."

Moyes was an isolationist appointment. An unadventurous appointment. He knew the English game. He knew Everton. He brought in an Everton way of doing things. He brought in Everton coaching staff, lock, stock and barrel (and also said goodbye to good inflencers such as the Dutchman Rene Meulensteen). This did not go down well with the much-garlanded United players: champion defenders such as Rio Ferdinand and Nemanja Vidic did not much fancy being taught how to play their positions by watching videos of Phil Jagielka.

Van Gaal is a much more *expansive* appointment. He has European knowledge and pedigree. Prior to his settling into the role at Old Trafford, Louis van Gaal just *seemed right* for Manchester United. Big and cunning and arrogant and broad-shouldered and visionary and successful enough for the toughest job in football. Cocky enough to believe he could fill Sir Alex Ferguson's boots, certainly.

And, what's more Van Gaal would be onto a winner from the off: United fans were *already* grateful to him: willing to give him time. Because he wasn't David Moyes. Because United had *already* been through so much upheaval. Because we'd already seen how bad things could get. Right-hand to Cantona, United fans would be pleased if he'd just play football the right way. That was all we wanted after the 2013-14 season of unrestrained mediocrity in which the Red Devils had failed to even qualify for the Champions League,

We all felt the same: according to United's own ticket office more people than ever before renewed their

Season Tickets in the close-season, in the wake of Van Gaal's appointment.

Behind the drawbridge of the fortress which is Old Trafford, the *players* felt the same. Robin van Persie had already claimed he would "walk on fire" for the new boss and had enjoyed a successful 2014 World Cup under his tutelage: one only had to witness the (slightly botched) high-five between the pair of them after Van Persie's wonderful diving header against Spain to know all about the mutual respect the pair had for each other.

Hell, even within the ranks of the back-room staff whose jobs might have been under threat from Van Gaal's staff there was great enthusiasm. Paul Scholes, who was uncommonly outspoken about the David Moyes era, wrote in his Paddy Power column: "Right now, Manchester United fans and myself cannot wait for Louis van Gaal to get the job started at Old Trafford. It wasn't a vintage Holland team he was managing and Van Gaal got them to the brink of a World Cup final. He's going to have to perform a similar operation at United after a shocking season in 2013-2014." Scholes felt Louis van Gaal would improve the Reds "by up to 25%" because he had a "touch of genius" that could make United "serious challengers" again.

Jamie Jackson contended that the United players (the ones who survived the cull, at least) would be "desperate to forget last season's debacle under David Moyes". He reckoned the players – who'd been disillusioned under the leadership of the Scot – would welcome the new manager's "tactical fluidity" as witnessed in the World Cup.

They would also welcome his broad-shoulders. Too often in 2013-14 Moyes sought to blame players for poor performances. Van Gaal during the World Cup made it plain the buck would always stop with him. Jackson noted that after his "golden willy" gamble in replacing Jasper

Cillessen with Tim Krul for the quarter-final's penalty shoot-out: "Van Gaal made the smart move of later stating that if the gamble had backfired he would have shouldered the blame. This worked as an exercise in long-distance man-management administered by Van Gaal, via South America, to Manchester. It sought to get United's players onside, by saying: 'Believe in my methods, and I will always take ultimate responsibility.'"

Darren Fletcher, for one seemed impressed. Fletcher, who Jackson noted "has been at United since he was 11" was a Ferguson acolyte (so much so that some of the United fanzines dubbed him Fergie's 'love-child'), cheered: "It's an exciting season with the new manager coming in. There are some new signings and a real buzz around the place again. Everybody's looking forward in great anticipation to the manager coming in and him getting his ideas across. I'm desperate to do well for the fans and to get the team back to where we belong."

And *without* Old Trafford, some of the leading lights of the world game were similarly sure of the viability of the United-Van Gaal match. Franz Beckenbauer said: "He would be perfect for Man United because he is an internationally experienced coach and he understands English football. He is experienced and he is ambitious. He has the personality. He has everything."

His former charge Ronald de Boer agreed: "Van Gaal is the best coach I ever worked with. He is the best chance for a team to have success," he told TalkSport in July. "Nobody really believed in this (Holland) team, but I said, 'if one man can change this team, it is Louis van Gaal'. It is the same for Manchester United. Sometimes you need a bit of luck, of course, like we (Holland) have had in this tournament and it will be the same at Manchester United."

De Boer did sound a note of caution, however: "In the long term you will have success with him, but do you have the patience? He could win the Premier League title, or maybe the Champions League (in his first season), but it is not really realistic, of course."

Another of those ex-United Dutch stars, Arnold Muhren, spoke to the *Manchester Evening News* regarding his confidence in Van Gaal, the "perfect man" to take the reins at Old Trafford. "For me Louis van Gaal is the complete coach. We talk in Holland about the big five and they are Rinus Michels, Johan Cruyff, Guus Hiddink, Dick Advocaat and Louis van Gaal. They are the best we have ever produced.

"Every player who has ever worked with him talks about him with great respect," continued Muhren. "He defends his players in public and that is one of the many areas Sir Alex Ferguson was so good at."

Indeed, Muhren was keen to discuss the Fergie-Van Gaal comparison: "I see a lot of Sir Alex in Van Gaal. He is strong in his decision making, has lots of experience and knows exactly what he wants. His attacking style of football is just what United want. He is very clear in the way he wants to play. He is very 'team' minded. Of course he likes individual players but they have to fit into a team structure. And he is not just interested in the senior players. He was always very hands on at Ajax with the youth academy. He wants to know about everything that is going on from the young kids upwards. He is always looking to promote young home produced players."

But Muhren too, issued a warning: "Wherever Van Gaal has been he has had a strong Dutch contingent with him and will also bring in a lot of Dutch players as well. He will want his trusted coaches in there to join him. But I also think he will see it as very important that he has some English influence there who know the club. As I said, he is the boss and is a strong personality but that doesn't mean he doesn't listen to people. He has his own opinions, has a strong mind but he is open to other ideas."

It would be hard for Van Gaal during his first, transitional season, Muhren acknowledged, but: "his personality is strong enough to deal with it(…). He is fit, very keen and it has always been his dream to manage in the Premier League. United is right for him and he's right for United."

In the wake of the World Cup, Van Gaal's stock was raised even higher, but even before it, Louis van Gaal was hot property. Jamie Jackson in *The Guardian* revealed Louis van Gaal said he came "'very close' to becoming Tottenham Hotspur manager before taking over at Manchester United. (…) Van Gaal said: "As a little boy I was a fan of Tottenham Hotspur with the team of Jimmy Greaves when he was the champion. Jimmy Greaves was my idol. So I was very close. I was a fan of Spurs during my childhood. Those fantastic white shirts and Jimmy Greaves."

And over the years – even in the wilderness years I speak of in this book - he'd never been short of job offers. He was on the short-list for the England job back in 2008, and had even been mentioned in dispatches for the Liverpool hot-seat once upon a time. And he'd *almost* had a shot at taking up the helm at United when Alex Ferguson announced his intention to retire at the end of the 2001-02 season. Even then, Van Gaal had declared: "It would always have been an honour to replace him."

And now, finally, he would get his chance.

And he'd bring with him what Barney Ronay called "a coherent, large-scale, fearless big-club methodology."

"This sense of a well-grooved elite level tactical model is again where Van Gaal stands apart from Moyes, albeit the sheer density of his blueprint may present a problem in itself," claimed Ronay. As outlined in a tactical presentation during his time at Barcelona. Van Gaal breaks football down into four phases, from non-possession, to about to gain possession, to actual possession and all the way back to playing without possession again. Within this, possession itself is not one but four things, a finely nuanced process that runs from slow-build possession, to pre-chance creation possession, to chance creation possession and, finally, to either scoring or failing to score a goal."

"There is a lot of theory here, a lot of posturing, a lot of academic control freakery," acknowledges Ronay. "How well experienced English footballers – not to mention the class of '92 coaching core – take to being forcefully re-educated along these lines will be fascinating to watch."

"Similarly, the overlap between Van Gaal's fierce – and at times very funny – intellectual snobbery promises to be a gripping subplot. This is a man who has fallen out spectacularly with one overbearing in-house father figure in Uli Hoeness. Who remains enduringly combustible in all his professional relations. And who – promisingly – has been known to explode with anger at being asked 'stupid questions' by journalists. Welcome to England, Louis. It promises to be anything but dull."

Which is what – I'm afraid – it was for large chunks of the 2013-14 season under Moyes. And United fans would give anything for it not to be boring.

The job is a huge undertaking, but Van Gaal made a solid start. Even when he was absent – in Brazil – his upheaval began. He instructed the club to clear out the dead wood, amongst them his compatriot, Alex Buttner. Buttner was never anything more than a squad player at United, and yet he clearly saw his role at the club differently. "Van Gaal never gave me the chance in the Dutch national team, despite being voted man of the match 14 times at Manchester United," he claimed in the Dutch paper *De Telegraaf.* "Apparently he is not very confident about me. So I think this is the right moment to leave." Buttner's agent Alexander Bursac says his client remaining at Old Trafford is "not an option".

"In the past two years, Louis van Gaal has ignored Buttner time after time so what kind of perspective does he have when Van Gaal becomes his new club coach?" he told Voetbal International.

Then there were the early arrivals: the young England full-back Luke Shaw pitched up at Old Trafford as the most expensive teenager in the history of the game, and Ander Herrera, a cultured midfielder, joined from Bilbao. Between the pair of them, United shelled-out nearly £60 million. A huge element of risk was involved in the signings of both players, but even on this United fans were not worried: no, they were simply glad to have avoided the same transfer shenanigans which had embarrassed the club the previous summer and left them scrabbling around in an unseemly fashion at the last minute, trying to drag someone – anyone – through the transfer window before it slammed shut.

And even from Brazil, Van Gaal was heavily involved in the appointment of the specialist youth coach Albert Stuivenberg. Jamie Jackson outlined Stuivenberg's credentials: "When previously in charge of Holland Under-17s, Stuivenberg guided the team to the 2011 and 2012 European Championship and his appointment underlines Van Gaal's determination to develop and harness United's youth structure.

Also: "Van Gaal has appointed Giggs as his No2, and brought in Frans Hoek to replace the discarded Chris Woods as the goalkeeping coach – as well as made Marcel Bout the opposition scout."

Assistant manager Giggs was left holding the fort while Louis van Gaal's Netherlands' extended run in the World Cup kept him in Brazil until after the dead-rubber of the Third Place Play-Off. Van Gaal had already given the former United ace his homework which included, according to Jamie Jackson "organising United's training sessions and adhering to a "blueprint" laid down by Van Gaal prior to the Dutchman taking over at United."

Giggs said: "He will relish and look forward to it. He has been at big clubs – Barcelona, Bayern Munich – and in my eyes he is now at the biggest club. He has a clear philosophy and is not afraid of taking over United." And he too was quick to draw comparisons between Van Gaal and Ferguson: the two men, he said, had the same "aura" about them. And the same willingness to make tough choices.

"Sweeping the old names out and ushering in the new suits Van Gaal perfectly," said Paul Wilson, in *The Guardian*.

Within these pages, Van Gaal has been shown to be many things: a brick with hair, a master tactician, a fundamentalist, an egoist, a joker, a crier; the man with the "golden willy". At United he will need to be all of those things and more: he'll need to be a new broom, he'll need to be a teacher (well, he's trained), a thinker, a visionary.

He *might* be a stepping-stone rather than a brick (as Daniel Cossai suspects).

He *might* be a disaster.

Or he *might just* change the fortunes of the greatest club on earth, and deliver a blueprint which will set in stone a new United way, a Dutch United way.

I began this book by talking about Brian Glover's wonderful take on the stereotypical PE teacher in *Kes*. It is worth noting that Glover's PE teacher's 'fantasy team' was Manchester United, and his fantasy player 'Bobby Charlton'. And whilst Louis van Gaal announced upon his unveiling as Bayern Munich that he was joining his "dream club", it is actually *United* which could be the stuff dreams are made of for the man with the "golden willy". At the Theatre of Dreams, if he is given time, he can build an empire.

An empire of dreams.

IX: VAN UNITED

PART 2 - THE 'HONEYMOON PERIOD'

MANCHESTER UNITED (JULY 2014 – NOVEMBER 2014: A DIARY)

During July and early August 2014 there was a football vacuum. We'd said goodbye to the World Cup – generally regarded to have been one of the best international tournaments in living memory - and we were waiting with bated breath for the start of what was anticipated to be one of the most hotly contested Premier Leagues since the Premier League began. We tried to fill this sports-shaped hole with the England-India test series, with the Commonwealth Games which played out in Glasgow, with the seemingly endless pipeline of transfer tittle-tattle.

None of them quite fitted right.

But generally one man could be counted on to command the headlines in the sports media at this time, satisfying in one fell swoop our craving for football news. And that man was Louis van Gaal. From the moment he swung into Old Trafford – Wednesday 16th July was the first 'official' day he clocked-on - Van Gaal was King Louis, the King of the Swingers, a Premier League VIP. He was a ubiquitous figure in Sky Sports news bulletins, on TalkSport, in both the tabloid and broadsheet press.

His shoulders were broad enough to fill the void. He didn't even need a holiday between leaving the World Cup and arriving in Manchester: "I don't need a holiday," he said. Holidays are for wimps, he implied, in the manner of a Dutch Del Boy. And the press loved him for that, for allowing him to continue the narrative of football, even when football wasn't happening.

The media built him up as a Mourinho-type figure upon whose every word they would hang. Journalists loved him – or at the very least were in awe of him. Hell, *The Guardian's* Jamie Jackson became a veritable Van Gaal acolyte so many articles on the Dutchman did he submit for publication. During July and August Jackson saw King Louis as the well which would never run dry. Every day there was a new story about King Louis, and if there wasn't, there was always an old one to rehash.

The media had craved a Mourinho type – controversial, outspoken, funny, arrogant, ridiculous – ever since Jose had left Chelsea back in 2007. The Mourinho who'd returned to the Stamford Bridge club in 2013 hadn't quite been the same. He'd been taken down a peg or three by his bitter experiences in Madrid. He returned worn-down, a little cowed, less arrogant. He wasn't so funny any more (if anything he'd become a weak caricature of himself). And Fergie had also left a great, whopping hole when he'd retired from United. David Moyes proved unable to fill that hole in 2013-14. So the media were desperate to hang their hats on *somebody*.

And Van Gaal was the ideal choice.

(Although not for everybody. Paul Wilson wrote in a *Guardian* think-piece that although "Louis van Gaal presses all the right buttons for Manchester United now that they have joined the supercoach circus after decades of doing things their own way" it was actually *Mourinho* they should have plumped for, a year previously when he was on the market after falling-out with practically everybody at Real Madrid (including, seemingly, himself). "Last summer, Mourinho's qualifications for the Old Trafford vacancy were clear. He too had won the league in different countries, taken two different teams to Champions League success, and as an additional bonus he had already proved himself a success in the Premier League. But he was overlooked because it was felt he would stick around for only three or four years before moving on. He was the restless type, would see himself as bigger than United, and he would make enemies and trouble along the way." Instead United had opted for the known-quantity of David Moyes and got par for the Moyes course: seventh place.)

You see, there was a sense that when Jose Mourinho left Chelsea in 2007 it was because Roman Abramovich feared the Portuguese had become bigger than his club, no matter how much money he (Abramovich) poured into it. The Mourinho circus was the story, always the story, never Chelsea's style of play, never the trophies they won. Players in the modern era are trained in media relations. Their soundbites *lack* bite (unless they're on social media, which is a whole different story). And so it is to *managers* the media look for their controversy, for snippets to feed the ever-hungry 24/7 rolling-news broadcasts which Sky and TalkSport demand.

Managers like Mourinho (and like Ferguson, and like Van Gaal, they hoped) were marketing tools for the new season. And on channels like Sky Sports, like BT Sport, history is forgotten; every new season is going to be the best ever; every new match is going to be the biggest game ever. Managers like Mourinho and Fergie and Van Gaal are dish-sellers; satellite TV subscription persuaders.

They are the news even when there is no news.

This can be a very dangerous thing. It can be the kind of thing which can come back and bite a manager on the arse if things start to go wrong. Because if you've been the news, the good news, and nothing but the good news for a long time, when you're the bad news, you won't be able to escape the bad news.

Still, in July and August, Van Gaal said all the right things. He was bullish ("For me, the challenge is always to come first, not fourth") and yet at the same time strangely humble ("I hope at Manchester United I can do my best... I *will* do my best. Whether that's enough for the fans I will wait and see, but I genuinely hope that will be the case.") He reached for familiar clichés ("We (the United players and I) have to sing from the same hymn sheet.") and created new ones ("When you analyse it, it's about *the click*.": Van Gaal stated the key to the success of his philosophy was this "click" between playing staff and manager. In his first press conference, there was so much talk of clicking, Fonzie might as well have been in the room, leaning against a jukebox). He even made up his own new way of scoring games. After a win on penalties against Internazionale in the pre-season tour of the United States (following a game which finished scoreless) he claimed: "I'm pleased. (...) We played well and conceded only one shot on goal. We created six or seven chances and that means it's 7-1."

He said the right things as far as United fans were concerned ("It's the biggest club in the world"; he even hinted at one point that the club was *too big*) and as far as the board and the United 'brand' managers were concerned ("I know already how important Manchester United is, but also how important the sponsors are").

By the same token, United gave Van Gaal *the big-sell.* They launched his tenure under the banner 'Re-United', announcing via a multi-channel media campaign (which incorporated social media, email, mobile, radio and MUTV) that the club were ready to fight back after a miserable 2013-14 campaign. I received an email, or a text, virtually every day which shouted the club's intentions from the rooftops. So, I imagine did many of the club's supposed 75 million 'fans' worldwide.

Re-United, as in: under Moyes it had been torn apart, cast asunder, and now required being drawn back together. The message couldn't have been clearer.

It was all so different from David Moyes' arrival. Paul Wilson noted in *The Guardian:* "Louis van Gaal's unveiling as Manchester United's second new manager in a little over a year took place in the same room as the installation of his predecessor, although things have changed quite a bit since David Moyes was given a club jacket and tie and sent smiling into his season-long funeral. (…) After 10 years at Everton Moyes did not need any introduction at Old Trafford, so he did not get one. King Louis got the works. Perhaps in symbolic recognition of their back-to-front mistake a year ago, United went to the considerable trouble of turning the whole room around to accommodate Van Gaal, who was ushered in by Sir Bobby Charlton and shown a seat behind a gleaming new desk."

"Behind him, for the benefit of all the photographers, a version of Van Gaal the club had prepared earlier appeared in inspiring pose in a background montage. Pictured in front of the Sir Alex Ferguson Stand, no less, flanked by new signings Luke Shaw and Ander Herrera as well as Wayne Rooney and Robin van Persie, Van Gaal gazed heroically upwards into the middle distance in the manner of a sovereign depicted on a banknote."

"Moyes," Wilson concludes, "never had any of that and neither did the currency of his managerial career lend itself to a five-minute video compilation of his previous triumphs such as the one United played by way of welcome."

At that initial press conference, Van Gaal summed up the challenge like this: "It is the biggest club because of world renown but in sport you are never the biggest unless you've proved it every season. You are not the biggest if last season you were seventh. Then you are not the biggest but are well known all over the world. In China and Brazil people talked about Man Utd when I was coach of the Dutch team. There is a lot of expectation. It is a great challenge because of that. Barça were No1 in Spain, Ajax No1 in the Netherlands and Bayern Munich No1 in Germany and now Man Utd No1 in England and I hope I shall fulfill the expectation." (A speech which recalled his metaphorical chest-thumping after Ajax's 1995 Champions League win in Vienna: "We are the best! We are the best! And not just of Amsterdam. But also of Rotterdam. And Eindhoven. And Europe… And now we are the best of the…. *world*!" And at Bayern: "Who has the best defence? FC Bayern! Who has the best attack? FC Bayern! And that's why we are *champions*! And not just in Munchen. Also in Gelsenkirchen! And also in Bremen. And in Hamburg! We are the best of Germany. And perhaps soon: of Europe!")

He added: "The owners and CEO have a lot of confidence in me and because of that they have come to me. I have explained my philosophy and they were excited and that is why I am here. That is why we have to see if I can fulfill the expectations and that of the fans. But in the world of football you cannot predict."

You cannot predict, but you *can* prepare. (Incidentally, Roy Keane, he who lived by the ethos of the six p's – proper preparation prevents piss-poor performance – would have *loved* LVG.) The media *lapped-up* stories of Van Gaal as disciplinarian: he ordered *double-training* on his very first day, dontchaknow. (The Dutchman led his first training session of the squad as late as 5:30pm.) The teenage-tyro, new-signing Luke Shaw, was made to train alone during United's pre-season tour of the States, because of concerns over his fitness, and this was headline sports news over and above the golds, silvers, and bronzes won up in Glasgow.

And when Van Gaal *literally* ripped-up the past - he ordered the training pitches at Carrington be torn up and replaced by "Desso, a synthetic-grass hybrid material" – this was the football-writers' dream of a metaphor. A new type of grass generated miles of newsprint. As did the fact the Dutchman dictated that *trees* – trees of all things - should be planted along the perimeter of the training pitches: suddenly Van Gaal had the football press talking like gardeners. (Incidentally, the pitches were the least of it at Carrington. Camera systems were installed in order that Big Brother Van Gaal could *spy* on his charges. Jonny Evans explains: "We have this system where he can watch us. He is saying: 'You should be five yards to the right'.")

All of this PR guff began to take its toll on Van Gaal as early as the first week of the US tour, in July. Jamie Jackson reported the Dutchman voicing his concerns regarding the fact that "commercial demands could hamper the team's success." Dragging the playing squad halfway around the world would help raise the club's profile in a key market, but it would also disrupt his preparation of the team. Van Gaal even took his criticism to United's in-house TV channel, MUTV: "Maybe it is too big a club," he said. "Not only in a sporting sense but also commercially. We have to do a lot of things that normally I don't allow. I have to adapt to this big club but I think also this big club has to adapt to Louis van Gaal. I hope we can have some balance to that."

Pre-Season: US Tour

Still, this did not seem to hinder the players too much as they took the field in front of 86,000 spectators at the Pasadena Rose Bowl – the stadium which hosted the 1994 World Cup final - for Louis van Gaal's first match at the helm. Jamie Jackson trumpeted: "The Louis van Gaal show is up and running and in the brightest of lights after a 7-0 trouncing of Los Angeles Galaxy." The Dutchman's new-look United produced a stellar display, admittedly against inferior opposition. Wayne Rooney starred, scoring twice; Ashley Young threw off his confidence issues of the previous two seasons to also net a brace; and most surprisingly, Bacup-boy Reece James, a young defender, also scored at the double. (Van Gaal seemed immediately fond of the youngster, calling him "our friend Reece James".) But the good news didn't stop there: new-signing Ander Herrera's performance glittered with promise, and the new formation, a Netherlands-esque 5-3-2/ 3-5-2 worked well.

Van Gaal said: "It is fantastic how they have performed today. When you see us train, you can expect something but not 7-0. It was a surprise, but they were beautiful goals and beautiful attacks. The result always matters. With such a result you get confidence. We introduced a new system and played twice on the training pitch, 11 v 11. It is not very much, but the boys are willing to pick up the information. Last week, 10 players who played tonight were not even at our training complex. When I see my team playing a new system, it is better to win 7-0 than to lose because the players will then doubt the system. But now I don't have that problem."

He added: "When you want to change a system, you must start at once. We don't have time to prepare for other things. The other system they can play is 4-3-3 and they have played it for many years. I can change it back if it doesn't work. With the quality of the players we have, I can play 4-3-3 with three strikers on the bench, but I want to play with two strikers. We have four number 10s, so the selection is not balanced in my eyes. I have decided to play this system because of the quality of the players. But if we lose, I can change back to another system."

So why the 3-5-2 system in particular, especially given Van Gaal's past preference for a 4-3-3? Well, his success in the World Cup with the Netherlands is one answer. Injury to Kevin Strootman forced his hand on this. But tactics expert Jonathan Wilson believes it goes further than this. Here's what he wrote in *The Guardian:*

"Although he used a 4-4-2 at times with AZ and Bayern, Van Gaal has tended to prefer to use three men in central midfield. Even with a 4–4–2, he tended to have one forward – Thomas Müller or Ivica Olic – who could drop back to become an additional midfielder if required. Three in midfield, even if one of them is a slight luxury such as Wesley Sneijder, offers security and flexibility. Besides which, looking at United's squad, Van Gaal can not have seen any potential pairing that would prove adequate in central midfield – a problem that haunted David Moyes last season and was a concern long before that."

"So he wanted three in midfield but how to do that when United's obvious strength is the front two of Robin van Persie and Wayne Rooney? They may not necessarily be great as a partnership, but they are both, when fit, clearly among United's four or five best players. Both have played wide in their careers, but neither enjoys it so to accommodate the pair, they have to be used as a central partnership. Perhaps in the long term there are better solutions, but there are other issues that require more immediate attention."

In other words Van Gaal's United star chart *had* to contain its two most shimmering talents. But Van Persie didn't even travel to the States. He'd been given extra time off to recover after the Netherlands' extended run in the World Cup. Still, in the wake of United's Death-Star style demolition of LA Galaxy, the team was on something of a high. Going into the International Champions Cup, a tournament engineered to raise awareness of the European game in America (so much so that *The Guardian* dubbed it the 'Expand the Brand' cup), the new-look Reds were quietly confident despite the level of competition they would face. Van Gaal's Red Devils had been drawn in a group with Italian giants Roma and Internazionale, as well as 10-time European Champions Real Madrid (though they at least avoided Manchester City and Liverpool, who were both drawn in the other group, alongside Olimpiakos and AC Milan).

And United began their International Champions Cup campaign with another tour victory, though this time with a less assured performance, against Roma. United prevailed 3-2 (having been 3-0 up), and yet again Wayne Rooney scored twice, but that *click* Van Gaal talked of didn't seem to happen, and the rest of the team laboured. Ander Herrera in particular put in a disappointing display. This bang, then whimper brought to mind the Netherlands World Cup campaign: in Brazil the Dutch had started with an explosive 5-1 victory against Spain, before they struggled to beat Australia 3-2 in their second group game. They did manage to beat Chile 2-0 in their final group match, but throughout the knockout stages failed to find the net in regulation time with anything like the frequency they had in the Spain win.

And indeed, United's second International Champions Cup (the more I write that phrase the more I think of *Thunderbirds*) game finished 0-0 against Internazionale (though United won on penalties). Van Gaal claimed he was pleased with the performance: "I was very pleased with our ball possession. It was much better and we covered our positions better. I was very pleased with my players tonight."

But you got the impression he was papering over the cracks a little. He'd had the opportunity to run the rule over the squad he'd inherited from David Moyes now. He described it as "broken".

"There are a lot of players that can play in the same position," he said. "It is not in balance. It's more difficult to succeed in a difficult situation than in a fantastic situation."

Which seemed rather like stating the obvious.

But, doubts regarding the quality of this "broken" squad notwithstanding, the LVG honeymoon period across the pond continued into their third International Champions Cup group stage match. The appeal of a game between Manchester United and Real Madrid, two of the biggest, most famous names in world football, is obvious even to an American audience. Indeed, a crowd of close to 110,000 turned out at Michigan Stadium (aka The Big House) on Saturday 3rd August: an all-time record for a "soccer" game in the US. (Van Gaal estimated the Reds had played in front of over "300,000" supporters during their tour to date.)

And United put in a big performance in The Big House. They took the lead with just over 20 minutes on the clock: "a slick sequence," wrote Jamie Jackson, "that ended in four smart passes that allowed Ashley Young to score the opener. Darren Fletcher prodded the ball to Wayne Rooney for the latter to engineer a one-two with the Scot. He played in Danny Welbeck who recycled the ball to Young, who slotted home."

Van Gaal said: "I think that in the news all over the world the broadcasters will show the first goal. It was a fantastic goal. All the team has touched the ball I think."

Although Gareth Bale dragged Madrid back into the game six minutes later from the penalty spot, Ashley Young doubled his tally before half-time; his cross-cum-shot wrong-footing Iker Casillas and looping into the back of the net. And Javier Hernandez applied the gloss by adding a third with ten minutes to go to send the majority of the United-supporting crowd home happy.

The win meant United had qualified for the International Champions Cup final, and a shot at Van Gaal's first trophy, 'Expand the Brand' cup or not, *friendly* competition or not. Their opponents? Arch-rivals Liverpool. *Because* it was Liverpool, this would be no meaningless friendly. Prior to the game Van Gaal described the Merseysiders as not United's "favourite" opponents. Which is some euphemism. Liverpool and United are the two principal members of a mutual loathing society which has been in existence for over a hundred years at a local level – just 30 miles on the East Lancs Road separate the two north west powerhouses – on a *national* level for over 50, as the two battled it out to occupy the top perch in English football, and on a continental scale as the reds of Liverpool and Manchester vied to out-do each other in terms of European Cup wins. And now the match would be played 1000 miles away from the north west, in Miami, baby.

In his match report in *The Guardian,* Steve Brenner called it: "a friendly only in name". "United," he noted, "started the stronger. On four minutes Hernandez (…) really should have opened the scoring when the Mexican striker failed to make proper contact with an excellent centre from the lively Young."

But on 13 minutes Phil Jones clattered into a rampaging Raheem Sterling and Liverpool were awarded a penalty which was converted by Steven Gerrard. It was a familiar, if disturbing sight for United fans: the last time the two rivals had met, Liverpool had been awarded *three* spot-kicks, two of which the former England captain had converted in a 3-0 victory at Old Trafford.

Yet United didn't let their heads drop. Despite some awkward moments – particularly for Jones and Smalling, two members of the new-look Van Gaal 'back three' – the Reds weathered the storm until half-time. And during the interval, the Dutchman made changes. He pushed the forwards – Rooney and Hernandez - further forward in order that they could press a Liverpool defence which looked just as clumsy as United's had, and moved Shaw and Young a good ten yards further up the pitch. This provided United with a renewed attacking impetus.

This would eventually pay-off – and how – ten minutes into the second period. Steve Brenner wrote: "on 54 minutes, Rooney drew United level. Hernandez's cross was deep and accurate and as the ball dropped over a flailing Martin Skrtel, the England forward was on hand to volley home. And within 120 seconds United were ahead, Mata's shot from 12 yards flicking off Mamadou Sakho and past Simon Mignolet following decent work from Herrera and Shaw in the build-up. It was some turnaround, and the celebrations by both clearly showed just what it meant – friendly or not."

It was left to youngster Jesse Lingard to complete the scoring late on. Lingard is from Warrington – midway between Liverpool and Manchester – but his goal, and his celebrations proved there were no divided loyalties. It was a cool, calm, collected finish, and it secured the first trophy of Van Gaal's reign. It wasn't the *calibre* of trophy United were used to – Barney Ronay described "a distinctly sheepish looking Darren Fletcher and Rooney holding up the International Trophy as though presenting to the cameras a dead fish washed up on the high-tide line" – but a trophy is a trophy is a trophy.

And "only time," wrote Brenner, "and defensive improvements," would tell if there would be "more in his grasp come May."

Wayne Rooney was certainly bullish post-match. "It's been a good few weeks, we've got a new manager who wants us to play a different style of football. We've had to adapt. We've had some good results against top opposition so we can be pleased," he said.

"I think the system suits the team, not only myself. The manager came in and had a look at the players we've got. He's done what he thinks is best suited for our team."

"He's a tough manager but he's been great since he came in. He's given us all a different way of looking at football, which we haven't had before. It's been great for us and hopefully that will continue."

"We wanted to win games, play well. And obviously we've done that. We've won a trophy as well. It's always nice to beat Liverpool. We're happy with the work we've done out here, now we go on to Valencia and then the season starts."

United fans would have been delighted to hear such glowing reports from Rooney, particularly as he was the man many commentators tipped to 'disagree' with Van Gaal's methods.

And yet the players would wake up the morning following the Liverpool win to headlines talking about a 'Van Cull': the Dutchman, it was said, had now had the time to run the rule over his players and was ready to let up to six players go. The most serious questions were being asked of Anderson, Smalling, Cleverley, Young, Nani, and Fellaini (though Young did himself no harm at all by performing well on tour. The new 3-5-2 formation meant United for the first time in living memory would line-up without wingers and there remained quite a few of them at the club. It soon became clear they must reinvent themselves – as an attacking full-back, as Young did - or else leave).

"I shall make judgments after this tour," Van Gaal had said. "I let all the players play and I know now more than before the tour. Now also it is a little bit soon to judge but in football you have to judge. You have to give a chance to the player to make a transfer when I see that his prospects to play are not so high. You have to say it in advance because it's too late after 31 August. I will tell players after the tour but to them not to you (reporters)."

Now, upon his return to Carrington, the *real* hard work would begin.

It wasn't all sweetness and light for Van Gaal and the media either. At another press conference at the end of July, the Republik of Mancunia reported Van Gaal's first signs of getting irritable with certain sections of the media (something he has a great deal of *previous* for). And though King Louis can be excused somewhat as the interrogator he got antsy with was Ian Ladyman, the *Mail's* famously Liverpool-fanatic reporter, it was clear Van Gaal was not 100% happy with the situation he'd inherited at United.

Ladyman asked: "What do you think of the challenge of having such a big club like Manchester City in the same City, a team that has also won the title?"

Van Gaal replied: "It does not bother me. Whether they are ten metres away or 30km away."

Ladyman pressed the issue: "What do you think of what Manchester City have done over the last three years?"

And again Van Gaal replied uncontroversially: "It is amazing because they were not a big club and now already Champions and they have also won the Cup in the last three years. They are knocking at the door but that is good for Manchester United also because where there is competition you can be proud when you are the champion at the end and maybe we will be the champions."

So Ladyman upped the stakes. He asked: "City fans would argue that they have knocked at the door and opened it and closed it and now you have to knock at the door again and try and get back through it?"

And *now* Van Gaal was starting to get riled. "If you like to say that, then you have to write it down! I feel that he (Ladyman) likes to say that."

A smirking Ladyman continued: "But that's their view – that they are on top…"

And Van Gaal snapped: "I have learnt the word 'entice'. You are enticing me. I said 'provoke' but Ryan (Giggs) said it should be 'entice.'"

Entice or not, it became clear that the Dutchman was concerned about the level of competition United would face, not just to win back the Premier League title, but even to make it into the top four Champions League spots. Although United had at least managed to make some additions to the squad – which was a damned sight better than in the previous season's summer transfer window – *others* had reinforced too.

Champions Manchester City had reinforced, bringing in centre-half Eliaquim Mangala for a whopping £32m, midfielder Fernando from Porto for £12m, back-up 'keeper Willy Caballero for £4.5m, and Bacary Sagna from Arsenal on a free.

Mourinho's Chelsea had – inevitably – strengthened too, spending big to bring in the former United transfer-target Cesc Fabregas for £30m, the Brazilian Filipe Luis for £16m, *Didier Drogba* on a free, and Diego Costa for £32m. In Costa, they'd finally secured the services of a striker who might not flatter to deceive (unlike Torres, Eto'o, Ba *et al* which had been their roster for the 2013-14 season, and in all likelihood the reason why the Premier League trophy went to the City of Manchester Stadium and not Stamford Bridge). They'd also brought back Courtois from a successful loan spell with Atletico Madrid.

Liverpool, despite losing Luis Suarez (as was always going to happen after *that* bite in the World Cup) had invested heavily, securing the services of Southampton trio

Adam Lallana (£25m), Rickie Lambert (£4m), and Dejan Lovren (£20m) as well as the maverick striker Mario Balotelli for £16m. More: Divock Origi (£10m), Emre Can (£10m), and Lazar Marcovic (£20m)also arrived in order to bolster what had been a small squad.

Hell, even the perennially parsimonious Arsene Wenger had loosened the purse strings and splashed out on Alexis Sanchez (£35m), Calum Chambers (£16m), Mathieu Debuchy (undisclosed), and David Ospina (£3m).

And it wasn't only the arrivals board at United which Van Gaal had to worry about. There was a great deal of work to do regarding the departures board at Carrington. Despite losing an entire, multi-trophy-winning defence in Evra, Vidic, and Ferdinand, not to mention those squad players who hadn't made the grade such as Buttner, Macheda and Bebe, United's squad was still too cumbersome - especially considering European football was completely absent from the fixture list for the season - and was not exactly teeming with players of the requisite quality to mount a title challenge.

Still, United concluded pre-season (in Van Gaal speak "preparation time") with spirits within the camp extremely high. There was a sense of giddy anticipation evident from everyone within the squad, even its leader LVG. In his programme notes prior to the Valencia friendly the Dutchman couldn't hide his excitement at the thought of walking out at Old Trafford as manager of the home side for the first time. "I know it will be a special moment for me," he wrote. "I have been here before, of course, as a manager with Barcelona and Bayern Munich, and I know just how difficult it is for visiting teams at Old Trafford. I am really looking forward to having you on the same side as my players."

After the game – which United won 2-1 thanks to a Fergie-time winner from forgotten man Fellaini – Van Gaal spoke in depth about his feelings on that first touchline walk. "I don't know the word," he said, pointing to his forearm. In Amsterdam it is "kippenvel". It means goosebumps.

Daniel Taylor wrote in *The Guardian:* "Van Gaal put his chin up, marched down the tunnel and, when he emerged into the fading light, it was with an expression on his face that suggested he liked the look of his new workplace."

This was Van Gaal the new broom, expected to sweep the place clean of the cobwebs of misery remaining from the 2013-14 season, under David Moyes.

Saturday 16th August 2014: United v Swansea City (1-2)

The David Moyes era at Manchester United was hardly an era at all. (More of an *erratum*). He was the Chosen One rather than the Special One. United were already doing a good job of airbrushing him out of the club's history, as though he was a nasty mole, or blemish (*that* Re-United multi-channel media campaign for example).

The differences between Moyes and Van Gaal are legion, but in one respect they are the same: they both began their United careers with a match against Swansea. Under David Moyes, United travelled to the Liberty Stadium for a late kick-off on the first Saturday of the 2013-14 season and ran out impressive 4-1 winners. Unfortunately for Moyes the Swansea game was only the start of a terrifying run of early fixtures – including Liverpool, Manchester City and Chelsea – at the end of which United had already imploded.

The fixture list would be far kinder to Louis van Gaal (certainly there were easier pickings than in the early games Moyes "enjoyed". This time around, United would face three of the newly-promoted teams in their opening five games in Leicester City, QPR and Burnley. Their other fixtures would pit them against last season's strugglers Sunderland and Swansea.

As such, United fans were quietly confident of a good start which would form the foundations upon which to build a season full of promise. Some felt that a top four finish – and therefore a Champions League place for the next season – was well within reach. Some supporters got *way, way* ahead of themselves and predicted United might challenge for the Premier League title. Buoyed up by the belief that the absence of European football might leave the path clear for a championship challenge (*a la* Liverpool last season) and with Scholes' "mad genius" new boss at the helm, reds were starting to believe again.

Swansea at home - on Saturday 16th August - would be push-overs, wouldn't they?

Well no. They wouldn't. After 90 minutes of football on the opening day of the season, that fragile bubble of confidence burst.

Those who talked of a 21st title had so much egg on their faces after Swansea ran out 2-1 winners. Those who calmly predicted a top four finish were left twitching uncomfortably after Swansea – who'd never won a game at Old Trafford in their history before 2014 – recorded their second win in just eight months. It was the first time since the early 1970s that the reds had lost their inaugural league game at home. And though the display showed more promise, more planning, than anything reds fans were forced to witness in the dark days of Moyes, it was still Swansea. At home.

Daniel Taylor, writing in *The Observer,* described the game as containing "a cloying sense of déjà vu". Fans had seen such "huffing and puffing" before. The team, he said, were "short of ideas", and "drastically in need of some more dynamism".

"Maybe now," said Taylor, "it should be clearer why Louis van Gaal has been telling anyone who cares to listen they should not be surprised if Manchester United's rehabilitation takes longer than they would ideally like. He had warned his new club to brace themselves for some difficult moments and here was the hard evidence that a change of manager at Old Trafford is not simply going to wash away the team's shortcomings."

This was an utterly demoralising defeat. Paul Wilson wrote in *The Guardian* that the poor fare served up by the team destroyed in one fell swoop the "feelgood factor" borne of the pre-season wins. He concluded – harshly – that "without results no manager is bulletproof". Which has to be the earliest call in history for a manager's head.

As to the manager: after the game, Van Gaal said: "It is very disappointing for the players, the fans, for me, my staff. When you have preparation time and you win everything (in pre-season) and then lose your first match, that cannot be worse. It is not good because we have built up a lot of confidence and it shall be smashed down because of this result. But we have to know it is only one game of many games and you shall not be the champion at this moment, you shall be the champion in May."

The Dutchman continued: "I have said before that because of our wins in the United States and against Valencia the expectation is so high, and I have seen in the first half a lot of players very nervous, making the wrong choices, and that is a pity. These players have to get used to that expectation because this is Manchester United. You have to cope with that pressure. I have said to them in the dressing room: 'I cannot say you didn't do your very best, unbelievable work, fantastic mentality, but reaching the level is difficult, not only running but using your brain and then you can play like a team.' In that, we have failed today."

Scott the Red, in his *Republik of Mancunia* Red Rants column, was damning. Not of Van Gaal, but of the United board and their apparent failure to address the glaring deficiencies of the squad. "Manchester United," he wrote, "finished last season as the 7th best team and have since lost several key players. Nemanja Vidic, the captain, Patrice Evra, the vice-captain, as well as two of the most experienced players in the squad, Ryan Giggs and Rio Ferdinand. When you consider that takes away three of our back four, as well as last season's only cover for left-back, Alexander Buttner, United would need to buy five players just to break even."

"United need to do more than break even though. Our squad was worse than Manchester City, Chelsea, Arsenal and Liverpool's last season, yet all four of those clubs have spent more money than us in the transfer window, and none of them seen as many first team players leave."

"Of course, in Louis van Gaal, United have a much better manager this season and that should ensure we see better performances from the players. But his quality isn't enough to bridge the ever increasing gap between us and the teams above us last season."

"We've already fallen three points behind thanks to the inability of the Glazers to make our money available and Woodward's incompetence to get a deal done. How much further will we fall behind before the fans begin to make a stand again? Moyes faced the brunt of the frustration last year but it is unlikely that Van Gaal will face the same fate. There's no questioning his credentials and his ability to make title winning squads. But there are huge question marks over the owners and CEO. If they want top four football this season they need to act now, before one dodgy season turns in to decline."

United did indeed act, and swiftly. The 24-year-old Argentine left-back Marcos Rojo was brought in to address some of the defensive deficiencies. He joined for a fee of around £16m from Sporting Lisbon. Rojo had been named by many critics as the best full back in the 2014 World Cup, and he became, according to Jamie Jackson, the first player bought by United who was "identified solely by Louis van Gaal since he became manager in the close season. Although the Dutchman signed off the deals for Shaw and Herrera, both players had been picked by his predecessor, David Moyes."

However the securing of one signature was still not enough to paper over the cracks in the Red Devils squad according to some football experts. Confidence was *still* "smashed". In a press conference prior to United's second Premier League appearance of the campaign, at Sunderland's Stadium of Light on Sunday 24th August, the Dutchman spoke of how quickly the club's fortunes (and his own) had changed. "Two weeks ago," he said, "I was the king of Manchester and now I am the devil of Manchester. It's the football world and it is especially the media in this football world. I think the fans of Manchester are intelligent. I've already said in all the press conferences that it shall be difficult in the first three months, for the players and also for the fans."

Sunday 24th August 2014: Sunderland v United (1-1)

So began another trying week for red supporters across the land. United did not lose in the north east, which was progress of sorts. And yet it was not necessarily the result which worried United fans, but the performance. There was very little cohesion: scant evidence of Van Gaal's masterplan starting to take effect. A Juan Mata strike on 17 minutes gave United an early lead. It was very much against the run of play. An equaliser from a set play by ex-Manchester City midfielder Jack Rodwell levelled the scores. And that was about it. Sunderland seemed happy enough with a point and United did not have the drive, the penetration, or the brains to find their way to a winner, despite dominating for the final twenty minutes.

Daniel Taylor suggested in *The Guardian* that there were "only fleeting moments here when they looked close to getting it right." His match report was pockmarked with words like "careless" and "clueless". Jamie Jackson, writing in the same newspaper, went further. He called the performance by an injury-hit reds side "dismal". "Van Persie and Rooney," he said, "were starved of chances."

Michael Cox analysed the game for *The Guardian* and blamed Van Gaal's system for this. "The build-up play was alarmingly slow," he said. "And Rooney and Van Persie spent much time coming short, with no one making the reverse run to provide penetration. Mata's goal showed his all-round midfield ability, starting the move from the centre circle before motoring into the six-yard box to finish, but overall he struggled to influence the game."

"It is with the attack, then, that Van Gaal may be most concerned. He is surely using this system to get Mata, Rooney and Van Persie in their favoured positions, because it does not suit the rest of the squad. If those three do not perform, playing 3-4-1-2 becomes pointless."

Cox concluded: "There are few reasons for optimism."

Van Gaal himself blamed injuries for the lack of attacking flair. "It is not usual that we have four injuries in midfield," he said. "Every club that has that has a problem."

But he too was perplexed by the poor passing displayed by the reds. "All too slow, all too fast, all too hasty," the Iron Tulip said, rather paradoxically.

The lack of pace in the team was startling. Only when Danny Welbeck entered the fray as a substitute did United have anything vaguely resembling their incisiveness of old. However, over that Bank Holiday weekend it emerged that the Red Devils were working hard behind the scenes to address that. Rumours began to emerge even before the Sunderland game that the Real Madrid winger Angel di Maria – a dead ringer for Speedy Gonzalez - was set to sign on the dotted line for a touted £59.7 million. It would be a new record British transfer fee, eclipsing the £50 million Chelsea paid to Liverpool to secure the services of striker Fernando Torres three years previously.

The angelic Di Maria had featured for Argentina during their run to the World Cup final in Brazil (though he'd been injured and ruled out of the final itself) and also received the man of the match award for his performance during Real Madrid's record tenth Champions League win in May. He topped the assists charts in *La Liga* during 2013-14 and was seen as key to increasing United's creative output. He was a big name with a big reputation: the finished article not just 'one for the future'.

Di Maria flapped his wings and flew in to Manchester on Tuesday 26th August, coughed for the doctors, and sealed the deal: an Angel signing for the Red Devils. And Van Gaal, "the devil of Manchester" had got his man. He compared the capture of Di Maria with that of Arjen Robben when he was at Bayern Munich: "I have bought him because he can play inside and on the wing, and that is handy for a coach," said Van Gaal. "When I was at Bayern Munich, on August 28 I also bought Arjen Robben, who could also play on the wing and inside."

Tactical analysis master Jonathan Wilson felt that Di Maria would be the perfect man for Van Gaal's new 3-5-2 system: "Angel di Maria (...) operates (...) on the left of a midfield three. Self-sacrificing and tactically intelligent, he was perfect for the role, going wide when Cristiano Ronaldo came infield, dropping back to cover when Marcelo or Fábio Coentrão charged forwards (for Madrid). He is also a master at leading counterattacks, with a keen sense of when to carry the ball and when to play the pass. Without a wide player beyond him, his role will be different at United, but it is easy to imagine him covering for a wing-back's foray or linking up with Rooney when he drifts left."

But, remarkably, United's smashing of the British record transfer fee was not even the biggest Red Devils story of the day. No, that was saved for the hellish fare United served up in the evening kick-off.

Tuesday 26th August 2014: MK Dons v United (4-0)

The lack of European football meant that United, for the first time in nineteen years, would play in the second round of the League Cup. They would face the Milton Keynes Dons, from the third tier of English football, at Stadium MK. The fates were not auspicious: back in 1995, nine years before the MK Dons even existed as a football club, the reds had been embarrassed at Old Trafford by lowly York City. The Minstermen ran out 3-0 winners against a supposedly second-string United side which included Paul Parker, Gary Pallister, David Beckham, Phil Neville, Lee Sharpe, Brian McClair and Ryan Giggs.

It couldn't get any worse than that, could it?

Actually, it could.

The following day's *Sun* led with the headline: 'Dons 4 Donkeys 0'.

The Daily Mirror led with: 'MK Dons 4-0 Man United: Yes you read that right as Van Gaal suffers stunning League Cup loss'.

United's match against MK Dons plumbed the depths. The *new* low by which all new lows should be measured. It was a humiliation. A disgrace. A nadir.

But not a shocker. No: Van Gaal claimed he'd seen it coming. And maybe he had. I mentioned auspices earlier, and the Dutchman had one of his own. This was Novelda in the Copa del Rey all over again. Novelda, who were "bottom of Segunda Division B – the Spanish third division", and who beat the mighty Barcelona during Van Gaal's second spell with the club.

Van Gaal, whose winless run as United supremo had now stretched to his first three competitive matches, said: "I'm not shocked because I know what can happen. We had nine injuries and played again within 48 hours (of the Sunderland draw). So I had to look at the second team and youth players for this match."

It might have been a second-string side, but the Reds team featured six full internationals, including David De Gea, Anderson, Javier Hernandez and Danny Welbeck. Jonny Evans was made captain for the night, and it was his sloppy pass which gifted the Dons their first goal. And after it, United never really recovered. *None* of those senior players stepped up to the mark. Not one. Indeed the only small crumbs of comfort provided to United fans were offered up by two young substitutes: the precociously talented Andreas Pereira, and James Wilson, who on 72 minutes provided *United's first shot on target* against a League One club.

David McDonnell's match report in *The Daily Mirror* stated that: "the early teething problems in his (LVG's) Manchester United tenure now a full-blown crisis". He called it "a shocking fall from grace".

All this talk of angels, demons, and falls: the defeat was Biblical, and in the wake of it, bookmakers quoted a price of 7-1 that Van Gaal would not make it to the last game of the season as United boss.

The Guardian's Jamie Jackson did offer some hope for United fans to cling to in the wake of the Iron Tulip's disastrous start: "The dropping of five points from the opening two league matches is a bad start as the Dutchman bids to restore the club's Champions League status by securing a top-four finish. Yet history shows this can be a pattern of Van Gaal's managerial career, and his sides recover. At Barcelona in the 1998-99 season the club stood

10th after 14 games and ended the campaign as champions. With Bayern in '09-10 Van Gaal's side were seventh after 13 matches yet won the Bundesliga. And even when eighth the following year after 13 games and on Van Gaal's sacking in April 2011, his legacy was enough for Bayern to still finish third."

But in the same newspaper, Paul Wilson argued that the Dutchman had to shoulder at least some of the blame for the defeat. "It might be occurring to Van Gaal right now that players in the English Premier League are not quite as adaptable or tactically aware as players he has coached elsewhere, and competitive games that allow scope for experimentation are not to be sneezed at. Van Gaal may not have been too bothered about the Capital One Cup, but he has to be concerned by a 4-0 hiding so early on his watch, and he has to take a share of the blame. If he was determined to play the kids, it might have been better to send them out in a formation to which they were more accustomed."

Wilson added: "Already Van Gaal is beginning to appreciate why the club are paying him so much money. It is not for his coaching expertise after all, at least not yet. It is for his impeccable sang froid as the television cameras close in on his stuffed frog expression, searching in vain for a flicker of emotion or annoyance as the players in his eyeline but out of shot mess up once again. Van Gaal is playing his part marvellously so far, bigging up the United supporters' loyalty in adversity and making a point of signing autographs on the way out, but he is here to be judged by events on the pitch, not for his PR skills on the sidelines. Good will is not infinite. He will have been hoping for a better start than this, and around now is the time for him to begin changing things."

Off-the-field change continued apace during the final week of August as the closing of the Summer transfer window drew ever closer. It began to feel like a real life game of Fantasy Football (which, incidentally, must have been what it would be like to have been a supporter of Manchester City or Chelsea over the past few years).

Over the weekend of 30th and 31st August, United confirmed the signing of one of Van Gaal's World Cup heroes. Daley Blind – the son of Danny Blind, who'd been on the Iron Tulip's coaching team in Brazil, and who'd also played under Van Gaal at Ajax (most notably in the Champions League success of 1995) – signed on the dotted line in a reputed £13.8m deal from Ajax. The versatile 24-year-old was one who fitted perfectly the Van Gaal ideal of a team-player, and, though the fee was seen to be rather on the expensive side – for such a sum United could have secured the services of a Weekly Curtain, or a Monthly Drape – he would still provide great value, according to Van Gaal.

The addition of Blind took United's summer spending to a heretofore unprecedented £145.7m. Previously, the Red Devils' highest-spending transfer window had been Summer 2007's, in which they'd brought in Anderson, Hargreaves, Nani, and Kuszczak (along with Tevez on loan) for a combined £62m. In 2011, and 2012, they'd spent relatively heavily (£53m and £43m) but these figures had been very much overshadowed by the spending of their rivals, especially that of the newly moneyed Manchester City and Chelsea.

Scott the Red compared and contrasted the spending of United, City and Chelsea over the past four years (since United sold Cristiano Ronaldo for £80m and replaced him with £21m worth of playing talent) for *The Republik of Mancunia*. Even taking into account the Red Devils' extravagance in the 2014 Summer transfer window, "over the past six seasons, Chelsea have spent £108.4m more than United and City have spent £180.65m more. When you then take in to account that United are the most profitable club in England, and one of the most profitable sports "franchises" in the world, it's insane that the club has been allowed to, season by season, fall behind its competitors."

But finally, it looked as though United had entered the same game as their competition.

How much this had to do with the presence of Van Gaal at the helm is a moot point. (But can you imagine Moyes signing Di Maria?) Sponsors too would have demanded large-scale investment in the squad. Still, for once, United weren't buying *ones for the future*. They were buying top level, quality players. At once the transfer window of 2014 felt like 2001, when United made the whole of Europe sit up and take notice when they dropped a cool £50m on (proven talent like) Van Nistelrooy and Veron, and also like 1996, when, in the wake of another major international tournament – Euro '96 in England – United brought in Ronny Johnsen, Karel Poborsky, Ole Gunnar Solksjaer, Jordi Cruyff, and Teddy Sheringham.

In order to make room for 2014's newbies, United off-loaded. The under-used and often over-promised Shinji Kagawa rejoined Borussia Dortmund on Sunday 31st August – a day before the transfer window closed - for £6.3m. Javier Hernandez flew out to Madrid for a medical prior to a one-year loan deal. Tom Cleverley left too, for Aston Villa, again on loan. More: rumours abounded that United were touting up to six more first team players for similar deals as the flying circus which is Transfer Deadline day ticked ever closer.

Saturday 30th August 2014: Burnley v United (0-0)

On the field, nothing changed. United headed to Turf Moor, Burnley, for a Premier League tie against the newly promoted club. Much was made of the presence of Di Maria in the United line-up for the first time since his

British record transfer fee. In their entire history, Burnley had spent less than United had on this one, galactico player. And Turf Moor must have seemed *stratospheres* away from the Bernabeu to the Argentine: behind the low-slung, old-style stands was a view of the town's dark Satanic mills, and behind that, the backdrop of the moors.

The game ended in a stale-mate. In *The Guardian,* Jamie Jackson, wrote that after this: "latest insipid (…) display (…) their (Manchester United's) struggles may no longer be news." "Perhaps," he suggested, "the players that the manager has at his disposal are finding their natural level. Which is bore-draws in Burnley. Which is falling even further behind the early pacemakers, Chelsea. Which is coming away from a newly-promoted team *such as* Burnley kind of pleased to get out of there without being humiliated *a la Milton Keynes.*

Jackson suggested nothing had changed since Moyes, that the whole *Re*-United thing was an illusion, that you could throw as many transfers as you liked at the club, but in essence, United remained as moribund as some of the Ozymandian old mills lying derelict in Burnley. He suggested that the Dutchman was not "inept" – "Van Gaal's glittering résumé means that charge cannot be leveled" but damned him with faint praise all the same: "the three years since he last managed a club may have left him playing catch-up to current modes."

BBC Sport's chief football writer, Phil McNulty, agreed. He witnessed: "little sign of (the players) getting to grips with Van Gaal's methods and new system as they were uninspired in the face of Burnley's organisation and spirit."

He added: "Van Gaal remained rooted to his seat in the dug-out, clutching a clipboard for the entire game and there was little urgency on the field either as United struggled for inspiration."

And he talked of the team – The Team, in Van Gaal's parlance – boasting an "unbalanced look". Certainly when you watched the Everton-Chelsea game which was televised later that evening, the contrast between United's 'level' and that of both Roberto Martinez's and Jose Mourinho's teams was stark.

There were few straws to clutch at. Di Maria's debut showed promise. According to Jamie Jackson: "the 26-year-old convinced in central midfield as an attacking force who can laser passes into Van Persie and Rooney, beat opponents with pace and trickery, and offer a scoring threat, as he did when he had a second-half shot stopped inside the area."

Van Gaal himself seemed rather deflated in the post-match press conference. "When you have two points out of nine that is not good enough and that is disappointing," he said. "The progress is there but a club like Manchester United have to win."

"At the moment it's certainly not a world-class team, but we have to wait and have belief that it will come," he concluded.

And so, August was over. The Dutchman had still not won a competitive match as manager of Manchester United. The progress he talked about was not exactly apparent to fans, and doubts about his *system* began to rear their ugly heads. Writing for *The Republik of Mancunia*, Zak Hann said: "What we've actually *seen* has not been good. Of the seven goals United have conceded, including all four against MK Dons, six of them were preventable. And those six (excluding Sunderland's Jack Rodwell's goal from the corner), it's sad to say, had something to do with the formation. For example, Swansea's first goal via Ki came from too much space in front of an exposed defence. Others, like in the cup game, came from defenders putting each other under pressure because of the positions they picked the ball up in and the lack of options they had anyway. Everyone's looked a little uncomfortable in the system. Jonny Evans and Chris Smalling are much better than this. Darren Fletcher can't influence a game even a little. Juan Mata, Wayne Rooney and a rusty Robin van Persie have generally been woeful up front. And here's another thing we've seen too often: David de Gea receives an awkward pass from a defender with little choice, delays his kick and goes deeper in an attempt to gain control, then hits it out of play."

Belief is a fragile thing. Van Gaal talked of how his players' belief in themselves had been "smashed" by defeat against Swansea in the season's opener at Old Trafford. Fans' belief had taken one hell of a knock during the entirety of the 2013-14 campaign. That flag, so often seen at the Theatre of Dreams and in the away end whenever United played in Rome or Mandalay: *Not Arrogant, Just Better*, seemed all kinds of far away from the attitude we *now* maintained (believing a draw at Burnley was *okay*, simply because it could have been worse: we could have lost; we could have been humiliated).

And yet, belief can be buoyed just as easily as it is "smashed".

When, for example, the team you have supported all your life and you think you know like the back of your hand ups and pulls a rabbit out of the bag, *surprises* you back into belief. On Transfer Deadline Day, Manchester United pulled off the coup of the Summer. It was the kind of transfer which has you reaching for your calendar to check its *September* 1st, not April 1st. The kind of against all the odds transfer which – for a moment – makes you forget all about systems and formations and who'll have to make way in order that there's space in the team and instead simply give a hoot of joy. The kind of transfer which you remember exactly where you were when you first heard about it (and then waggled your finger around in your ear to check whether your ears were functioning correctly). For me, it felt like the moment we signed Mark Hughes back, the moment Andy Cole joined from Newcastle, the moment United signed Eric Cantona from Leeds, the moment the little witch, Juan Sebastien Veron joined from Lazio.

And what made it doubly great was the fact our new signing chose United.

There is no doubt about it: the Colombian Radamel Falcao resides in that top bracket of international stars, just below the big two of Cristiano Ronaldo and Lionel Messi. Daniel Passarella, who coached Falcao in South America, at River Plate, compared the Colombian with one of the best strikers Europe has ever seen. "He's like Van Basten," said Passarella. "He scores goals, he attacks on all sides and he heads like a god." There'd been rumours that the divine Colombian was getting ready to leave Monaco all summer. Monaco had already sold off their other crown jewel, another Colombian James Rodriguez, who'd starred in the World Cup largely due to Falcao's injury-absence, and Monaco's owner, the Oligarch Dmitry Rybolovlev made no secret of the fact he was looking to recoup some money following a divorce settlement of £2.6 *billion* earlier in the year. But if Falcao was to follow Rodriguez out of the exit door from the principality, surely his destination would be Chelsea, or Manchester City. Liverpool, still cash-rich following the Suarez sale, were also rumoured to be interested.

But City seemed to hold all the aces. The fact they'd allowed Alvaro Negredo to leave on loan meant there was a vacancy in their squad. And when a source close to Falcao leaked the news that the Colombian was booked on a private jet to Manchester on the morning of Transfer Deadline Day all the evidence pointed to Falcao rocking up in a sky-blue shirt for the 2014-15 season. Indeed, the back page of Monday 1st September's *Manchester Evening News* listed Falcao as almost certainly on his way to City. United, they reckoned, weren't even a consideration.

But by 9am, Sky Sports News giddily reported the Old Trafford club had stolen a march on their rivals, and it was in fact to *Carrington* Falcao was headed. BBC Sport's Simon Stone soon picked up the story, and spoke of Manchester United blowing "deadline day 2014 apart with this deal." Daniel Taylor, in *The Guardian,* claimed it was "a jolt for the football world". Scott the Red, on *The Republik of Mancunia* United blog could scarcely believe it. "Incredibly," he reported, "Manchester United have managed to loan Radamel Falcao from Monaco for the 2014-15 season."

The deal moved swiftly towards its climax. Daniel Taylor called it "an agreement of uncommon speed that demonstrates, again, United's determination to spend their way back to the top of their sport." It was indeed a loan deal - United agreeing to pay a reported £6m up front to secure the 28-year-old's services for the season – but the Reds would have the option to sign the striker permanently at the end of the season, once doubts about the after-effects of the knee injury which had kept Falcao out of the World Cup had been allayed. But those doubts about his injury were the *only* doubts about the deal. His goal-scoring record in Europe was astonishing. At Porto, he bagged 34 in 43 games in his break-out season after signing from River Plate, and then a Ronaldo-esque 38 in 42 in his sophomore year. A big-money transfer to Atletico Madrid followed, but even in *La Liga,* the goals flowed: he scored 36 goals in his first season and 34 in his second. Then came the false-start of the £50m move to Monaco. Falcao had a less than happy time in France, not least in suffering the injury which kept him out of the World Cup, but he still managed a goal ratio of better than one in two.

Upon his unveiling, Falcao said he was looking forward to working with his new manager. "Yes, I am very excited for that. (Louis) van Gaal is a very good trainer with a lot of experience. I want to do the best for the team, for him and for the supporters."

The transfer was a shock for myriad reasons. Firstly because he hadn't gone to City, or Chelsea. Secondly because he topped-up United's summer-spending to an incredible £150m, a record for an English club during a single transfer window. Thirdly because United hardly needed another striker, with Rooney, Van Persie, Welbeck and the young tyro James Wilson on the books, as well as a plethora of number 10s and the new British record transfer, Angel di Maria (yet still remained lacking in more defensive areas). Fourthly because of Falcao's injury record. Writing for *The Guardian,* Jonathan Wilson picked up on the Van Basten comparison, but took it one, chilling step further. "Lurking behind the Van Basten comparisons is the thought that injury ended the Dutchman's career at 29. Falcao turns 29 in February."

Finally, it was a shock because Falcao was 28. A few years ago, United had made it club policy never to buy *anyone* over the age of 26. Securing the Colombian's signature was final confirmation that United had recognised the need – rather belatedly, some might say – that they had to suck it up and enter the same 'competition' as Manchester City and Chelsea. They needed to buy ready-made, proven players from the top tier of football, not 'ones for the future'. They needed the best and they needed them now.

Football finance expert David Conn talked of how: "Shocked out of eight merry years re-financing and brand-sweating, United's US owners, the Glazers, have had to sanction their eager executive and former banker, Edward Woodward, to tear up years of restraint."

In signing Falcao, United began acting, finally, like the world's biggest sporting 'franchise', throwing their weight around just like we'd witnessed our rivals doing over the previous five to ten years.

They'd become ruthless: as Falcao came in through one door, Danny Welbeck – who'd been at United since he'd been 9-years-old – left out the other, for £16m to Arsenal. (Gary Neville questioned the decision, calling it "strange"). More: *The Guardian's* Daniel Taylor claimed Welbeck wouldn't be the only one to suffer. "The people in charge at Old Trafford decided long ago that a frontline including the considerable talents of Wayne Rooney and Robin van Persie was not dynamic enough for a club of their ambitions," he wrote. Even David Moyes had recognised the need for change: he'd looked at another South American plying his trade in France. Edinson Cavani had long been on the United radar and Moyes was reported to have told Ed Woodward, United's chief executive, during one strategy meeting that the Uruguayan would "score goals for fun" in the Premier League.

United got as far as arranging a meeting with Cavani's agent, but in the end, Moyes decided the alleged £65m the Reds would have to stump up to Paris Saint Germain would simply have been better spent on other areas of the team.

But Louis van Gaal is most certainly not David Moyes. You get the impression Moyes would have been kept up nights worrying about what Daniel Taylor described as United's "jumbled priorities", the "imbalance" in the team and the "lopsided" look to the squad. Yet Van Gaal seemed energized by the new additions to the squad, like some literate and principled version of Sky Sports News favourite wheeler-dealer, Harry Redknapp.

"It was never United's intention, one suspects, to arrange a mass emergency air drop of proven talent into Carrington," said Paul Hayward, in *The Telegraph*. "Reinforcements were always going to be bought, but the scale of the spending reflects the team's poor start after a misleading pre-season tour of America. This is where Van Gaal comes into his own. Few managers possess the skill to integrate so many players so quickly, but LVG set about the task with relish, finding a shape to accommodate Wayne Rooney, Robin van Persie and Juan Mata."

Yet a familiar van Gaal nemesis, Johan Cruyff, was quick to ask his own questions regarding United's top-heavy squad. When asked for his gut-feeling in regard to Van Gaal's prospects in Manchester, he said: "I don't know because they almost bought and created a new team. So now you have to fix it together – the team itself. It's not a question anymore about the quality of the players, or are they good enough. But to make a mixture of good players is very difficult."

"The big problem," he said, "is to manage all these players. It's the same thing with Barcelona. They now have Suarez, Messi, Neymar – how do you play them together? If you see them individually then they are great players. It's the same at Manchester United. Individually they are great but they have to play like a team."

"Then you get another problem," he added. "They are all famous. They earn a lot of money both on and off the field. How can you create a team and bring all these egos together? The main goal for Manchester United is for them to play well – and not have a player saying, 'I play well, I scored two goals'. Because if I score two goals but three goals go into our net then we lose. They provide Van Gaal with a lot of good players but he has to turn them into a team. And you can't arrange the chemistry of the team in two weeks. It needs time."

Basically, Cruyff's problem was with United's new *galacticos* policy, and the term *Van Gaal-acticos* had already become the media catch-phrase of choice during the two-week international break which separated United's stalemate at Burnley, and a home tie with Queens Park Rangers on Sunday 14th September. Suddenly, United had become England's Real Madrid, and there was a great deal of anticipation regarding how Van Gaal would shoe-horn his full and dizzying array of attacking talents onto the pitch for what would be a grand new start for Manchester United.

And how.

Sunday 14th September 2014: United v Queens Park Rangers (4-0)

After the false-start of the first three league games of the season (and that 4-0 reverse in the League Cup against MK Dons) this, finally, was the real thing. Henry Winter reported in *The Telegraph* that "this felt like United's season finally jump-starting, the Van Gaal era really kicking into life." In the same newspaper, reporter Paul Hayward went even further: "seldom in England's top flight has there been such a strong sense of starting all over again," he wrote.

And Van Gaal's ultra new-look United played to the occasion, running out 4-0 winners, delighting an expectant75,000 spectators at Old Trafford, and in one fell-swoop reminding everyone of the *old* United. They were "quick, incisive and demonstrated a speed of thought that was simply too much for a team with QPR's limitations," said Daniel Taylor.

Henry Winter agreed. Though the Red Devils are "still a work in progress under Louis van Gaal (…) the signs of progress are substantial and thrilling. (…) There was a new mood to the team, a real belief flowing through them, barring the occasional aberration. This was more than a win for United, more than three points. (…) This was a formidable statement of intent, a reminder of their replenished resources, and reviving ambition."

Paul Hayward said: "the most salient detail is that watching United was exciting again after a long period of bafflement".

Every one of the new signings gave a good showing. Marcos Rojo looked tough, and, barring a couple of mistakes, showed why United's left-side could become feared throughout the land again.

His compatriot, Angel di Maria, with whom Rojo had developed such a good understanding in Argentina's procession to the World Cup final, made a goalscoring home debut and played a role in each of the other goals too, reminding us that he wasn't the King of the Assists in *La Liga* last season for nothing. He also displayed a piece of *galactico* magic in scooping through a delightful through-ball to Van Persie which recalled another pass by another United catalyst in another era: Cantona's sand-wedged ball to Irwin against Spurs in the 1992-93 season.

Daley Blind showed himself to be the type of defensive shield in midfield that United had lacked since that succession of injuries forced Owen Hargreaves' out of the reckoning.

And Falcao made his bow, midway through the second half, to the delight of an ecstatic crowd. He almost scored too, after the hapless QPR 'keeper Rob Green spilled a Blind shot right into his path, but the Colombian couldn't lift the rebound over the onrushing ex-England international.

Even the old boys had a good day: Wayne Rooney bagged his 175th Premier League goal, and with it, drew level with Thierry Henry in third place in the All-Time Premier League goalscoring charts.

Louis van Gaal said of the result, and the attacking talent at his disposal: "This result is fantastic but we can do much better. I have worked for more than 35 years and I have always played attack and all my teams have scored the most of the league. So I hope at the end of this league, we shall have scored also the most. But the purpose of our goal is to be in the first three because we have to qualify ourselves in the Champions League. The most important thing is trajectory. We are building a process and we have to play in a certain style."

"I said before the game let us make a new start," he said. "That is important as, after Sept 1, after the transfer period, we can now work on a team-building process and make ourselves better every week. The most important thing from today is that we created goals. In the other matches we were the better team on the pitch but we didn't make goals. Now we have made four goals and that gives a boost to every player. This is special because it is also the birthday of my wife Truus. I have already given her a present, but she said the biggest present shall be the victory and we gave it to her."

Van Gaal was smiling. Truus was smiling. The players were smiling. So were the fans. Daniel Taylor wrote: "Old Trafford, for the first time in a while, felt like a happy, optimistic place".

And yes, Henry Winter was right to sound a note of caution: "Amidst all the euphoria stirred up by Di María and the Gaalacticos, United supporters will readily acknowledge that Queens Park Rangers were the meekest of guests, wall-flowers in white, at the Old Trafford party."

But still, this felt like a party, a brushing away of the cobwebs of the meek failure of 2013-14 and a cause for hope for the future. The Old Trafford crowd was in full voice all afternoon. Here, Paul Hayward said: "Money did more than talk. It sang songs of reassurance to a previously frightened crowd."

United were, for 90 minutes one mid-September afternoon – a full 16 months since the departure of Sir Alex Ferguson, over £200 million later – back. And, seemingly, they were cured.

Sunday 21ˢᵗ September 2014: Leicester v United (5-3)

Or maybe not. Maybe the QPR result was simply a dead cat bounce. Certainly there was something decidedly sickening about United's next result against another newly-promoted side in Leicester City. And United's shock defeat had media commentators feverishly writing off Van Gaal's side all over again.

On paper, the Reds' 5-3 defeat at the King Power Stadium should have been as nauseating as anything fans were forced to suffer under David Moyes. Statistically, this was the lowest of the low. Twice United led by two clear goals, twice they were pegged back. It was *30 years* since United had lost in any competition having raced into a two-goal lead.

They won the match *twice,* and still managed to lose.

And, meaning no disrespect to Leicester, whose fans could be seen pinching themselves in the crowd as goal after goal rolled in – *four* for the home side in 21 second-half minutes - this wasn't a top side. This wasn't a Chelsea, with Diego Costa blazing a trail up-front. It wasn't Manchester City, and Sergio Aguero. It wasn't even Liverpool and their 'Super' Mario. It was Leicester, and, as Jamie Jackson noted, "Jamie Vardy, a former Stocksbridge Park Steels, Halifax Town and Fleetwood Town attacker".

This was Leicester, against whom United had racked up ten successive wins prior to the capitulation on Sunday 21ˢᵗ September.

This was Leicester, and it was the first time in United's long and glorious history that they'd conceded four or more goals to a newly-promoted side.

This was Leicester, for Christ's sake, and United's reverse signalled the club's worst-ever start in the history of the Premier League. Van Gaal's side now had just five points from the opening five games, having secured the full three points on only one occasion. You'd have to track back twenty-two years to find a league table with United positioned so lowly after five matches: the Reds were 12th.

And 12 was, coincidentally, another black-magic number for the Old Trafford club. The five goals Leicester put past David de Gea meant United had let in 12 goals in six games under King Louis. It had taken David Moyes' United side 11 matches to concede the same number.

The Guardian's Midlands football correspondent Stuart James noted: "This was the first time in 853 Premier League matches United have surrendered a two-goal lead and lost… Once upon a time United were famed for their own acts of escapology but nothing is quite how it used to be."

Nobody wants records like that. Records like that were supposed to have been consigned to the era of the wrongly Chosen One.

The script wasn't supposed to read this way. It was supposed to be easy. This was, as Jamie Jackson noted LVG "the man whose CV boasts a European Cup, seven titles in three different countries and a reputation for being a tactical genius" against the journeyman manager Nigel Pearson. This was over £150 million of new talent against a set of players who had, in the main, plied their trade in the Championship the previous season.

Then again, we should have known there'd be goals.

In *The Guardian*, Michael Cox wrote: "It is difficult to remember a recent Premier League game with six strikers on the pitch at the kick-off and, while football is essentially about trying to outscore the other side, it is rare for two sides to interpret that objective quite so literally."

Those United fans who'd been so starved of excitement during the David Moyes regime, and who'd claimed they wouldn't mind losing in 2014-15 as long as they got a bit more swash for their buckle, and a few more goals to celebrate, were left wondering whether they could cope with a season in which there'd be so many swings, so many twists in the tail, so much uncertainty. But then again, one only had to rewind and play Angel di Maria's wonder goal – "think Karel Poborsky at Euro '96", said Stuart James - which made it 2-0 in order to be convinced that at least we were concentrating on the right area of the pitch at last.

Still, critics from outside the club were out in force to condemn United's approach. ESPN's Craig Burley said: "If it was excitement that Manchester United wanted when the Glazer family finally opened the piggy bank, they have it. The stultifying, ponderous fare of the season's opening weeks has gone, only to be replaced by chaos. A year ago, David Moyes was struggling with a squad to which he was only able to add Marouane Fellaini. Van Gaal has enviable granted riches, such that United only faintly resemble an Alex Ferguson team: Only David De Gea, Rafael, Jonny Evans, Rooney and Van Persie remain from the 2012-13 title winners. For the moment, too, the results are not that much different."

Even those with firm United links weren't shy of voicing their opinion. Former Red skipper Gary Neville said: "There's no doubt Manchester United are soft-centred. They're not tough enough. Going forward they're a lot better than they have been in the last 12-18 months and that's a positive. But in the first half, every ball that got played forward from distance, a Leicester player won it, whether it was the first ball or the second ball. Credit to Leicester and Vardy and Ulloa – they really ran them ragged. It wasn't intricate play or world-class football, it was just hard work. Grit, hard work, with a bit of quality mixed in with it and United couldn't deal with the physicality of that team."

And yet. And yet statistics, raw facts, the record books; none of them show that this was a game which turned on one incident. When United were in control of the game at 3-1 (Van Persie had scored with a header from a Falcao cross, Di Maria had scooped in his 'worldie', and Ander Herrera had added a third just after Falcao had rattled the crossbar with a strike which, had it gone in, would have put Di Maria's in the shade) and up stepped Jamie Vardy, he of the glittering career with Stocksbridge Park Steels, Halifax, and Fleetwood Town.

Scott 'the Red' Patterson of *The Republik of Mancunia* takes up the tale behind the stats: "On Sunday, Manchester United suffered a humiliating 5-3 defeat at the hands of newly-promoted Leicester, despite looking as though they had the three points wrapped up with an hour played. The star of the show and the man stealing all the headlines is Jamie Vardy, someone who was playing non-league football less than three years ago, and now, through determination, ability and desire, has ripped United apart."

"It's a romantic story," he continued, "but one that isn't strictly true, despite that being the angle reported in the press the following day. With United cruising at 3-1, Vardy shoved Rafael da Silva to the floor then ran in to the box. Rafael jumped to his feet, amazed that Mark Clattenburg didn't blow his whistle for a clear foul, before catching up with Vardy. Without the Brazilian even putting in a challenge, Vardy fell to the floor, and a penalty was given. Some reports have referred to this as a "dubious decision", as that fits the narrative of the underdog superstar, but the fact is he dived."

A disgusted Scott added: "The momentum shifted and two minutes later Leicester were equal. United have no one to blame but themselves for conceding that goal, but the home team were only in a position to draw level thanks to Vardy's cheating. To wrap up the points, Vardy pushed another United player off the ball, this time Tyler Blackett. The United defender managed to catch up with him after being fouled, but was unable to make a clean challenge, so conceded a penalty."

"Vardy was named in BBC's Team of the Week, without a single mention of his cheating," Scott observed. "Had Ashley Young, or another frequent diver who is singled out for criticism in the press, done the same as Vardy, he would have been crucified in the media the following day, not held up as a superstar."

Once we'd gotten over the disappointment of that final half-hour, there were other reasons for United fans to feel slightly positive. Louis Van Gaal certainly remained confident United could finish third. "When you are 3-1 ahead after 60 minutes you have to win. Then we are two points off second in the table. Because of the loss we are sitting here and you are talking like that and questioning me like that. But if we had won this game it was a different story. We can overcome and the season lasts more than one day."

Tim Simon, writing for *The Republik of Mancunia*, offered further encouragement: "Before the game changed on an absolutely dreadful penalty decision from Mark Clattenburg, United looked like a side ready to set the Premier League alight with their array of attacking talent. Angel Di Maria's captivating performance in midfield was enough in itself to gets United fans hysterical with excitement whilst having the luxury of leaving Juan Mata's creative talents on the bench and watching Radamel Falcao's full debut in a Red shirt would both have been unthinkable just a month ago."

"Di Maria's remarkable chipped finish in the first half almost defied the laws of physics but had the Colombian hit-man's own instinctive lob dipped one inch further, it would have arguably topped it," said Simon. "If we rewind six months to the latter stages of David Moyes' nightmare reign as United manager, there was no room for such excitable thoughts. The team was heartless, gutless, had little creativity and lacked sheer mobility all over the pitch. The humbling 3-0 defeats to Manchester City and Liverpool at home and the abject 2-0 losses to Olympiakos and Everton away from Old Trafford showed that a massive overhaul was needed at the club. Moyes, his coaching staff and several senior first team stalwarts had to go so a new manager could re-build a broken team which had laboured to a seventh-placed league finish."

"That is exactly what happened in the summer as Van Gaal along with six new summer recruits arrived at the club," he added. "The problems never going to be fixed within a couple of months of the new season and you would have to be pretty naïve to think it would have been. A squad that has undergone such a huge re-build needs time to gel and get used to the way each other play. Unlike Moyes, Van Gaal obviously has a long-term plan and he should be given time to implement it. There just isn't enough patience in the game these days."

And before we put the Leicester game to bed, and consign it to the realms of nightmare, we should remember one more salient statistic. The last time Leicester City beat the Reds was in 1998. United went on to win 10 of the 11 matches which followed. How United responded to the defeat would be crucial in determining whether the 5-3 would be remembered as a mere blip, or whether it was the symptom of a sickness which had spread far more widely.

The players, certainly, seemed determined to 'cure' themselves. They self-medicated with a team meeting. Robin Van Persie revealed: "We have to deal with it. We had a proper look at it next day. Sometimes it was a bit confronting and it was a long meeting. One hour or something. We went from there, started again this week and have put a couple of really good sessions in. Everyone feels ready to face West Ham. When you look at the defensive mistakes, it starts somewhere else. That's where we looked at as well. It's not just the one mistake which happens.

There's a mistake before the mistake and before the mistake, maybe positional wise. Everyone knows where we have to improve."

It was left to Van Gaal to have the final word, as is his wont. "We give a lot of information to the players and you have to work out that information," he said. "I have said that before. There shall be a moment in the season when this information is too much – maybe at this moment it is too much for the players, but I have already said it's more about advice. You have to be yourself, you have your own identity. But that's very difficult because we are starting with a new team, a new relationship between players, so that's why it needs time. But I don't want to say that all the time because all the fans are very tired of hearing that sentence."

Yet again, critics from outside the club were eager to weigh in with their own opinions. Sam Allardyce claimed David Moyes had not been given the time, or the backing by the club which Louis van Gaal was enjoying at Old Trafford. "If I was sat at home in David's shoes I would be wondering why they didn't spend the £150m with me," Allardyce said. "There was a complacency by United in not going out and delivering the signings David felt he needed. Now there's a panic on. He will obviously look at what he might have done better but he should have got the players he wanted and he tells me he didn't get any of them."

Saturday 27th September 2014: United v West Ham United (2-1)

Moyes first 5 games brought a haul of 7 points – two more than the Dutchman had achieved during the same spell - however they also included defeats to hated rivals Manchester City and Liverpool. In Moyes' sixth league game, United lost at home to West Brom. That *could* have happened for Van Gaal too, in a decidedly shaky second half showing against Allardyce's West Ham.

But it didn't.

A second sending-off in consecutive matches – against Leicester young Tyler Blackett had seen red for a professional foul; against the Hammers captain Wayne Rooney was giving his marching orders for a tackle which Van Gaal dubbed "too unfriendly" – saw the Red Devils up against it for the final half-hour, but the Dutchman's charges held firm in a way they hadn't in Leicester.

Van Gaal was pleased with the determination and character his players showed in battling to cling on to the three points. "You have to fight, fight and fight and I'm very pleased with the attitude of my players. They have fought until the end and after the match I told them when you do that you shall always be rewarded with a good result."

Rooney was the perceived villain of the piece. His wild kick at Downing put the win in jeopardy but he was the United hero early in the game, netting a crisp volley in the third minute to set the Reds on their way to what looked like it might be a routine victory. Van Persie had added a second too, but just before half-time a West Ham side - which looked bigger than their United counterparts to a man - scored with a free-header from a set play and suddenly the leftover Leicester jitters came out to play once again. Suddenly fans feared the Reds might let yet another seemingly unassailable two-goal lead slip.

Daniel Taylor said in *The Observer:* "There will come a time when Manchester United get rid of this unwanted knack of making life implausibly difficult for themselves but, plainly, that time is still some way off and for a long while here there was the very serious risk they might sieve away a two-goal lead for the second time in a week."

"Van Gaal's men did at least show a spirit of togetherness during those final exchanges," he added, "and there was a wonderful clearing header from Paddy McNair on a day when the 19-year-old rookie, signed from Ballyclare Colts four years ago, appeared in a patched-up defence."

McNair's appearance gave the lie to those pundits and journalists who'd claimed United had sold their soul, following the sale of Danny Welbeck. As Scott the Red noted in The Republik of Mancunia "after just seven games in charge, Louis van Gaal has given debuts to seven youth team players at Manchester United. For four of those, their debuts were in Premier League games. Tyler Blackett, Jesse Lingard, Paddy McNair and Tom Thorpe have all represented United in the league, while Saidy Janko, Andreas Periera and Reece James have played in the League Cup. Last season, just three players from the youth team made their debut, Adnan Januzaj, Tom Lawrence and James Wilson, and two of these were when Ryan Giggs took charge of the final four games of the season."

Sunday 5th October 2014: United v Everton (2-1)

Indeed, Van Gaal's fabled faith in youth was again in evidence a week later, as he achieved his first back-to-back victory with a home win against those typically tricky customers Everton. Rob Dawson wrote in the MEN: "Van Gaal's decision to sell Danny Welbeck to Arsenal might have raised some eyebrows. But the United XI that finished the game against Everton included three academy graduates 20-years-old or under - Paddy McNair, Tyler Blackett and James Wilson."

But McNair, Blackett and Wilson were not the names which made the headlines in the wake of the Reds' 2-1 win. No, that honour was reserved for goalkeeper David de Gea. The young Spaniard had suffered more than most during United's often chaotic defensive performances at the start of the season, so he must have been immensely proud of his display in keeping out the blue half of Merseyside. Not only did he save a penalty in stoppage time in the first-half, he also pulled off a hat-trick of show-stopping saves in the corresponding added time in the second half. Of those saves, Van Gaal said: "He did very well in the last 15 minutes, three shots outside the box, always difficult because a lot of players are in front of him so his view is not always good but when you stop those kind of shots you are very good."

The Manchester Evening News' Stuart Mathieson rated De Gea a perfect 10 for his performance. In his match report, Mathieson said: "Leighton Baines had a 14-from-14 100 per cent success rate from the penalty spot prior to facing De Gea but United's keeper won the 12-yard shoot-out."

In *The Guardian,* Jamie Jackson called De Gea's penalty save the "perfect psychological moment", occurring right on the stroke of half-time as it did.

Angel di Maria was another stand-out performer, adding another goal and another assist to his rapidly growing portfolio at Old Trafford. Mathieson wrote the Argentine is: "almost dragging performances out of this tentative transitional Reds side" with his routine of blistering runs, tasty tricks and incisive passing. It was, as Andy Hunter would have it, "another incisive, classy performance" from the British record transfer, prompting some to claim he was worth every penny of his near £60 million fee.

His fellow South American Falcao also had a good day at the office. Despite missing a number of chances, he didn't let his head go down and continued to make dangerous runs. And he was eventually rewarded with the winning goal just after Everton had pegged United back at 1-1.

Make no mistake about it, the match was, as Tim

Simon would have it on *The Republik of Mancunia* United blog, "most definitely Louis Van Gaal's biggest test as United boss to date". Despite the fact Everton had "started the season poorly themselves, sitting in a lowly 17th position in the Premier League and coming off the back of a lengthy trip to Russia to face Kuban Krasnodar in the Europa League on Thursday night" the Toffees remained a force to be reckoned with, and Red fans had bitter memories of a number of recent clashes with Everton (particulary that 4-4 draw when David Moyes' Everton which handed Manchester City the initiative in the 2011-2012 title race and then, in 2013-14 when Moyes was United boss, Everton's double at the Red Devils' expense: the first of those games had seen Everton win through a late, late goal from Oviedo; the second of which, at Goodison, had been the trigger for United to sack Moyes).

United had passed that test – just.

It was, said Stuart Mathieson, by no means a perfect performance. The Reds were: "still wobbly when anyone puts them under pressure." But, just like against West Ham, they'd held out. Rob Dawson, also of *The Manchester Evening News,* said: "Louis van Gaal has admitted Manchester United are 'not playing well' - but he's warned the rest of the Premier League to watch out when they start clicking."

"Van Gaal," he wrote, "was critical of United's second-half performance during the 2-1 win over Everton at Old Trafford, and thanked David De Gea for making three fine late stops and saving Leighton Baines' first-half penalty. The Dutchman admitted he wasn't happy with his team's display after the break - but warned that when they started playing well for 90 minutes instead of just 45, they will become a fearsome prospect."

Van Gaal said: "We are not playing good but we are already fourth in the table. What is coming when we are playing well? It is now our second game when we are not good in the second half. Maybe last week we had an excuse but I said to my players it is not an excuse 11 against 10, it is more easy to keep your organisation then because it allows to play compact. We didn't do it last week and now we didn't do it this week."

But a win is a win is a win. Those critics from outside the club who'd pointed to the statistical evidence that United remained a spent force (in more ways than one) couldn't ignore the fact that the club were now in the Champions League places for the first time in over a year. Andy Hunter called it a "potentially significant afternoon in United's season". And Jamie Jackson claimed the win made it "a satisfying occasion all-round for United" as they went into the international break on the back of three wins in four games. In reality that tally should have read four in four, that poor refereeing decision at Leicester notwithstanding.

But for now, the league table at least told Reds fans the team were heading in the right direction. It was especially important to put points on the board after a difficult start and a potentially gruelling October and November. The Everton match-up heralded the start of a difficult run of fixtures for the Reds which included early pace-setters Chelsea, champions Manchester City, and a potential rival for a spot in the top four in Arsenal over the next five games. Van Gaal had repeatedly banged the drum, telling fans they should only judge him after three months. Those fixtures would mark time's-up for the Dutchman and once they were over we'd have a better measure of how he was performing as United supremo. They'd also define the club's ambitions for the season.

For now, fans were simply delighted we'd witnessed three wins on the bounce at Old Trafford. Tim Simon wondered whether Old Trafford was becoming a fortress again. "The victory means it is now three wins in a row at Old Trafford for United. Just like old times. This never happened under Van Gaal's predecessor David Moyes and it is a statistic which will please the 63-year-old as he made it one of his primary aims when he took the job to restore the fear factor that has gone missing at the Theatre of Dreams."

Home league fixtures are a club's bread and butter, and if you don't get that right, you're on a hiding to nothing. In 2013-14 United stumbled from disaster to catastrophe at Old Trafford, but hopes were raised we'd be in for some better fare after the three wins in the Indian Summer of 2014.

So whilst fans were happy, those outside the club with headlines to write and newspapers to sell were still painting Van Gaal's inaugural three months at Old Trafford as something of a mixed bag. The jury was still out in Van Gaal's trial by media. Nick Ames said, in his typically measured way, in *The Guardian:* "Louis van Gaal's early months at Manchester United have elicited plenty of noise – to the extent that their fourth place in the Premier League table seems like a trick of the light. But there it is: they are in a Champions League position despite mishaps such as those against Swansea and Leicester. While it still seems a little slung together, and they have not been particularly convincing except against an awful QPR, the platform is there and it is evident that – even if coherence is some way down the line – Van Gaal now has enough match-winners to get them out of tight spots."

Jamie Jackson, as is his wont, went way over the top, bringing every single aspect of the Dutchman's management under the microscope. His topics for conversation ranged wildly from the team hotel ("Van Gaal has proved a stickler for punctuality, politeness and decorum at the Lowry Hotel, where the squad gather before each home match.") to training ("Since arriving Mr Van Gaal has shown a clear vision for the Aon training complex that has resulted in a £3m investment.") *The Guardian's*

Manchester United correspondent raised doubts about the burgeoning injury list, as though *that* was the Dutchman's fault: "One serious frustration has been the number of injuries – up to 10 players have been unavailable – with many of these occurring during training. Mr Van Gaal has admitted puzzlement at this but is working hard to address the problem."

Overall, Jackson's mid-term report judged the Dutchman a B-. Not great. Certainly not *Fergie*. But not Moyes either. "All in all," he said, "Mr Van Gaal has made an encouraging start – and it should also be noted this has been done while giving debuts to seven homegrown youngsters – and a title challenge is still a distinct possibility."

Talking of Fergie. Sir Alex Ferguson addressed the crowd before the Everton game at high-noon on Sunday 5th October. The previous season, the media had been keen to paint him as some kind of pantomime villain, this constant presence looming over Moyes' shoulder, frowning when things went wrong. This year, Fergie had been present in the crowd during the disaster at Milton Keynes Dons, so he could have been forgiven for being similarly displeased with Van Gaal. However, Ferguson told MUTV: "Louis van Gaal has made a lot of changes and, thinking about that, actually maybe he's doing the right thing, to clear the decks and build his own team. Because he's got the experience and coaching ability to do that. The way he's approached it I think has been brilliant." He described Van Gaal as a "formidable" man with the "stubbornness and the determination" to put things right at Old Trafford.

Moyes himself was wheeled out by the media, like some injured war hero, like Banquo's ghost. Ostensibly he was there to talk about his 'recovery' after the trauma of managing Manchester United. But the timing of it cannot have been by chance, coming at exactly the time Van Gaal invited all-and-sundry to cast their judgment upon him.

Everyone, it seemed, had an opinion.

Monday 20th October: West Bromwich Albion v United (2-2)

And Van Gaal had never been short of an opinion either. The Dutchman was certainly in bullish mood prior to their clash against West Bromwich Albion at the Hawthorns on Monday 20th October. In a pre-game press conference he compared his start at United to his start at Bayern Munch. After a decidedly sticky start in Germany, his charges won 4-1 in Turin against Juventus (see Chapter VI: "Death or Gladioli": Bayern Munich (2009 – 2011)) and that result proved the spark for a highly successful season in which the German giants reached the Champions League final as well as winning the German league and cup double.

"Do you remember when we had our revival?" he said. "We won 4-1 at Juventus, a fantastic game, and that gave us that psychological benefit."

A similar result for United against West Brom, or during the tough spell of games which followed, might do the same for his new club. The catalyst, he said, "can be any match but it cannot be every training session because a training session is different to a match, believe me. You cannot simulate the match rhythm. We try to, but it's different."

He denied United would enjoy the benefits of playing fewer games than their direct rivals for the Champions League places due to United's failure to qualify for the competition. "When you can play the Champions League, especially the Champions League but also the Europa League, you can compare yourselves as a team with the better players, with a higher level," he said. "When you are in the Champions League and it's going well and you beat opponents, you are coming in a flow and then it's not so bad to play all the matches."

The international break had stopped United full-flow. They went into it off the back of two wins on the bounce. But for the width of a post, Louis van Gaal's charges might have recorded their third consecutive victory and regained fourth place in the Premier League. But for an 87th minute equaliser the Reds would have been – at least as far as the media were concerned - back in crisis again. West Brom had not beaten United at the Hawthorns in 30 years, since the heady days of Cyrille Regis *et al.* And yet they came within three minutes (plus injury time) of doing just so.

It was that kind of topsy-turvy affair on 20th October, when United and West Brom drew 2-2 in what Stuart James called "a pulsating match" in his *The Guardian* report. And while United and the Baggies have form when it comes to providing all-action affairs such as these – witness the incredible 5-5 draw on this very ground in Sir Alex Ferguson's final game in charge of the Reds – United still *should have won.*

This should have been their catalyst.

After conceding early – a Sessegnon bolt from the blue after only eight minutes – David de Gea was not troubled again until the 66th minute, when a long punt downfield saw Saido Berahino in the clear and at his ease to finish. Otherwise the Red Devils were all over their Midlands counterparts. Van Gaal likes his teams to play dominant football, and those two goals notwithstanding, United did exactly that. And it was borne out in possession statistics. Stuart James' *The Guardian* report noted that United "enjoyed 63% of possession and had 22 shots to Albion's eight."

And it was possession, generally, in the right areas of the pitch. United poured forward in a style which was reminiscent of Kevin Keegan's Newcastle (a comparison which had been doing the rounds in the media during recent weeks). Unfortunately, they defended like Keegan's Newcastle too, with the freshly-returned-from-injury Phil Jones a Darren Peacock- alike disaster-waiting-to-happen and both Luke Shaw and Rafael caught out positionally for the West Brom goals.

One thing was clear. In the World Cup, Van Gaal impressed with his substitutions (think Tim Krul for the penalty shoot-out against Costa Rica) but prior to the West Brom game the jury was still out as to what effect – if any – the Dutchman's changes had made to any Manchester United match. At the Hawthorns, he was brave enough to haul off the ineffective (and clearly not match-fit after a rib injury) Ander Herrera.

And his choice of a replacement was a controversial one amongst United fans.

Sky TV's cameras had repeatedly lingered on the United bench throughout the first half, particularly after West Brom had taken the lead, and with the first half still in play, they focused on what looked like an altercation between Van Gaal – on the first row of seats on the bench – and the unpopular Belgian Marouane Fellaini. Fellaini was seen by many as a hangover from the David Moyes regime. He'd had a terrible first season at Old Trafford, losing so much confidence that at times it seemed he could barely move without a stray elbow swinging into an opponent and seeing him penalised. He could hardly trap the ball either, let alone pass it, and seemed positionally unaware.

It turned out we weren't bearing witness to a Dutch-Belgian row. We were watching LVG handing out his instructions to the lanky Belgian in the second half. Van Gaal had clearly seen a weakness in West Brom which he could exploit using Fellaini's height, by utilising him in his full-on, rampaging siege-tower mode.

And how. Two minutes after appearing as a half-time substitute Fellaini pulled out his trademark move. At Everton Fellaini's chest-control was thought to be the best in the Premier League, but United fans had seen scant evidence of it in a Red shirt. But the way he instantly pulled down another hopeful Di Maria cross on his chest belied any lingering confidence issues. He took a touch right, taking him away from the attentions of his marker, and then blasted a thunderbolt past Myhill. It was his first goal for United in 24 games; a Gary Birtles-type run, and it came over a year after he'd signed for the club.

It was some impact. Some substitution.

In an interesting side-note, Stuart James' match report observed: "It was clearly not what one of Albion's media staff had in mind. "Fellaini has now taken his tracksuit off, fortunately he has a Man Utd strip underneath," was the message posted on their official Twitter account moments before the Belgian came on for Herrera. An hour after the game it had been retweeted more than 17,000 times.""

And Alan Smith, writing in *The Guardian,* had his own take on that 'altercation' between LVG and Fellaini just before half-time: "In the first half Van Gaal engaged in a frank exchange with the Belgian on the bench, like a headteacher telling off a misbehaving pupil. Whatever was said had the desired effect on him initially. For a side shorn of physicality, Fellaini's 1.94m frame was a welcome tonic."

We'd seen similar from Van Gaal many, many times before.

Still, from then on, Fellaini was brimming with self-belief. He won every header, every tackle. His energy drove United forward, and for a twenty minute spell, West Brom simply could not get out of their own half; their own *penalty area* at times. United were relentless. Dominant. Like the United of old.

Crosses zipped across the six-yard box and only narrowly eluded a United touch which would surely have brought another goal. Di Maria, ably abetted by Luke Shaw, gave the West Brom full-back twisted blood. Over the course of the match United won 11 corners. West Brom won none.

That tells the story of this game. As does the fact that most of these corners came during United's second half onslaught.

The only let-up for the Midlands club was the Berahino goal.

And that seemed to drive United on still further. They *knew* they needed to get the points, with Chelsea and Manchester City on the horizon.

Van Gaal oh-so-nearly pulled off another masterstroke when he brought Falcao on as substitute. The Colombian was instrumental in drawing defenders away from Robin Van Persie in order that he could engage in an intricate spot of ball-juggling on the edge of the box and then an arrow of a shot which had the West Brom 'keeper Boaz Myhill beaten all ends up. But not the post.

West Brom were hanging-on. They survived a couple of penalty appeals, and United kept going. Surely a goal would come. Could Manchester United score? The Manchester United of old would always score... And after all, they had Robin Van Persie, Adnan Januzaj, and Radamel Falcao on the field of play (the excellent Angel di Maria having departed injured: a dead-leg).

In the end, the second equaliser came from as unlikely a source as the first. And again it was a player netting his first United goal; defensive shield Daley Blind found a rare yard of space on the edge of the West Brom penalty area and passed the ball calmly into the net in order to spare the blushes of his Dad Danny Blind's pal, Van Gaal. Blind, a £13.8 million capture from Ajax, had not enjoyed his best game in a United shirt before the goal. And he hardly had form as a goalscorer: he'd scored just one for Ajax in the 2013-14 season, despite being made the Dutch footballer of the year (his total career goals in club football is now just four). But he'd quietly grown in importance to

Manchester United, and the equaliser against West Brom brought about great relief for fans and *Gaalactico* team-mates alike.

In the end, a draw was bearable for United fans if only because they'd witnessed some fantastic, dominant, attacking football. But the return of a single point for all that effort expended seemed unjust, and it left the Reds with just 12 points from the 24 on offer in the eight games thus far in the season, and *still* to win a match on the road. They'd drawn with Burnley, Sunderland, and West Brom, and suffered embarrassing reverses at MK Dons and Leicester. Goals weren't exactly in short supply: since the advent of the *Gaalacticos* they'd scored at least one in every game they'd played. However the *goals against* column made for unhappy reading. They'd conceded seven in their past two Premier League clashes alone.

It was clear where the problems lay. And where they didn't.

Defensively, United still looked like a mistake waiting to happen. They seemed to lack organisation and leadership at the back. Hardly surprising given the fact that old heads such as Vidic and Ferdinand were away in the summer and that this, as Tim Simon noted for *The Republik of Mancunia,* was Van Gaal's "fifth central defensive pairing in the first eight league games". But still, there was enough quality on show in the back-line for the Reds to have been better than this.

Attacking-wise United continued to find the net, however neither goal was scored by a striker. Tim Simon called it "a night to forget for Robin Van Persie and Juan Mata, who both failed to have an impact on proceedings." Van Persie in particular – that volley against the post notwithstanding – looked "laboured". Wayne Rooney was much-missed, as much for his energy as for his goalscoring, and Radamel Falcao should arguably have started in Van Persie's place were he not suffering from jet-lag after

Colombia's trip to Canada in the international break.

As for the plus points. There was of course Fellaini's cameo. The Belgian, as Simon noted, "completely changed the game", and though he "may not be a regular at Old Trafford this season (…) it is good to see that he may have something to offer the club, even if it is a route one, Plan B option off the bench."

And there was also the angelic form of United's new number seven, Di Maria. At times at the Hawthorns, the Argentine was unplayable. He'd already proved himself to be invaluable to Van Gaal's team, but now United looked as though they were relying on him too heavily. "It is obvious," said Simon, "that United are beginning to rely heavily on his phenomenal flair and invention. Gary Neville pointed out post-match that United are currently relying on great "moments" to get results rather than a consistently dangerous attacking performance and it has been Di Maria that has generally been that spark in recent games. It is a new side, who are still getting used to the way each other play but the reliance on Di Maria is slightly worrying. The Argentine looks like he will make something happen every time he touches the ball but whilst it is amazing to have that world class midfielder in the side, the other players around him have to start producing too. Looking at the positives, Di Maria has the ability to tear any defence apart from either a central area or a wide position and it is fantastic to have someone like that at Old Trafford."

So, a topsy-turvy game and a topsy-turvy performance from the Reds. Simon Burnton, in *The Guardian's* minute-by-minute text commentary of the game, summarised like so: "If Manchester United could ever be encouraged by a draw at West Brom secured by an 87th-minute goal having twice fallen behind and despite having a paper-thin defence that habitually stands way too far from its own goal, this was perhaps it. They got themselves some serious momentum at times, demonstrated some admirable bouncebackability, and massively dominated all but the most important of statistical metrics (the scoreline, obviously). Their midfield was good, particularly after Fellaini came on and before Di Maria went off, but there are problems both in defence and in attack, where Van Persie didn't do very much. Chelsea and Manchester City might show up their deficiencies even more starkly. Still, small steps and all that."

Van Gaal's analysis was similar: "Two points lost – I think we were the better team. I am very disappointed about the result. You can say we were two times behind but I don't think that West Bromwich Albion has created many chances – I think zero. And we gave the two goals away. I think we dominated the game – that's what I want as a coach, as a manager – but the manager doesn't want a result like 2-2. I said that to my players, I cannot be happy."

When quizzed as to whether he should sacrifice some attacking flair to make the team more solid, Van Gaal said: "I don't think that is the solution. I have already explained that a lot of times. It was two errors (against Albion). And also in the past, because I think we could have eight points more and then we are up (the table)."

Still, he admitted United needed to improve prior to the Chelsea, City, and Arsenal games. "Now we have to play against Chelsea. In the Netherlands they say that is another cookie, another biscuit. It is another level and we have to see if we can beat them."

And he still wouldn't concede that his United charges had no chance in the title race either. Asked whether Chelsea were catch-able, he said: "That's possible but it is difficult to say because I am then arrogant. But I have done it a lot of times."

Sunday 26th October 2014: United v Chelsea (1-1)

Of course, United *catching* Chelsea wasn't the main media story in the build-up to the long anticipated clash. Instead, much of the focus in the days preceding the game at Old Trafford fell upon the managerial heavyweights of Van Gaal and Mourinho, who would be pitting their wits against each other for the first time in England. Their only previous meeting as managers had come in European club football's showpiece game, the Champions League final (in 2010, when Mourinho's Internazionale beat Van Gaal's Bayern Munich 2-0 at the Bernabeu, Madrid). But the pair had a long, shared history all the same.

They first became acquainted in 1997, when Van Gaal took over from Bobby Robson as manager of Barcelona (see Chapter II – Welcome to "Vietnam": Barcelona (1997-2000)). Indeed, as an interesting side-note, in 2014-15 there was a sense that *all* roads led back to Barcelona circa 1997-2000. Football tactics expert Jonathan Wilson noted that not only did Van Gaal have Mourinho on his staff at Camp Nou, also his midfield was populated with, at various times during his reign, Pep Guardiola, Luis Enrique, Phillip Cocu, Ronald Koeman, and Frank de Boer: "or, to put it another way (…) the present managers of Barcelona, Bayern Munich, Manchester United, Chelsea, Ajax, PSV Eindhoven and Southampton.".

Anyway, back to '97. When LVG arrived as the new coach, Mourinho's position at the club was a fragile one. Without Robson's protective wing, Jose had become something of a sitting duck at Camp Nou. Indeed, he'd become a figure of ridicule.

Ian Ladyman described the situation in a *Daily Mail* article prior to the United-Chelsea match-up: "Sir Bobby Robson's relationship with Mourinho is well chronicled. What is less well known is that a young man in whom Robson saw so much potential was beginning to be lampooned a little at the Nou Camp when his mentor was moved aside to make way for Van Gaal."

"Robson loved Mourinho," Ladyman continued. "The Portuguese was much more than a translator to him — he was a confidant and a trusted scout. But in the boardroom at the Nou Camp that was what they rather sneeringly called him. *El Traductor.*"

"Van Gaal changed all that," noted Ladyman. "Encouraged by Robson to keep him on, the innovative Dutch coach then took the leap of faith that his predecessor subsequently admitted he had been reluctant to take without harder evidence of Mourinho's true capabilities.

'Sometimes I think I was the only guy left who believed in Jose,' said Van Gaal. 'When Bobby left, Mourinho was angry. His position would be disappearing. But I was impressed with his personality so he was kept on, initially for a year. When I told the club he had to stay, they weren't pleased.

To start with he was still just a translator but gradually he became as valued as my other assistants. We did a lot of positional play in sessions. Then you can see if someone can really coach. He could.'"

In the end, "Mourinho, barely into his mid-30s," became "Van Gaal's 'No 3 assistant'". Van Gaal "promoted him to the point where he took training sessions and gave match-day team talks."

And he might have been the *third assistant,* but Mourinho and Van Gaal had become a "good cop/ bad cop" partnership straight out of Hollywood movies. Ladyman explained: "Former Barcelona winger Simao, signed by Van Gaal in 1999, recalled: 'Van Gaal would get mad at anything. Everywhere. Everything. He was very demanding. He banned telephones. You had to watch out. Mourinho, though, was different. He was very relaxed, making jokes. In the morning he would give me the newspaper and talk to me about the news. He was very attentive.'"

"Theories of what Van Gaal and Mourinho initially saw in each other abound. There are, however, clear similarities," said Ladyman. "Neither man achieved as much as they would have liked as players and both were teachers. Perhaps crucially, though, Van Gaal knew that coaching assistants could make the step up if they were good enough, having done exactly that at the age of 35 under Hans Eijkenbroek at AZ Alkmaar and then again under Leo Beenhakker at Ajax in 1990."

And, importantly, neither relied upon the sheer weight of reputation they'd built up as a player in order to acquire authority within a dressing room. Neither was a Cryuff.

Their partnership was not solely limited to their working relationship. Ladyman said: "In Sitges, the upmarket resort 25 miles south-west of Barcelona, the two men lived barely 15 yards from each other in an apartment block. Often, they would meet around their dining tables to talk football."

At Old Trafford on Sunday 26th October 2014, they'd be around 15 yards apart on the touchline as their two sides faced-off.

And yet, despite this close proximity in the hot-house atmosphere of the Premier League, the relationship between the pair was *still* defined by mutual respect and admiration. You got the sense that here there'd be no pushing and shoving or encroachments into the opponents' technical area as had recently occurred in the Chelsea-Arsenal game. You got the sense there'd be no post-match *brouhaha* regarding handshakes, missed or otherwise. Indeed, after conducting their obligatory pre-match interviews in the media area of the tunnel at the Theatre of Dreams, both men sought each other out to enjoy a hug which had many commentators rushing to their laptops to find out the exact dictionary definition of "bro-mance".

The Daily Mirror's David McDonnell described the hugs – there were two in the tunnel and a further one pitch-side – as a "love-in". "If they were a frisky couple, such public displays of affection, would have yielded the response 'get a room'," he wrote.

It played out a lot like the Mourinho-Ferguson relationship, in fact. Mourinho is often painted as arrogant, aloof from many of his fellow managers (witness those missed handshakes at Aston Villa, which so enraged Roy Keane, and the frequent flare-ups between the Portuguese and his French counterpart, Arsene Wenger) and yet, with Fergie and Van Gaal, Mourinho proved himself to be deferential. Respectful. Humble, even.

It was a two-way street. Van Gaal said: "I am always portrayed as the arrogant Louis van Gaal but now I am humble. Because now he is better than me." Indeed, he said, "Mourinho was the first one I texted when I got the United job," said King Louis. "He was the first one to text me back. He said he was jealous of my list of clubs."

For his part, Mourinho said of Van Gaal: "They (United) have one of the best managers in the world. I think they are in good hands. Louis, with time, will make a fantastic team."

And if there was something old-fashioned about the relationship between the two managers of these ultra-modern, superpower clubs, there was something old-fashioned about the game, too. At least about its outcome: after a strong first-half showing from United, Chelsea took the lead early in the second-half through that old warhorse Didier Drogba, who scored his first goal of his second spell for the Blues at the ripe old age of 37. And then Chelsea made like boa constrictors, tried to squeeze the life out of the match. But, in Fergie-Time, United grabbed an equaliser.

If the old United were back, Chelsea were back, in

the form of the old Leeds United, committing repeated cynical fouls and sharing them out amongst the team as a function of a deliberate spoiling strategy on the part of Mourinho. Tactical rotational fouling, they call it, and Chelsea – in fact *all* Mourinho sides – are the past-masters of it. Referee Phil Dowd issued 10 yellow cards during the game, seven of them to Chelsea players. Two of them to the *same* Chelsea player, Branislav Ivanovic, who was given his marching orders deep into stoppage time for a clip to the heels of Angel di Maria.

From the resultant free-kick, Fellaini won the header, and though Chelsea's Courtois blocked this, he could do nothing about the rebound, which Robin Van Persie smashed home the leveller. His "celebration (…) felt like a release of pent-up emotion" said Daniel Taylor.

And United fans celebrated it like they'd *won* the match. And it felt like a win. It felt like the old United were back. It felt like this might have been the turning point to the season which LVG kept talking about (with those Bayern-Juve comparisons).

"Now, perhaps, Louis van Gaal has a better understanding why Sir Alex Ferguson used to boast no other side on the planet had Manchester United's penchant for late drama," said Daniel Taylor. "They were in the fourth minute of stoppage time when Robin van Persie pulled back his left foot to rescue them and here was another moment to punish anyone who risks heading for the exits when United are chasing a game and the clock is still ticking."

"George Best tried it as the 1999 Champions League final moved into extra time, with the score at 1-0 to Bayern Munich. Their latest feat of escapology ranks further down the "football, bloody hell" scale but it was still some moment and the celebration from Van Persie told its own story. He was off, running to the crowd, peeling off his shirt, throwing it high and screaming to the skies. It felt like an explosion of pent-up emotion and that small moment revealed a lot, perhaps, about this club's inner frustrations."

And yet, the comeback had hardly been anticipated.

This was Chelsea, the best team in the league, not West Brom. We could not see a repeat of Daley Blind's late, late show at the Hawthorns coming, let alone see it coming from the unlikely source of his fellow Dutchman Van Persie, who'd previously missed two very presentable chances and had looked yet again out of sorts.

And it was Chelsea. Even when United had the ascendancy – in terms of winning titles – against the Blues, Chelsea had always been something of a bogey side for the Reds. And before the game, United had recorded just six wins out of the last 22 clashes. And Chelsea looked stronger, fitter, *bigger* to a man.

It didn't look like the impossible would be made possible. The four minutes added on were not characterised by wave after wave of United attacks crashing down on the Chelsea defence. "Unlike so many other United comebacks there had been no real sense this one was brewing," said Taylor. "Chelsea were not completely coasting but United's response to going behind had been poor and the league leaders were on the verge of moving six points clear of Southampton and eight from Manchester City. United were looking desperately short of ideas. In Van Gaal's words: "We lost our heads."

They seemed to have run out of ideas and they seemed to have run out of energy too. After scoring, Chelsea made the pitch big. They made United run and run and run. They broke up play before the Reds could build any momentum. And it looked as though another disappointment in this most uneven of seasons would be coming our way.

Enter Robin Van Persie and exit hopelessness.

Enter delirium, exit doubt.

Luke Shaw, a veritable United newbie but one of

the Reds' outstanding performers on the day (and reportedly a Chelsea fan during his formative years), said he'd never experienced anything like it: "It's a feeling I've never felt before. The whole crowd got up and you saw how much it meant to all of us. We all jumped on each other. It was crazy, the fans, the stadium sort of erupted. It was a great feeling and I was proud to be involved in that."

Of course, in the maelstrom of emotion which followed this second late equaliser in a week, fans could have been forgiven for forgetting that United drew with Chelsea at Old Trafford under David Moyes too. Early in the 2013-14 season, the Blues had visited the Reds while Mourinho was still bedding-in for his second spell in the Stamford Bridge hot-seat. His starting line up that night lacked a single striker and it was said – after the fact – that he overestimated the opposition. He didn't make the same mistake here.

But still, the ammunition was there for the neigh-sayers to make their claims that £160 million down the *Swannee*, United were in fact *worse* off than last year. Certainly in terms of results in corresponding fixtures the Red Devils were six points down on 2013-14 – the worse swing in the entire Premier League – and those lavish, crowing celebrations marking Van Persie's equaliser here seemed – to some – to be over-egging the pudding somewhat.

United had only drawn, at home. This was not Barcelona in 1999.

Their reward for scoring so late was a mere point, and it would leave them in eighth place, behind Liverpool and Arsenal, let alone Manchester City and Chelsea.

But in 2014-15 the mood was wildly different to that of 2013-14's United-Chelsea draw following the final whistle. A last minute equaliser can do that. Mark Odgen in *The Telegraph* said that although United remain "a contradiction under Louis van Gaal (…) at least the mood music has a rousing finale these days. For the second time in six days, United snatched a draw from the jaws of defeat: Fergie-time is back, with sheer persistence and determination securing a crucial point against the league leaders."

This was a great psychological result for United - and the performance was good too.

It was a performance which inspired, which pumped us up.

It was a performance which had us thinking bigger. Though the belated nature of the goal meant there was a case to be made for Chelsea having dropped two points, there was also an argument to be made that United had deserved more than a point. Statistically, the Reds were on top. Even counting Chelsea's dominant spell immediately after scoring, United had the best of the possession statistics. They had more than twice as many shots both on and off target.

Gary Neville named the Chelsea 'keeper Courtois his man of the match on Sky Sports.

Jacob Steinberg on *The Guardian's* minute-by-minute match report said this was: "undoubtedly the best Manchester United performance under Louis van Gaal" and the mood amongst fans was more optimistic than at any other time in the past 18 months.

Jamie Jackson talked of how after the result – and statement performance - United are "heading skywards and Van Gaal means business".

Talking of skywards, Mark Ogden talked of how, at United at last "blue sky is now beginning to creep into view behind the grey clouds". There was, he said, "something different in the air at Old Trafford, despite the black-and-white reality that it was actually better, at this stage, under a man doomed to be sacked after just ten months in charge. The difference? Belief is one quality that has returned and, with Van Persie driving home an equaliser against the league leaders three minutes into stoppage time, so has that United quality of going right on until the end."

Only Van Gaal sounded disappointed. He thought United did more than enough to win the game. And, he said: "I think Jose Mourinho knows that also."

And he wasn't utterly convinced by the performance either. "I have said that to the boys. It was not our best performance and that is a pity because at this moment you have to show yourself against the better teams but in spite of that we have created a lot of chances – much more than Chelsea. They have created one chance in the first half and before the goal there was the Hazard chance which David de Gea stopped fantastically. The corner kick for Drogba's goal was a lack of communication and that is why they scored. That is always the difference in such games."

Of course, Van Gaal may well have been playing mind-games with his squad, firing them up for the next big test, the following weekend at Manchester City.

Jamie Jackson talked of how Van Gaal's words were those of "a perfectionist who always demands extra. As his team walked through the mixed zone nearly all of them refused to be interviewed, with many avoiding eye contact. Van Persie's late goal made it seem as if Chelsea had been beaten. So the downbeat demeanour suggests Van Gaal had delivered a sobering message for his players to carry into preparations for Sunday's 168th Manchester derby at the Etihad Stadium."

Sunday 2nd November 2014: Manchester City v United (0-1)

United fans would certainly *hope* the manager would get the team up for the derby. Over the past three or four years – with the notable exception of the 3-2 win at the Etihad when Van Persie scored the winner in 2012-13 – United's performances against the noisy neighbours had been characterised by flaccid fearful tactics. There hadn't been a committed game plan in sight; certainly nothing like the bold and inventive blueprint LVG set up for the Chelsea game.

United's performances against City in 2013-14 were nothing short of disgraceful. They were hammered 4-1 at City in Moyes' fifth game in charge, and arguably the team never recovered from that. They lost 3-0 in the corresponding fixture.

But Van Gaal's team were a "united United" according to Jamie Jackson. Almost the entire matchday squad had watched *El Classico* on the TV the night before the Chelsea game. And Van Gaal talked of how the team had taken away some useful information about team-shape from watching the Real-Barca clash. "We were at the Lowry hotel and we had a TV screen in our dining room and I invited the players to watch the second half. Seventeen out of 18 players were there and I have never experienced that before so I was very pleased. I said to the players you have seen what they have done because, for example, Barcelona with Luis Enrique is always pressing from behind and even the home side Real were playing from behind. They drop in and are very compact. But after Real scored the second goal the match was over because Barcelona don't keep compact like they did in the first half. It was deadly. Because of that my team, despite the 10 minutes when they lose their heads against Chelsea, we were always in our shape."

This is classic Van Gaal: always teaching. Always prompting. Always looking to improve the system and the shape of the team.

However, you can put in place all the blueprints you like, you can talk up the psychology of games and 'turning points' of seasons all you like, but you can't legislate for the actions of one stupid boy.

Before the Manchester derby on 2nd November Van Gaal had spoken about the importance of his players keeping their heads. So you can imagine him wearily shaking his head like a latterday Captain Mainwaring when Chris Smalling experienced two rushes of blood to the head in the space of ten first-half minutes and found himself on the receiving end of two yellow cards which saw him dismissed, and United's chances of recording their first victory against the noisy neighbours since the championship season of 2012-13 disappear in the blink of an eye.

Despite the superlative-strewn build-up to the game on Sky Sports, the derby was, like United-Chelsea the week before, hardly a match for *El Classico*. (Barney Ronay instead called it *El "Collapsico"* derby in *The Guardian).* Feverish, intense, and ultra-competitive *sure,* but ultimately there was a real deficit in quality.

Barney Ronay called it: "a high-tempo, high-drama mess of a match between two well-resourced champion teams that have divvied up the Premier League title between them for the past four seasons." This was, he added: "a group of high-class players charged at each other for 90 minutes here with all the cool, collected precision of the world's most outrageously talented pub footballers trying run off a Jagerbomb hangover. Elite-level football is often described as a game of chess, but this was closer to a late-night round of contact dominoes."

The match was littered with individual errors. You could hear the nerves of the players jangling over and above the (initially) raucous chanting of the Mancunian faithful. This was understandable: City went into the game off the back of three games without a win (including two defeats) and United, the £160 million player injection and last gasp smash-and-grab against Chelsea notwithstanding, still hadn't recovered the arrogant swagger of seasons past.

Wayne Rooney, returning from a suspension which had seen him miss almost the entire month of October's competitive football, carelessly gave the ball away the first three times he received possession of it.

Angel di Maria's performance was patchy. Throughout the first half he appeared a shadow of the superstar speed merchant Reds fans had already come to know and love.

The Blue half had their own problems: Yaya Toure – a big player in derbies past – couldn't get into the game. Fernando was anonymous. And, with David Silva missing through injury, it left their midfield looking rather outnumbered by United's in the opening quarter of an hour. This was reflected in early possession statistics which showed the Reds as the dominant side, though opportunities on the opposition goal remained scarce.

The crowd became restless as 'derby' tackles flew in. Referee Michael Oliver twice showed leniency in refusing to brandish a yellow card to a home player and this led to no little frustration on the part of United when holding midfielder Daley Blind received the first booking. Jovetic and Toure had both committed similar fouls and yet had only received talkings-to by Oliver. And Wayne Rooney in particular was infuriated when Oliver's inconsistency was highlighted yet again just two minutes after Blind's booking when he refused to caution Pablo Zabaleta for what was certainly a bookable offence.

Of course, Manchester City would have their own complaints about Michael Oliver's performance. They could point to three close-call penalty shouts which they had turned down during the 90 minutes. But it was the referee's decision to dish out the second booking of the game to *another* United player – Chris Smalling: Van Gaal's "stupid" boy – which would change the course of this game. Smalling prevented Joe Hart from taking a quick punt upfield and was yellow carded for his troubles. And then, minutes later, he dived in on James Milner. He didn't take the ball, and Oliver now had no choice but to dismiss the

United centre-half with ten minutes (including injury time) of the first half still to play.

"It was Smalling's dismissal that changed everything" said Daniel Taylor in his *The Guardian* match report.

And indeed it was. United's rearguard already had something of a makeshift look to it - wide midfielder Antonio Valencia was deputising for the injured Rafael at full-back – and Smalling's departure forced Van Gaal to shuffle his deck still further. He was forced to sacrifice Adnan Januzaj – whose pace had already worried City's back-line – and bring on midfielder Michael Carrick at centre-half. Carrick had been out since May and was playing his first competitive football of the season.

It was backs to the wall. Especially when, early in the second half, the *other* centre-half, Marcos Rojo, was stretchered off with a dislocated shoulder: that left youngster Paddy McNair as Van Gaal's only possible replacement. "Your challenge," said Paul Hayward in his *Telegraph* column, "is to name a more unlikely, ill-fitting and patched-up Manchester United back-four than the pair of midfielders and two 19-year-olds who ended up defending David de Gea's net against the league champions and noisy neighbours on the other side of town."

"How the club of Steve Bruce and Gary Pallister, of Jaap Stam and Rio Ferdinand, have had to embrace such extreme ad-libbing is now the most pressing question in Louis van Gaal's jerky first campaign," he pleaded.

On the Sky Sports commentary Gary Neville said that it would be one of the most famous defensive displays if United's improvised back-four managed to hold out against the City onslaught which defined the fifteen-minute spells either side of half-time for the full 90 minutes. As it was they displayed admirable staying-power as City laid siege to the United goal. But the stalemate couldn't last and finally Sergio Aguero broke the deadlock and United hearts.

It was his sixth goal in seven games against United.

And watching Red fans could have been forgiven for worrying about another collapse against their city rivals when that goal went in. After all, it is in the instincts of Manchester United to chase lost causes even when everything seems set against them. It was this determination which had seen them slump to the awful 6-1 defeat at Old Trafford in October 2011, when another 10-man United team had sniffed a chance of getting back into the game when a late Carrick goal brought them back to 3-1, and instead City broke relentlessly and racked up a further three goals.

But this time, United's 10-men took control of the game and *almost* forced their way back into the match. Certainly they had Manchester City worried: the Blues dropped deeper and deeper, inviting United on to them. They lost their composure, resorting to long balls hoofed out of defence to clear the danger. Joe Hart skewed the ball straight out of play from a goal-kick. Aguero was withdrawn, and Fernandinho brought on in his place, inviting United onto City still further. It was a substitution which bore parallels with Chelsea's introduction of Mikel John Obi the week before. *That* change had given United added impetus; the idea that Chelsea had settled for 1-0 stinging the Reds into a response.

And it *nearly* worked here too.

United drove forwards. Rooney tested City's backline with a fantastic pacy and powerful run which was reminiscent of the Wayne Rooney who'd first burst onto the scene in Euro '04 in Portugal. Van Persie slalomed through the Blue defence and almost beat Joe Hart at his near post. Di Maria came close with two free-kicks and Fellaini might have scored from at least one headed chance which came his way.

One illustration of the way the momentum of this match was heading came late on in the game when after a clash with City's 'keeper Hart, Wayne Rooney remained prone in the Blue penalty area. United had possession and City urged them to kick it out in order that *Wayne Rooney,* the devil incarnate as far as City fans are concerned, should receive treatment, but *United* were keen to keep playing, to keep on attacking. To keep the ball.

"Remarkably United's 10 men almost salvaged an improbable draw during a late, spirited challenge," said Daniel Taylor, in what was otherwise a very Blue-tinted match report. "They showed great competitive courage in that period and there were chances for Robin van Persie, Angel Di Maria and Marouane Fellaini to punish City for defending too deeply and not being more clinical with their opportunities at the other end."

"United's supporters will be heartened by the performance of their own team, who managed the notable feat of both collapsing and simultaneously not collapsing, all-but falling to pieces for 20 minutes either side of half-time, but still playing out the match with commendable spirit exemplified by the chugging determination of Marouane Fellaini in central midfield," said Barney Ronay.

And Paul Hayward offered United fans similar consolation in his own match report for *The Telegraph::* "Against the league's two best teams United have shown signs of recovery. Flashes of verve against Chelsea last Sunday lit the path to the sky blue half of town, where they survived three strong penalty claims and came snapping back at the new kings of Greater Manchester in the last 20 minutes. To see United indignant about being a goal down – and not deterred by numerical inferiority – was to feel a stirring of the olde Old Trafford spirit."

But that spirit did not ultimately bring about an equaliser this time. For the first time since the advent of the *Gaalacticos* the Reds had failed to score.

Instead it was left to City to – almost by default – grab the bragging rights in the city of Manchester once again. And Daniel Taylor noted: "It was City's sixth win in their last seven league meetings against United, including four in a row for the first time since 1970". The heady days of 1990s had never seemed so far away: those glory days in which United ruled Manchester, remaining unbeaten during the entire decade and 14 games.

1986 seemed even further away, and yet defeat left United - points-wise – in their worst position at this stage of the season since 1986-87, when Sir Alex Ferguson took over from Ron Atkinson in the Old Trafford hot-seat. Worse, it left the Reds without an away victory all season, and languishing back down in 10th place level on points with West Bromwich Albion and Newcastle United, neither of whom had had anything like the scale of investment we'd seen at the Theatre of Dreams and both of whom had been labelled as crisis clubs during 2014-15.

Defeat left a bitter taste in the mouth and it also left them way off the pace set by quick-out of the blocks Chelsea. United had secured only half of Chelsea's 26 points, last minute equaliser or no last minute equaliser.

And not just Chelsea. Daniel Taylor in his match report called it "a derby that left Manchester United a long way back in Manchester City's wing-mirrors and, in the worst moments, straying dangerously close to being their own worst enemy."

And yet, United's showing was by no means humiliating or embarrassing. Certainly it wasn't anything like as painful as some recent clashes against City have been - particularly 2013-14's two clashes which finished as an aggregate 7-1 to City.

Paul Hayward said: "Given the turmoil of the past 12 months, United's fans will draw encouragement from the battling urges displayed against Chelsea and City. Recoveries often start with heightened intent. It would take an alchemist, though, to forge a title-winning defence from the resources available to Van Gaal, whose attempts to make the front of the team sing are undermined by crashes and bangs at the back."

They were undone in the end by the 5th red card of 2014 for United. This was more than any other Premier League club had received. Playing with 10-men for so long against the champions was never an advisable course of action, and Reds fans were forced to consider what might have been, were it not for the stupidity of Smalling.

Van Gaal, who was announced as one of the nominees for FIFA World Coach of the Year (for his work with the Netherlands), during the week prior to the derby, said: "The sending off is not one of those things. As a player you have to control your aggression. I didn't see the first yellow but the second you know as a player you have a yellow, so you have to handle it differently. I said that to the players. In the derby you have to be careful. The second yellow card was stupid. You cannot do what he has done with the second yellow card. That is not very smart. What can I say?"

"The sending off had a big influence on our opponent but also ourselves," he continued. "Despite having 10 men we played better in the second half than the first and that is because of the willpower of the team. We created a lot of chances, they fought until the last moment, but City had a very good goalkeeper. We are very close but we have to improve."

It is a common myth that Sir Alex Ferguson *always* supported his players in public, keeping any criticisms in-house. If Fergie felt he needed to dish out a "message" to a particular player, he was never afraid of using the media in order to get his point across. Though Van Gaal's reaction to the Smalling sending-off was initially surprising – "the sending off is *not* one of those things" – the jarring nature of this public criticism in fact followed a pattern. It had now become a common theme for the Dutchman to give his players a reality check in each and every press conference or post-match interview. Witness all those references to his players being "stupid", "small", not "thinking". There was a very real sense that the Iron Tulip was trying to rule with an iron fist; trying to make his players afraid of him. Though he might not have used a hairdryer, Van Gaal was behaving in a very Fergie-like way. *Don't get too big for your boots, because you're not big men, not by any stretch of the imagination. Don't think you'll be forgiven, let back into the fold after that appalling individual error. Don't think I'll just blame it on the team. You must take it on the chin…*

Still, the headlines the next day would all read of United's growing crisis, but, as Scott the Red noted in *The Republik of Mancunia* the signs of improvement *were coming.* "Despite playing with ten men for an hour, United for dominated for large periods of the game, and finished the day with an impressive 48% possession of the ball."

Certainly Van Gaal was proud of (nearly) every one of his players. "I said to the boys their willpower and labour were unbelievable and they can be very proud. The fans know the boys are willing to give everything for the shirt of the club. But at the end of the game, we have zero points. In this sport, it is always the goals that count. We were so close in spite of playing with ten men."

Tim Simon's post match summary of the derby for *The Republik of Mancunia* was similarly glass-half-full. "United," he said, "may have had their worst start since 1986 and sit in a lowly 10th position in the table after 10 games but there have been several signs that they are improving. The campaign began with several makeshift teams and a lack of new signings which certainly contributed to the poor form. Since the new boys came in, there has been a distinct improvement with several individual errors costing them points in recent games."

"There were more signs in the derby that United were returning to some form. You can tell that Van Gaal's ideas have started to hit home and the performances are getting much better. United dominated large periods of the games against Chelsea and City and were unlucky to come away with just one point from those two fixtures. Expect results to pick up over the next ten games and United to continue to improve as the season progresses."

Still, Louis van Gaal was forced to field several probing questions about the Reds' position prior to the next game, at home to Crystal Palace on Saturday 8th November. At his usual Friday press conference, the Dutchman was a rather "chastened" version of his former self. *The Guardian's* Barry Glendenning spoke of how LVG ("with his One Flew Over The Cuckoo's Nest hair, cast-iron self-regard and heroic indifference to what anyone else thinks of him") had always been an awesome figure but was now "unrecognisably contrite (…) opting to demonstrate *something* resembling humility as he announced he was "feeling lousy for everyone that we have 13 points from 10 games.""

It couldn't last, of course. In almost the next breath, the old King Louis swaggered back. "In a return to the heartwarming bullishness with which his audience is more accustomed," said Glendenning, "Louis did at least point out to all present that, contrary to popular opinion, his injury-ravaged, inexperienced and occasionally slapstick defence is actually tighter than that of the Premier League leaders, making the very salient point that "when you don't count the five goals of Leicester City, we have conceded less than Chelsea". Sadly, he missed a trick by failing to follow up with the revelation that when you also don't count the two goals of Swansea, the one goal of Sunderland, one or both of the two goals of West Brom, the one goal of Chelsea and the one goal of Manchester City, his team are unbeaten and sitting pretty on top of the Premier League!"

But it was the Iron Tulip's final statement which sent social media into overdrive. "Even in the face of this hypothetical success," commented Glendenning, "Louis insists there's even more actual success to come, although it might take the length of his contract. "I said from the beginning that the process shall take more than one year – it will take three years," he said. "I hope, because that is always dependent on a lot of things. I think when we make it happen that we'll win a lot of matches in a row." Having thus far steered United to victory in two matches in a row just once and one match in a row just twice, Van Gaal must be grateful that football club owners and patrons are famously renowned for their serenity and patience in the face of poor results. If he's in any doubt, he can just reflect on what happened to David Moyes."

Where once the Dutchman had talked about United clicking in three months, suddenly he was revising upwards. It would be three years now. Jamie Carragher was one voice of many on Twitter when he questioned Van Gaal's maths.

But Van Gaal found a staunch defendant in Scott 'the Red' Patterson in *The Metro*.

"United don't have enough points and nobody can argue with that," said Scott. "Van Gaal hasn't denied that. The manager won't even allow the injuries to be used as an excuse. When you consider that United have been forced to play 37 different players this season, compared to Manchester City's 26, Chelsea's 23 and Southampton's 18, nobody could criticise Van Gaal for suggesting that injuries have contributed to our current position. However, what Van Gaal has talked about, from his first press conference to his most recent one, is the time it will take to transform United. Not in points or league position, but in mentality, performance and philosophy."

"If you can't see a drastic change in all three of those things with Van Gaal in charge compared to the David Moyes months, you should probably give up football now," he added. "That doesn't mean that United are performing well enough or winning the games they should, but to suggest that the current 'process' isn't a huge improvement on what we endured last season is bonkers. It beggars belief that this point would even need to be made, let alone hammered home, but United are heading in the right direction and any sensible fan should have patience that outlasts three months."

Talking of patience, my Dad, Ray Kirby, is not exactly blessed with that quality where the Reds are concerned. But he too was keen to add a little realism to the debate. "In the new football world of spend, spend, spend, United are five years behind Manchester City and ten years behind Chelsea. Both have bought players continuously, until they've struck on ones that win. So United have missed out on those generations of great players. If Van Gaal catches that up in three years – *not three months* - he really will be 'the best'".

Saturday 8th November 2014: United v Crystal Palace (1-0)

Red fans required patience in abundance against Crystal Palace. Though Louis van Gaal's second-half replacement of Adnan Januzaj with Juan Mata had an instant impact, with the Spaniard netting United's winner within moments of taking the field, the Red Devil's performance was not suggestive of a team which had turned the corner. In *The Guardian,* Jamie Jackson called it an "unconvincing victory" and a "disjointed affair". On *The Republik of Mancunia,* Tim Simon called it "laboured".

Whilst United "hoarded possession", enjoying 72% over the 90 minutes, the build-up was slow and proper goalscoring chances were at a premium. An out-of-form Robin van Persie ploughed a lonely furrow as the single-striker in a 4-4-1-1 formation which saw Wayne Rooney play a very withdrawn role. And though United kept a rare clean sheet, there were still some wobbly moments at the back. The defensive line was hardly helped by the fact this was already United's eleventh different combination at centre-back in twelve games.

Jamie Jackson suggested United's players must be "confused" by the constant system changes. Van Gaal had now tinkered to such a degree that they'd played 5-3-2, 4-4-2, 4-4-1-1 in the opening three months of the season and he was quick to admit that this constant chopping and changing was not ideal.

"It's too much, I think, I agree," he said. "But I'm looking for the balance and when you see the last four matches we have had more balance because we haven't conceded many goals. Nevertheless, we don't score so much. With the other system we scored a lot of goals."

The performance, then, was hardly satisfying. But most critics and fans were prepared to allow that the result was. "As long as Liverpool, Manchester City and Arsenal continue to stutter, there is hope in the quest for a Champions League berth," said Jamie Jackson. "United are only two points from West Ham United and Swansea in fourth and fifth respectively."

Tim Simon agreed: "Following good displays against West Brom, Chelsea and Manchester City but only coming away with a total of two points due to stupid individual defensive errors, the three points were a necessity this weekend. It did not matter how United were able to get them, as long as they did. It may not have been a pretty win but the 1-0 success brought three welcome points as United's rivals faltered this weekend. (…) The clean sheet came as a welcome boost too, particularly with the well-documented defensive problems in mind."

And while United headed into the international break in *not exactly* the same rude health they'd entered the last one – on the back of two straight wins – they'd at least ended a run of three matches without a win and had risen once more to seventh in the table, above Liverpool, Everton and Spurs, three sides which were considered to be the Reds' rivals for those four Champions League places.

Though the international break might have seen the Reds come up for air after a tough run of competitive fixtures, the fortnight spell between games saw no let up in the media's hunger for stories about the big boss, Louis van Gaal.

First, Karl-Heinz Rummenigge didn't exactly extend the olive branch to his former Bayern manager in a widely-quoted interview which made all the English papers. "As soon as he presented his autobiography in a snobby restaurant, I knew hard times were ahead. Louis van Gaal was not always easy-care. He wanted to 'Vangaalise' our club. He has a huge ego," the Bayern chairman knife-twisted.

Then the first in a new wave of books regarding the Iron Tulip (of which this book is one) was released. Dutch journalist Hugo Borst's Van Gaal biography (*O Louis! In Search of Louis van Gaal*) hit the shelves and Roddy Doyle – fresh from co-writing Roy Keane's controversial new biography - reviewed it for *The Guardian,* judging it to be a "savage" reading of the United supremo.

"Last May," said Doyle, "just before Louis van Gaal was confirmed as the club's new manager, a man from the BBC asked him what he knew about Manchester United. "That is a stupid question, I think," Van Gaal replied. "It is a stupid question." I'm with him: it is a stupid question. Questions, stupid and not so stupid, and Van Gaal's response to them, are at the heart of *O, Louis.*"

Doyle continued: "The book, translated by David Doherty, is very good but it is as much about its author,

Hugo Borst, as it is about Van Gaal. Its success is largely dependent on whether the reader can find Borst as interesting – as engaging, as irritating, as quotable, brilliant, monstrous and human – as his subject. The answer to that changes from page to page – yes, no, maybe, no, yes, maybe, no, no, Jesus no, no, maybe. It's like reading about a match that goes into extra time and endless mucky replays, between Borst and Van Gaal or, more accurately, Borst and Borst. Borst, the Van Gaal lover versus Borst, the Van Gaal hater; Borst, the man who wants to be Van Gaal's best friend versus Borst, the man who wants to annihilate Van Gaal; Borst, the gobshite, versus Borst, the astute, passionate, sometimes brilliant, football writer. It's a great game for the neutral. But those of us who love our football know that there is no such thing as neutrality."

"We already know Van Gaal – or think we do," said Doyle. "He goes back... Yet he arrived in England like a new thing. He arrived before he'd even arrived – if that can make sense. He was an immediate genius, before he'd selected a starting 11. He was the man who saved Manchester United, months before the current season started. He's in Manchester now and, with his dark suit and clipboard, he looks like a wedding planner. But the wedding isn't going to plan. The groom's a twit, the bride's mother is drinking her gin by the neck, and the Tom Jones covers band has turned up without a singer. But he's still Van Gaal. We know the face, the history, the accent, the arrogance."

Doyle picked up on some wonderful turns of phrase as employed by Borst. This is Borst on Van Gaal the player, for example. He "had all the mobility of a slug on sandpaper". And this is Borst on the Van Gaal philosophy, his 'blueprint': "there was a whiff of the sacred about it. There's something spiritual about Louis van Gaal, just like the Dalai Lama, Charles Manson and Stephen Fry."

Yet ultimately, Doyle found the book "unsettling" (and Doyle, remember, was required to spend countless hours in the company of the glacier-eyed and fresh from a-month-camping-in-the-woods bearded Roy Keane during the writing of *Roy Keane: The Second Half*).

"Football journalism is clearly a blood sport in Holland," said Doyle, "so much of what is written and cited in this book is shocking. Assessments of Van Gaal by other journalists and, among others, a spin doctor and a psychiatrist – also a star of the TV reality show, Holland's Worst Husband – are often close to cruel. Botox gets a mention. So does Stalin. And there's a short account of a phone call between Van Gaal and "the depression-stricken goalie", Robert Enke, that left me wanting to choke Borst."

The international break might have left *Van Gaal* wanting to choke a few people too. In a piece entitled 'Premier League: biggest winners and losers from the international break', *The Guardian's* Jacob Steinberg and Paul Doyle discussed the Iron Tulip's frustrations as so many of his United stars returned from international duty crocked.

"Louis van Gaal just cannot catch a break and the last thing United's manager needed was for David de Gea, Daley Blind and potentially Angel di Maria and Luke Shaw to return from international duties with injuries. While De Gea, United's most impressive player this season, has an outside chance of playing against Arsenal after dislocating a finger with Spain, the knee injury that Blind suffered in Holland's victory over Latvia is thought to be more serious. Di Maria will have a scan on an injured leg while Shaw was taken off against Scotland with a tight groin."

Saturday 22nd November 2014: Arsenal v United (1-2)

This meant that LVG would have to send another makeshift defensive unit out to face Arsenal for the late kick-off on Saturday 22nd November 2014. Of those *Gaalacticos* signed in the summer transfer window, only Luke

Shaw and Angel di Maria would be deemed fit enough to play. Rojo, Blind, Falcao were all injured. So was Evans. So was Phil Jones.

Chris Smalling was back, the suspension he'd earned for *that* red card at Manchester City now over. Though *some* United fans might have been forgiven for thinking it might have been better had he remained on the sidelines.

And *facing* the cobbled-together backline would be one of the men ousted by the Van Gaal revolution, one Danny Welbeck. It seemed written in the stars Welbeck would score, thereby giving Van Gaal one more name for his *To Choke* list.

And during a dire first-half showing from the Reds, the minds of United fans couldn't help wandering back to the heady days of Summer when we were given that fresh injection of optimism when all that lovely money was spent on the team. (Actually, though United spent, spent, spent in August, and the absence of European football meant the Red Devils announced a 10% drop in revenue when they reported their quarterly figures in the week of the Arsenal game, they also reported a 10% decrease in the wage bill: for those people who *still* harped on about how David Moyes never enjoyed the same support – resource-wise – as his successor, *under Louis van Gaal the wage bill was 9.9% lower.)*

But at the end of the day, United ran out 2-1 winners at the Emirates. It was the first away win under Van Gaal (at the seventh attempt). And in securing the three points, United jumped back into fourth place in the league, a lovely five points ahead of Liverpool, leapfrogging Arsenal in the process.

In many ways, United had played the perfect game, luring Arsenal into a false sense of security and then smashing-and-grabbing the win. In many ways, Van Gaal was a tactical genius. But such reviews are somewhat revisionist. They are written *in light* of the fact United *did* win, continuing their fine historical form against their north London rivals to just one defeat in the last 15 matches in all competitions.

They do not tell the whole truth. Which was an uncomfortable one. Because for what seemed like an age, the Reds were in disarray. In his match report for *The Guardian* David Hytner said United were: "almost impossibly awful for the opening 35 minutes". They were as bad as they were in the equivalent clash in the 2012-13 season, which fell just days after the Reds had sealed their 20th league title. In *that* game United played as though they'd been out on the razz for days. They were all over the place, stumbling over each other, misplacing passes, puffing and panting in the wake of quicker, more powerful opponents.

And so it appeared here. "The United manager," wrote Hytner, "looked anything but the tactical genius as his players hoofed and bumbled."

Of course Van Gaal's hand was forced. Injuries meant he *could only* send out what Daniel Taylor in his *The Guardian* report called "a scratch team". With "Tyler Blackett, Paddy McNair and Chris Smalling making up the defence" the Dutchman tried to make up for the shortfall in quality by upping the *quantity* ante, favouring "a return to the 3-4-1-2 system that most United followers must have hoped had been seen off in conker season."

And then Luke Shaw, the young full-back who'd looked arguably United's best player during the past two games, limped off too, meaning United really were down to brass-tacks: Ashley Young came on in his place. This meant that United now had two wingers filling the full-back berths (Antonio Valencia was on the right).

In *The Daily Mirror* Joshua Evans suggested that Van Gaal should have rectified the obvious defensive weaknesses during the summer transfer window instead of shelling out all that dough on attacking players. "Although

Arsenal and United both spent heavily in the summer transfer window, the cold reality is that they're light years away from the Premier League's very best. Their shortcomings - and by that, I principally mean their defensive frailties - are there for everyone to see. And the decisions of Arsene Wenger and Louis van Gaal to neglect that part of their respective teams is... jaw-droppingly bewildering."

And yet, in the same paper, Aaron Flanagan talked called this Van Gaal's "most emphatic result as manager of Manchester United". The manager's "game plan was executed to near perfection" he added. "Clinical and effective, Van Gaal had won a game by executing a thought-out game plan, performed to ruthless perfection by his team."

According to him: "Van Gaal has his mojo back."

So which is it?

Was Van Gaal lucky?

Or was it all the game-plan?

(As Roddy Doyle might say, the "answer to that changes from page to page – yes, no, maybe, no, yes, maybe, no, no, Jesus no, no, maybe.")

Certainly after the game Van Gaal was keen to claim the victory was a *told-you-so* moment for those who'd doubted his system, his formation, his team selection. Oliver Holt described the Dutchman's post-match interview: "Bombast mixed with the confidence of a big victory and turned parts of his post-match address into a tub-thumping sermon. "I told them at half-time that when we keep the ball, when we show confidence, then we shall create many chances," Van Gaal explained, beaming at the room and pausing now and then for dramatic effect."

"On inviting Arsenal on to them – as United had in the first-half, to worrying effect – Van Gaal said: "Yes, it was a risk. But I was sure Arsenal wants to attack and to press us. Then, you know Arsenal is giving a lot of space away. And then Mertesacker and our friend Monreal have to defend. That's why I put Di Maria against Mertesacker and Van Persie against Monreal. That's why I changed for Wilson. More pace. So, yeah, that's what you're thinking in advance of a match and when it ends like this you can be happy."

One thing was for sure: United had fought tooth-and-nail for the win. On BBC Sport's website, Chris Bevan called this "a battling display" from the Reds but admitted the match had comprised "long spells of dominance by the Gunners" (United only had 39% of possession). Similarly Oliver Holt said "they (United) defended dutifully and redoubtably".

In the first-half United ceded possession and territory to an Arsenal side who began at "whirlwind pace", drawing save after save from 'keeper David de Gea.

In the second-half United took the lead "in bizarre circumstances". *The Guardian's* David Hytner described it: "Kieran Gibbs scraped himself up after being clattered by his goalkeeper, Wojciech Szczesny, and jutted his left foot at one of those low Antonio Valencia blasts, the full-back's head was spinning. Almost in slow motion, the ball flicked off his boot and set a course for the far corner of the net. Gibbs slumped back down."

It might have been lucky. It might have been a mess of deflections, a discord of collisions, and totally against the run of play... But that was the *point* of it. *The Daily Mirror's* Aaron Flanagan said: "It was a perfect example of what Van Gaal has lined United up to being. Ruthless, determined and resilient. Pouncing on their first big opening."

After the goal. "Arsenal's desperation to find an equaliser meant they left themselves increasingly open at the back," said Bevan.

Arsenal were frantic. Tactics and formation went out of the window. They committed too many players forward. Gary Neville suggested on the Sky Sports commentary that United – "if they have anything about them" – would ruthlessly expose the gaps Arsenal left behind them as they poured forward. He suggested United would score "within five minutes". It took longer than that, but Dr. Neville's prognosis would eventually prove correct.

"Rooney ran clear to add a second goal and Di Maria should have scored a third when he raced unchallenged from inside his own, only to chip wide," said Bevan.

The breaks – when they came - were rapier-like. Quick, incisive, going straight for the jugular. They were reminiscent of so many recent United goals against Arsenal (think the Rooney-Ronaldo breaks in the Champions League clashes, or the Rooney-Nani rampages in Premier League fixtures) and it was true Van Gaal – just as Sir Alex Ferguson had done before him - overloaded the attack with pace (Van Persie notwithstanding) in order to utilise the counter-attack as a deliberate tactic.

The Rooney goal came with 85 minutes on the clock, and yet there was still time for late drama. *Lots* of time, as we were soon to learn. United fans had to suffer through a nervy eight minutes of stoppage time (and then an additional two minutes on top of that, which took the game-time up to *100 minutes)*, and when the Arsenal substitute Giroud smashed home on 94 minutes, a number of nails were shredded, a large amount of gum gnashed.

But *that* defence held out, and the Reds took the victory.

Not everyone was convinced though. David Hytner observed: "after the unexpected breakthrough, United were able to exploit the manner in which Arsenal over-committed. The visitors came to look secure and they threatened on the counter, which led Van Gaal to sell his first away win at the club as a tactical triumph."

Such an important win shouldn't have *needed* to be sold, and yet there was Van Gaal trying to convince, convince, convince. Because he must have known how close to the wind his United charges had sailed. In that terrible first-half they could have been obliterated. Defensively, they were very shaky.

Going forward they weren't much better. Indeed, there was a telling stat. United took the lead (through a Gibbs own goal) and were 1-0 up despite not having recorded a shot on target. Rooney's goal on 85 minutes would eventually be that first shot on target, and what a goal it was, but, as Daniel Taylor was at pains to point out, *both* United and Arsenal looked like "faded old champions".

It was abundantly clear to all who'd witnessed United's triumph that Van Gaal's United remained a team in transition, a work in progress. However *at least there was progress,* and an idea of what they were transitioning into. Had the Reds *lost* against Arsenal, United would have once more been plunged into crisis. He would have been subjected to (more) endless comparisons with David Moyes, who coincidentally re-started his own managerial career at almost the same time, over in Spain.

Moyes had taken over at the helm of struggling Real Sociedad. He had secured a point away from home in his debut game. He pronounced himself pleased with the 0-0 draw.

You got the impression Louis van Gaal was never entirely pleased. That he was always hoping for improvement, for development, for a better team.

Van Gaal asked to be judged after three months, and then three years, and, over the course of this final chapter, you'll have been able to chart the ups and downs of his "honeymoon period" in the United hotseat. The Dutchman's results on the pitch have been mixed. But off the field, a revolution has been taking place, and soon it will bear fruit.

Van Gaal, as Ray Kirby notes, "has been brilliant at spotting, and largely shipping out, the no-hopers: Kagawa, Cleverley, Buttner, and Hernandez. The jury is still out on whether Welbeck was one of them, but at the time of going to press, Welbeck was in danger of losing his striker's berth at Arsenal due to that same goals-to-chances ratio which convinced Van Gaal Welbeck was not a world class number nine. The chances are that Young, Mata, Smalling and Evans (and perhaps even Phil Jones) will be the next batch of players who Van Gaal will make his mind up about."

Of their replacements Rojo, Blind, Falcao, and Di Maria looked to have made promising starts, though injuries to the first three may have clouded the picture somewhat. Falcao's signing completely changed the mood at Old Trafford, just as Van Persie's did two years ago, but though he has been brilliant when he has played, his injury worries cast doubt on whether he will ever find consistent, top form again. Luke Shaw looks to have been an unqualified success; a taller Evra. And though Di Maria's form has dipped, his pace still rattled Arsenal.

Van Gaal has made a new player of Fellaini, and he's brought in a healthy number of United youngsters, in the form of Blackett, McNair, Wilson *et al.* But he faces a major headache over the form of Van Persie, who seems a shadow of the player he was two years ago, when he made the difference between United and City, and winning the title and finishing second. As Ray Kirby says, "It is a myth than Van Persie was one of the stars of the World Cup. What he did was score one of the best goals ever. In most matches he was peripheral and rarely got a kick, hence he had to be substituted. Sound familiar?"

In January, the transfer window will open again and it is hoped that, in the words of Steven Gerrard "we will go again". A centre-half, perhaps a right full-back, will do nicely for now. Perhaps if Kevin Strootman proves his fitness, a box-to-box midfielder too. None will come cheap, nor should they. United have tried to do things 'on the cheap' for a number of years now, and it's why the squad got into such a bad state in the first place. The Reds bought too many players who weren't of United quality, even if they were 'ones for the future'. In order to catch up, they need proven stars. Now.

Though the media jury is still very much out on Van Gaal, this latter-day Brian Glover, this "slug on sandpaper", this brick with hair, most right-thinking United fans are on board with him. We know he is dragging the club in the right direction. We know it will take time.

And for now, we're enjoying the ride.

Andrew Kirby
November 2014

ACKNOWLEDGEMENTS

You might say that, as a Manchester United fan whose knowledge of Louis van Gaal was largely restricted to what I'd witnessed of him in the opposing dug-out in a handful of Champions League games, embarking on the massive project of writing a *book* about the man was somewhat arrogant.

As arrogant as Van Gaal is said to be? Maybe.

But there it is. I like a challenge.

Still, once I began on my research and the project – the 'blueprint' if you like - began to spiral out of control, I began to wonder whether I hadn't bitten off more than I could chew.

In the end, those who knew him better reined me back in.

I must say a great thank you to the fans, the writers, the forum-contributors to both TotalBarca.com and Bayernforum.com whose wealth of knowledge, whose eagerness to share great stories, whose tips and hints, have helped make this book altogether more readable. And altogether more factually correct.

I'll own up right here, right now, to any mistakes made. Everything those guys sent me was excellent.

Here's an (embarrassing) example of how much they helped me. When I first wrote to Bayernforum.com, they got back to me almost straight away, agreeing to help me out. And it is a measure of how little I'd gotten to grips with my subject that it fell to Mark at the Bayernforum to tutor me in the correct way of spelling Van Gaal's *name* of all things.

He reminded me: "By the way, when you spell his surname, if you also include his first name (Louis), the 'v' of 'van' should be in lowercase, but when you have his surname alone it should be with a capital. That is: "Louis van Gaal blah, blah, blah. Van Gaal blah, blah, blah".

Which meant that I had to trawl through almost an entire manuscript, a whole bloody *fleet* of vans, setting things straight. By the end of it, I never wanted to see another van in my life. But at least I had things right.

Mark put me in touch with Daniel Cossai, whose article on Van Gaal's blueprint had first prompted me to contact Bayernforum.com. And I must say that Daniel's broad range of knowledge of European football in general, and his understanding of Bayern Munich in particular have considerably improved the Bayern section of this book. Daniel's grasp of high-level tactical detail was first rate, but it was his willingness to talk intelligently and passionately about football which truly inspired me. Daniel and I chatted regularly over email and his wealth of knowledge allowed me to bring Van Gaal at Bayern to life.

Alexandra Jonson, a freelance journalist based in Barcelona, provided me with similar assistance when it came to penning the Barcelona sections of this book. Blue and red runs in Alexandra's veins, it is clear, and what she doesn't know about Barcelona isn't worth knowing. She regularly attends Barça B games at the MiniEstadi, as well as youth team matches. As with Daniel, our email conversations began about Van Gaal and his influences on Barcelona and Bayern Munich, but soon spread to all aspects of world football, and it was very interesting to get a European perspective on the goings-on at Old Trafford from a couple of very interesting folk who hadn't exactly been brainwashed by the Re-United PR machine which cranked into overdrive almost as soon as the HGV known as LGV chugged into Manchester.

Both went above and beyond and I thank them for it.

I'd also like to thank my Dad, Ray Kirby, for his help in proof-reading this book and also for chucking in his own "two-penneth-worth" on United, which turned out to be quite a lot. Dad doesn't have a lot of patience where United are concerned (and if you've ever watched a match *near* him you'll know what I'm talking about) but he has time for Van Gaal, and not only because the Dutchman shares his view on recent United sides being too "small", too "powerless", too "stupid" to compete...

Talking of patience, you might have noticed this book ends rather abruptly. It finishes unfinished. That is the nature of that beast which is top level football today. I could have gone on writing about Van Gaal indefinitely, and with each week – hell, each day – that passes, scores of new stories about the man and his team would have been produced and required to be incorporated into these pages. A constant production-line of football stories – especially those regarding Manchester United – are required in order to satiate the always-hungry football-loving public.

So I had to draw the line somewhere.

And I thought the win against Arsenal was a crucial point. It had the potential to be the turning point in the Reds' season – the 'spark' which Van Gaal constantly spoke of. It was a second consecutive win and landed United in fourth place, which was pretty much the target for the season; Champions League qualification.

And yet at the same time, it might have been a false dawn, of which there had already been so many in 2014-15.

One thing was clear though, whichever way it went for the Dutchman, United supporters were confident he had the courage – the stones – to see it through. To re-make United into the team they once were. To create. He had the courage to force the heretofore tight-fisted board to part with a great deal of money in his first transfer window in order to address glaring deficiencies in the squad, and he'll have the courage to do it again in future transfer windows.

I like to think that in a couple of years time, I'll revisit the Van Gaal story – I've loved writing about him. I'd like to think that by then there'll be a glorious story to tell which will bookend this story nicely.

But for now, this is the end of the beginning of the Dutchman's story in Manchester. What comes in the second chapter could be magnificent.

Thanks for reading this book,

Andrew Kirby
Author

BIBLIOGRAPHY

Books

The Professor: Arsene Wenger, by Myles Palmer, Virgin Books, Thursday 7th August 2008

Football - Bloody Hell!: The Biography of Alex Ferguson, by Patrick Barclay, Yellow Jersey, Friday 14th October 2010

The Subtle Difference, by Philipp Lahm, Verlag Antje Kunstmann GmbH, Thursday 15th November 2012

I am Zlatan Ibrahimovic, by Zlatan Ibrahimovic, David Lagercrantz, and Ruth Urbom, Penguin, Thursday 5th September 2013

Fear and Loathing in La Liga: Barcelona vs Real Madrid, by Sid Lowe, Yellow Jersey, Thursday 26th September 2013

Stillness and Speed: My Story, by Dennis Bergkamp, Simon & Schuster, Thursday 26th September 2013

Alex Ferguson My Autobiography, by Sir Alex Ferguson, Hodder & Stoughton, Thursday 24th October 2013

The Managers: Football's Greatest Managers, by Jon Reeves, New Holland Publishers, Saturday 1st March 2014

Louis van Gaal: The Biography, by Maarten Meijer, Ebury Digital, Thursday 24th July 2014

Newspapers, Internet & Magazines

'McAteer strikes to stun Dutch', by Clive White, in *The Telegraph*, Saturday 1st September 2001

'Van Gaal leaves Barca', from BBC Sport website, Tuesday, 28th January, 2003

'Van Gaal resigns from Ajax role', from Uefa.com, Wednesday 20th October 2004

'Van Gaal resigns from post at Ajax' from CNN.com, Wednesday 20th October 2004

'Van Gaal to take charge at Alkmaar', from CNN.com, Friday 14th January 2005

'Red-faced: Manchester United's cup shocks over the years', on *Daily Mail* online, Thursday 27th September 2007

'Van Gaal: My football philosophy', from Fifa.com, Monday 7th January 2008

'Bayern appoint Van Gaal as coach', from BBC Sport website, Wednesday 13th May 2009

'Bayern expect top marks from football professor Van Gaal', by Ryland James, in The Sydney Morning Herald, Friday 15th May 2009

'Van Gaal honoured with "Rinus Michels Award"', from The Alliance of European Coaches' Associations News, Wednesday 10th June 2009

'In his biography Van Gaal inadvertently proves his lack of empathy', by Auke Kok, on NRC.NL, Wednesday 7th October 2009

'Stereotypes of Physical Education Teachers', by Lyn Newton, from the Families.com blog. URL: http://www.families.com/blog/stereotypes-of-physical-education-teachers

'Bayern Munich 2-1 Man Utd', by Sam Lyon, on BBCSport.co.uk, Tuesday 30th March 2010

'Louis van Gaal: the manager who would be king', by Ian Herbert, in *The Independent,* Wednesday 7th April 2010

'Man Utd 3-2 Bayern Munich(agg. 4-4)', by Phil McNulty, on BBCSport.co.uk, Wednesday 7th April 2010

'Robben tips balance Bayern's way', by Andy James, for UEFA.com, Wednesday 21 April 2010

'Olic treble takes brilliant Bayern to Madrid', by Matthew Spiro, for UEFA.com, Tuesday 27th April 2010

'Milito ends Inter's long wait', by Andrew Haslam, for UEFA.com, Saturday 22nd May 2010

'Bayern win Cup to clinch Double', from BBC Sport website, Saturday 15th May 2010

'Bayern want Van Gaal extension', by Ben Collins, from Skysports.com, Tuesday 25th May 2010

FAI History Chapter 40 - World Cup 2002 Qualifying, from the Football Association of Ireland official website, Wednesday 12th October 2010

'Lahm's outspoken autobiography causing controversy in Germany', by Nick Amies, for *DW,* Thursday 25th August 2011

'How Bayern Munich has followed in Barcelona's footsteps in the chase for European domination', by Daniel Cossai, on Bayernforum.com, Sunday 18th December 2011

'The Netherlands: From FIFA finalists to fractured football team', by Abhishek Iyer, for BigFourza.com, Monday 18th June 2012

'Van Gaal returns for second Netherlands spell', by Berend Scholten, from UEFA.com, Saturday 7th July 2012

'The Louis Van Gaal dream fulfilled', by Alexandra Jonson, for TotalBarca.com, Wednesday 28th November 2012.

'Van Gaal's vision seeks to recreate football Utopia', by Mohamed Moallim, *FourFourTwo.com,* Tuesday 19th November 2013

'World Cup 2014: Louis van Gaal relishing second chance to exorcise the ghost of Holland's 2002 nightmare', by Elko Born, in *The Telegraph,* Wednesday 22nd January 2014

World Cup Preview 2014 FourFourTwo.com, April 2014
'United candidate Van Gaal was Fergie's inspiration', by Stuart Mathieson, in the *Manchester Evening News,* Wednesday 23rd April 2014

'Muhren backs Van Gaal for Reds - with Giggs to help him', by Stuart Mathieson, in the *Manchester Evening News,* Wednesday 30th April 2014

'Imagining Louis Van Gaal', by Phil, on Livelifeunited.com, Sunday 11th May 2014

'Manchester United: what can they expect from manager Louis van Gaal?', by Jamie Jackson, in *The Guardian,* Monday 19th May 2014

'Louis van Gaal: Manchester United turn to an anti-Moyes disciplinarian', by Barney Ronay, in *The Guardian,* Monday 19th May 2014

'Manchester United's Louis van Gaal: Arrogant, dominant and innovative (and that's what he says about himself)', by Ian Chadband, in *The Telegraph,* Monday 19th May 2014

'Louis van Gaal's Manchester United will amuse, charm and entertain', by Daniel Harris, in *The Guardian,* Tuesday 20th May 2014

'Van Gaal has Total Football masterplan for United', by James Robson, in *The Manchester Evening News,* Wednesday 21st May 2014

'Louis van Gaal may just be the perfect manager for Manchester United', by Christian Nerlinger, in *The Guardian,* Saturday 24th May 2014

'Robin van Persie: I am just a kid with one wish … to play football', by Leo Verheul, in *The Guardian,* Thursday 29th May 2014.

'Louis van Gaal came 'very close' to managing Tottenham Hotspur', by Jamie Jackson, in *The Guardian,* Tuesday 3rd June 2014

'Ibrahimovic Criticises Manchester United Boss Louis van Gaal's Managerial Style', by Eduardo Fernandez-Abascal, from *International Business Times,* Thursday 5th June 2014

'World Cup History: The Netherlands', by Luca Gunby, in *Forza Italian Football,* Wednesday 11th June 2014

'Louis van Gaal's new broom has Holland flying under radar in Brazil', by Paul Wilson, in *The Guardian,* Thursday 12th June 2014.

'Holland's World Cup win over Spain wasn't the return of Total Football - Louis van Gaal has created something new' by Jonathan Liew, in *The Telegraph,* Saturday 14th June 2014

'Holland's Louis van Gaal keeps players grounded after crushing Spain', Press Association, Saturday 14th June 2014.

'Holland top Group B after Leroy Fer header helps break Chile's resolve', by Owen Gibson, in *The Guardian,* Monday 23rd June 2014

'Holland's Arjen Robben looks like a player fulfilled at World Cup', by Amy Lawrence, in *The Guardian,* Monday 23rd June 2014

'From Costa Rica to Holland, five World Cup teams with element of surprise', by Michael Cox, in *The Guardian,* Thursday 26th June 2014

'Louis van Gaal's tactical genius moving Arjen Robben to the right won the day', by Michael Cox, in *The Guardian*, Sunday 29th June 2014

'Football transfer rumours: Arturo Vidal in £48m Manchester United move?', by Rob Bleaney, in *The Guardian*, Tuesday 1st July 2014

'Louis van Gaal shows golden touch as Tim Krul antics spook Costa Rica', by Owen Gibson, in *The Guardian*, Sunday 6th July 2014

'Louis van Gaal brings Albert Stuivenberg to Manchester United', by Jamie Jackson, in *The Guardian*, Sunday 6th July 2014

'Why Louis van Gaal did exactly what Sir Alex Ferguson should have done', by Scott the Red (The Republik of Mancunia), for Metro.co.uk, Sunday 6th July 2014

'World Cup 2014: Argentina Players Sing *Bad Moon Rising*', from Huffington Post.co.uk, Monday 7th July 2014

'Louis van Gaal to improve Manchester United by 25% says Paul Scholes', by Jamie Jackson, in *The Guardian*, Tuesday 8th July 2014

'Louis v Lionel: Van Gaal and Messi may be a meeting of mastery at World Cup', by Barney Ronay, in *The Guardian*, Tuesday 8th July 2014

'Holland – Replacing Clockwork Orange with Pragmatism', by Michiel Jongsma, for Republik of Mancunia.com, Wednesday 9th July 2014

'Argentina win penalty prize to push past Holland and into World Cup final', by Daniel Taylor, in *The Guardian*, Wednesday 9th July 2014

'Louis van Gaal – a managerial heavyweight', by Scott the Red, for Republik of Mancunia.com, Wednesday 9th July 2014

'Holland's stifling tactics divert support to leave Arjen Robben isolated', by Owen Gibson, in *The Guardian*, Thursday 10th July 2014

'Netherlands vs Argentina match report World Cup 2014: Messi and Robben fail to shine as Sergio Romero breaks Dutch hearts', by Sam Wallace, in *The Independent*, Thursday 10th July 2014

'Netherlands vs Argentina comment World Cup 2014: Nigel de Jong sets tone as muzzled Lionel Messi meets match in Dutch defence', by Miguel Delaney, in *The Independent*, Thursday 10th July 2014

'Manchester United job does not scare Louis van Gaal, says Ryan Giggs', by Jamie Jackson, in *The Guardian*, Thursday 10th July 2014

'Louis van Gaal: lucky or brilliant? Manchester United won't mind either', by Jamie Jackson, in *The Guardian*, Thursday 10th July 2014

'Van Gaal: Excitement for United job means holiday isn't needed', by Scott the Red, for Republik of Mancunia.com, Sunday 13th July 2014

'World Cup 2014: Louis van Gaal wants Man Utd to emulate Dutch', from BBCSport.co.uk, Sunday 13th July 2014

'Louis van Gaal flies in to put his mark on Manchester United', by Jamie Jackson, in *The Guardian,* Wednesday 16th July 2014

'Louis van Gaal says challenge at Manchester United is to finish top', by Jamie Jackson, in *The Guardian,* Thursday 17th July 2014

'Louis van Gaal shows brand awareness at Manchester United coronation', by Paul Wilson, in *The Guardian,* Thursday 17th July 2014

'Louis van Gaal the right man at the wrong time for Manchester United', by Paul Wilson, in *The Guardian,* Saturday 19th July 2014

'Manchester United training pitches relaid on Louis van Gaal's orders', by Jamie Jackson, in *The Guardian,* Tuesday 22nd July 2014

'Louis van Gaal fears Manchester United are too big for their own good', by Jamie Jackson, in *The Guardian,* Wednesday 23rd July 2014

'LvG: Beautiful goals and beautiful attacks', by Scott the Red, for *The Republik of Mancunia,* Thursday 24th July 2014

'Manchester United hammer LA Galaxy as Van Gaal's reign starts with bang', by Jamie Jackson, in *The Guardian,* Thursday 24th July 2014

'Manchester United hold talks with Napoli over Marouane Fellaini exit', by Jamie Jackson, in *The Guardian,* Monday 28th July 2014

'Luke Shaw lucky to play in Manchester United friendly, says Louis van Gaal' by Jamie Jackson, in *The Guardian,* Wednesday 30th July 2014

'Van Gaal already battling with the press', by Scott the Red, for Republik of Mancunia.com, Wednesday 30th July 2014

'Brendan Rodgers: I loved the way Louis van Gaal's Barcelona played', by Philippe Auclair, in *The Guardian,* Thursday 31st July 2014

'Jonny Evans out to become Manchester United's main man at the back', by Jamie Jackson, in *The Guardian,* Thursday 31st July 2014

'Manchester United impress against Real Madrid in front of record crowd', by Jamie Jackson, in *The Observer,* Sunday 3rd August 2014

'Atletico want Manchester United's Javier Hernandez and Shinji Kagawa,' by Steve Brenner, in *The Guardian,* Monday 4th August 2014

'Wayne Rooney praises 'tough' Louis van Gaal's start at Manchester United, by Steve Brenner, in *The Guardian,* Tuesday 5th August 2014

'Manchester United beat Liverpool after second-half revival', by Steve Brenner, in *The Guardian,* Tuesday 5th August 2014

'Early rushes of Louis van Gaal era meet with approval of United masses', by Barney Ronay, in *The Guardian,* Tuesday 5th August 2014

'TOP FIVE: Endearing Things Louis van Gaal has done at Manchester United So Far', by Paul Ansorge, for *The Republik of Mancunia,* Saturday August 9th 2014

'Marouane Fellaini has last say to give Louis van Gaal win at Old Trafford', by Daniel Taylor, in *The Guardian,* Tuesday 12th August 2014

'LvG's first programme notes as United manager', by Scott the Red, for *The Republik of Mancunia,* Tuesday 12th August 2014

'Coaching's greatest seminar: how Louis van Gaal shaped five top managers', by Jonathan Wilson, in *The Guardian,* Wednesday 13th August 2014

'Paul Scholes labels Manchester United's Louis van Gaal a 'mad genius"', by Simon Burnton, in *The Guardian,* Thursday 14th August 2014

'Swansea upstage Manchester United in Louis van Gaal's Premier League bow', by Daniel Taylor, in *The Observer,* Saturday 16th August 2014

'Louis van Gaal concedes that he needs to find 'better players' soon', by Daniel Taylor, in *The Observer,* Saturday 16th August 2014

'Glazers and Woodward risk leading club in to decline', by Scott the Red, for *The Republik of Mancunia,* Saturday 16th August 2014

'Premier League: 10 talking points from the weekend's action', by Paul Wilson, in *The Guardian,* Monday 18th August 2014

'Argentina defender Marcos Rojo set to join Manchester United for £16m', by Jamie Jackson, in *The Guardian,* Tuesday 19th August 2014

'United spend club-record £72m in transfer window' from ESPN: Football.co.uk, on Thursday 21st August 2014

'New system leaves Manchester United's world-class attack looking limp', by Michael Cox, in *The Guardian,* Sunday 24th August 2014

'Jack Rodwell's Sunderland equaliser spoils Manchester United's day', by Daniel Taylor, in *The Guardian,* Sunday 24th August 2014

'Angel di Maria and the problem of Manchester United's central midfield', by Jamie Jackson, in *The Guardian,* Monday 25thAugust 2014

'Manchester United's MK Dons Cup humiliation no surprise to me claims boss Louis van Gaal', by David McDonnell, in *The Daily Mirror,* Tuesday 26th August 2014

'MK Dons 4-0 Man United: Yes you read that right as Van Gaal suffers stunning League Cup loss', by David McDonnell, in *The Daily Mirror,* Tuesday 26th August 2014

'Manchester United humbled by MK Dons after Will Grigg hits double', by Richard Rae, for *The Guardian,* Tuesday 26th August 2014

'Manchester United crisis: five reasons to still be cheerful ... and concerned', by Jamie Jackson, in *The Guardian,* Wednesday 27th August 2014

'STATS: How much have United spent in comparison to Chelsea and Manchester City?', by Scott the Red, for *The Republik of Mancunia,* Wednesday 27th August 2014

'Louis van Gaal must share the blame for Manchester United horror show', by Paul Wilson, in *The Guardian,* Wednesday 27th August 2014

'Why is Louis van Gaal so hell-bent on using 3-5-2 at Manchester United', by Jonathan Wilson, in *The Guardian,* Friday 29th August 2014

Burnley 0-0 Manchester United, by Phil McNulty, for BBC Sport: Football, Saturday 30th August 2014

'Draw at Burnley shows Manchester United still struggling with system', by Jamie Jackson, in *The Guardian,* Sunday 31 August 2014

'The Month: Van Gaal thinks August is overrated', by Zac Hann, for *The Republik of Mancunia,* Sunday 31st August 2014

'Even his Children call him Sir,' by Uli Hesse, in *FourFourTwo* magazine issue 243, September 2014

'United Sign Falcao!' by Scott the Red, in *The Republik of Mancunia,* Monday 1st September 2014

'Radamel Falcao's arrival at Manchester United poses formation questions', by Daniel Taylor, in *The Guardian,* Monday 1st September 2014

'Manchester United transfer spree reveals extent of Old Trafford upheaval', by David Conn, in *The Guardian*, Monday 1st September 2014

'Radamel Falcao promises Manchester United will have 'a great season'', by Jamie Jackson, in *The Guardian*, Tuesday 2nd September 2014

'Powerful Radamel Falcao – El Tigre – is ready to roar for Manchester United', by Jonathan Wilson, in *The Observer*, Saturday 6th September 2014

'Johan Cruyff: How will 'militaristic' Louis van Gaal manage all the egos at Manchester United?' by Donald McRae, in *The Guardian*, Friday 12th September 2014

'Manchester United 4 QPR 0: Radamel Falcao makes debut but it's Angel di Maria who lights up Old Trafford', by Henry Winter, in *The Telegraph*, Sunday 14th September 2014

'Manchester United 4 QPR 0: Louis van Gaal targets Champions League and insists his team can improve', by Mark Ogden, in *The Telegraph*, Sunday 14th September 2014

'Manchester United 4 QPR 0: Angel di Maria leads way as new signings suggest bright future awaits', by Paul Hayward, in *The Telegraph*, Sunday 14th September 2014

'Manchester United coast to first win of season with defeat of QPR', by Daniel Taylor, in *The Guardian*, Sunday 14th September 2014

'Leicester City and Jamie Vardy stun Manchester United in eight-goal thriller', by Stuart James, in *The Guardian*, Sunday 21st September 2014

'Leicester win duel of the diamonds against a stunned Manchester United', by Michael Cox, in *The Guardian,* Sunday 21st September 2014

'How Louis van Gaal's tactics were exposed by Leicester's Nigel Pearson', by Jamie Jackson, in *The Guardian,* Monday 22nd September 2014

'Three Points: Man United fall apart at Leicester', by Craig Burley, for ESPN.com, Monday 22nd September 2014

'Manchester United humiliation: Nine stats to concern Louis van Gaal', by Telegraph Sports Staff Writers, *The Daily Telegraph,* Monday 22nd September 2014

'Why Jamie Vardy should be seen as a villain rather than a hero after Leicester City's defeat of Manchester United', by Scott 'The Red' Patterson, for *Metro,* Tuesday 23rd September 2014

'Offering a rational outlook to United fans. There are plenty of reasons to be positive…', by Tim Simon, for *The Republik of Mancunia,* Thursday 25th September 2014

'Manchester United vs West Ham: David Moyes should have been given £150m like Louis van Gaal, says Sam Allardyce' by James Orr, in *The Independent,* Thursday 25th September 2014

'RvP reveals team meeting took place after Leicester defeat', by Scott the Red, in *The Republik of Mancunia,* Friday 26th September 2014

'Louis van Gaal confident he can solve Manchester United injury crisis', by Jamie Jackson, in *The Guardian,* Friday 26th September 2014

'Louis van Gaal describes Wayne Rooney's red-card tackle as 'unfriendly'', by Daniel Taylor, in *The Observer*, Saturday 27th September 2014

'Manchester United scrape past West Ham after Wayne Rooney sees red', by Daniel Taylor, in *The Observer*, Saturday 27th September 2014

'Van Gaal's gives debut to six youth team players', by Scott the Red, for *The Republik of Mancunia*, Saturday 27th September 2014

'Radamel Falcao opens account to help Manchester United sink Everton', by Jamie Jackson, in *The Guardian*, Sunday 5th October 2014

'Van Gaal critical of United but warns there's more to come', by Rob Dawson, in *Manchester Evening News*, Sunday 5th October 2014

'Five things we learnt from United 2-1 Everton', by Tim Simon, for *The Republik of Mancunia*, Sunday 5th October 2014

'Man United 2 Everton 1: Five things we learned', by Rob Dawson, in *Manchester Evening News*, Monday 6th October 2014

'Manchester United's No1 David de Gea leaves Tim Howard in the shade', by Andy Hunter, in *The Guardian*, Monday 6th October 2014

'Sir Alex Ferguson praises Louis van Gaal's start at Manchester United', by *The Guardian* staff writers, Thursday 9th October 2014

"Could do better' – Louis van Gaal's report card at Manchester United', by Jamie Jackson, in *The Guardian*, Wednesday 15th October 2014

'Premier League: 10 things to look out for this weekend: Manchester United's fragile momentum will be tested at West Brom', by Nick Ames, in *The Guardian*, Friday 17th October 2014

'Louis van Gaal: a win at WBA can spark Manchester United's title challenge', by Jamie Jackson, in *The Guardian*, Sunday 19th October 2014

'Daley Blind earns Manchester United point with late goal at WBA', by Stuart James, in *The Guardian*, Monday 20th October 2014

'Five things we learnt from West Brom 2-2 United', by Tim Simon, for *The Republik of Mancunia*, Tuesday 21st October 2014

'West Brom 2-2 Manchester United: five talking points', by Alan Smith, in *The Guardian*, Tuesday 21st October 2014

'Manchester United can still catch Chelsea, says Van Gaal after draw', by Stuart James, in *The Guardian*, Tuesday 21st October 2014

'Sir Alex Ferguson: David Moyes's Manchester United failure not my fault', by Daniel Taylor, in *The Guardian*, Tuesday 21st October 2014

'Louis van Gaal and Jose Mourinho used to live 15 metres apart... now when Manchester United face Chelsea at Old Trafford, they'll be separated by 15 metres on the touchline', by Ian Ladyman, for *The Daily Mail*, Saturday 25th October 2014

'Manchester United's Robin van Persie nicks point off 10-man Chelsea', by Daniel Taylor, in *The Guardian*, Sunday 26th October 2014

'Louis van Gaal: Robin van Persie was 'stupid' for taking his shirt off', by Jamie Jackson, in *The Guardian*, Sunday 26th October 2014

'Old Trafford gloom starting to evaporate under the reign of boss Louis Van Gaal', by Mark Ogden, in *The Telegraph*, Sunday 26th October 2014

'Mourinho and Van Gaal's love-in put to one side as the apprentice overtakes the master', by David McDonnell, in *The Daily Mirror*, Monday 27th October 2014

'Manchester United head in right direction with Van Gaal's roadmap', by Jamie Jackson, in *The Guardian*, Monday 27th October 2014

'Sergio Aguero strike wins derby for Manchester City against 10-man United', by Daniel Taylor, in *The Guardian*, Sunday 2nd November 2014

'Val Gaal: These players are prepared with give everything for the United shirt', by Scott the Red, for *The Republik of Mancunia*, Sunday 2nd November 2014

'Manchester United are never going to win anything with such an ill-fitting, patched-up back-four of misfits', by Paul Hayward, in *The Telegraph*, Sunday 2nd November 2014

'Louis van Gaal: stupid Chris Smalling cost Manchester

United against City', by Jamie Jackson, in *The Guardian*, Sunday 2nd November 2014

'Manchester City triumph in Premier League's Collapsico derby', by Barney Ronay, in *The Guardian*, Sunday 2nd November 2014

'Five key thoughts following United's 1-0 loss to Manchester City', by Tim Simon, for *The Republik of Mancunia*, Monday 3rd November 2014

The Fiver, by Barry Glendenning, in *The Guardian*, Friday 7th November 2014

'Louis van Gaal is making progress at Manchester United, forget his comment about it taking three years', by Scott Patterson, in *The Metro*, Saturday 8th November 2014

'Manchester United substitute Juan Mata ends Crystal Palace resistance', by Jamie Jackson, in *The Observer*, Sunday 9th November 2014

'Louis van Gaal concedes Manchester United system changes are not ideal', by Jamie Jackson, in *The Guardian*, Sunday 9th November 2014

'Five key thoughts from United 1-0 Crystal Palace', by Tim Simon, for *The Republic of Mancunia*, Sunday 9th November 2014

'O, Louis review – Roddy Doyle on a savage biography of Louis van Gaal', by Roddy Doyle in *The Guardian*, Thursday 13th November 2014

'Premier League: biggest winners and losers from the international break ' by Jacob Steinberg and Paul Doyle, in The Guardian, Wednesday 19th November 2014

'Manchester United announce 10% drop in revenue in first quarter' in *The Guardian*, Tuesday 18th November 2014

'Arsenal 1-2 Manchester United: Wayne Rooney seals smash-and-grab win for Louis van Gaal's men', by Aaron Flanagan, in *The Daily Mirror*, Saturday 22nd November 2014

'Arsenal 1-2 Manchester United' by Chris Bevan for *BBC Sport*, Saturday 22nd November 2014

'Arsenal 1-2 Manchester United: 5 things we learnt', by Joshua Evans, in *The Daily Mirror*, Saturday 22nd November 2014

'Arsenal dominant but dazed as Manchester United expose profligacy', by David Hytner, in *The Guardian*, Sunday 23rd November 2014

'Manchester United's Wayne Rooney nets breakaway goal to beat Arsenal', by Daniel Taylor, in *The Observer*, Sunday 23rd November 2014

'Man United's win over Arsenal could be the turning point in their season – and the top four beckons', by Oliver Holt, in *The Daily Mirror*, Monday 24th November 2014

Well Worth A Look Links

1. A series of pictures of tortoises that look like Louis Van Gaal: http://www.thepoke.co.uk/2014/06/03/tortoises-that-look-like-louis-van-gaal/

2. King Eric is returning to Old Trafford. Here Van Gaal recreates (for the benefit of the fourth official) an attempted kung-fu decapitation of Jari Litmanen by Milan's Marcel Desailly in the 1995 Champions League Final: https://www.youtube.com/watch?v=0-s6tO01hVE#t=48

3. *The Guardian's* Louis van Gaal Gallery: http://www.theguardian.com/football/gallery/2014/aug/05/the-gallery-louis-van-gaal

4. A detailed analysis of Louis Van Gaal's coaching philosophy (with video): http://defendingwiththeball.wordpress.com/2014/05/26/louis-van-gaal-tactical-philosophy/

ALSO BY THIS AUTHOR:

Fergie's Finest: Sir Alex Ferguson's First 11, by Andrew J Kirby, Endeavour Press Ltd. 8th May 2013

Search for it on Amazon

Sir Alex Ferguson was one of the greatest football managers of all time. Over 26 years in charge of Manchester United, his passion for winning and tactical flair made them the most successful club in the Premier League. Under his guidance, United won an eye-watering 38 trophies, including 13 league championships.

But who were the greatest players of the Ferguson era? Over 185 players debuted for United under Ferguson and more than 200 players wore the red jersey for Fergie. They included legends of the modern game from David Beckham to Ryan Giggs, from Roy Keane to Bryan Robson, and from Eric Cantona to Cristiano Ronaldo.

But which were the Greatest Eleven? Is Robin Van Persie the greatest striker? Or Ruud Van Nistelrooy? Was Paul Scholes the best player in the heart of the midfield? Or Bryan Robson?

In this fascinating study, Andrew Kirby selects the ultimate 'Team Fergie'? With interviews from football writers and former players, this book considers the leading contenders for each position in Sir Alex Ferguson's First Eleven.

It is the one book that every Manchester United fan - and indeed every football supporter - will want to read.

281

ALSO BY THIS AUTHOR:

The Pride of All Europe: Manchester United's Greatest Seasons in the European Cup, by Andrew J Kirby, Endeavour Press Ltd, 23rd June 2014

Search for it on Amazon

Manchester United was the first English team to make the foray into the European Cup, participating in the tournament despite the express disapproval of the Football League.

They were also the first English winners of the trophy.

Over the years, United's European adventures have spanned tragedy – the 1958 Munich Air Disaster – and triumph – three European Cup wins – and have provided no shortage of memorable stories.

Despite United being only the eighth most successful club in the competition's history, the United name is irrevocably linked to the European Cup. This book explores the reasons why.

With interviews from fans, personal anecdotes and excerpts from football archives, this book looks back at the history of the club and their greatest – and worst – moments.

'The Pride of All Europe' celebrates Manchester United's triumphs in European football, concentrating on ten key stories from the twenty-five seasons and six decades the club has participated in the Europe's premier competition, interspersed with brief, first-hand fan accounts of those fabled United "Euroaways."

In this detailed study, Andrew Kirby dissects the rich history of Manchester United in Europe.

9275780R00163

Printed in Great Britain
by Amazon.co.uk, Ltd.,
Marston Gate.